LANGUAGE

in Thought and Action

BY S. I. HAYAKAWA

IN CONSULTATION WITH Basil H. Pillard ANTIOCH COLLEGE

HARCOURT, BRACE AND COMPANY   NEW YORK

Foreword

This book began as a revision of *Language in Action*, published in 1941. Events since that date have naturally caused me to re-examine the whole of that earlier book. Some statements to be found there, unhappily, have been given a sharper, tragic significance by ensuing events; some statements, on the other hand, especially those in which it was asserted that the semantic discipline could be applied to the solution of many social and individual problems, now appear to me to have been somewhat oversimplified. I still believe that such application is possible; but it is not quite so easy as I am afraid I made it sound. The deeper I got into the task of revision, the graver the deficiencies and omissions seemed to be. The attempt to repair these deficiencies has resulted in something more than a revised *Language in Action*. So much has been changed and so much has been added that more than half the material in the present volume is new.

Two tasks confront the student of semantics. The first is the refinement of the basic formulations of the science. This task is, naturally, highly technical and of deep concern to specialists. The second task, no less urgent, is that of translating what is already known in semantics into usable terms. Today, the public is aware, perhaps to an unprecedented degree, of the role of verbal communication in human affairs. This awareness arises partly, of course, out of the urgency of the tensions everywhere existing between nation and nation, class and class, individual and individual, in a world that is changing with fantastic rapidity. It arises, too, out of the knowledge on the part even of the least reflective elements of the population that enormous powers for good or evil lie in the media of mass communication. Thoughtful people in all walks of life feel, therefore, the need of systematic help in the huge task that confronts all of us today, namely, that of interpreting and evaluating the verbally received communications that pour in on us from all sides.

But the task of providing that help is not an easy one, because the principles of semantics are extremely abstract, while the situations in which semantic guidance is needed are appallingly concrete. I have long known that the task of a student of semantics who would help others cannot simply be that of enunciating general propositions, however true they may be. His task is to live and act, in as many situations as possible, with the semantic principles always in the back of his mind, so that, before he recommends them to others, he may see how they may (and may not) be applied to actual human problems. The years that have intervened between the publication of *Language in Action* and the present work have given me many opportunities to explore further and to test more thoroughly the general principles of linguistic interaction here set forth. During the last eight years I have, in addition to my usual tasks of writing and teaching and lecturing, spent a period of study and observation at the Menninger Clinic and Foundation at Topeka, Kansas; I have been an art student at the Institute of Design under the direction of that excellent artist and inspiring teacher, the late Laszlo Moholy-Nagy; I was for four years a columnist of the Chicago *Defender*, a Negro weekly, and during those same years was a regular book-reviewer for *Book Week*, the literary supplement of the Chicago *Sun;* I did some first-hand research in folk music and jazz; I served on the board of directors of a co-operative wholesale and was president of a small chain of co-operative grocery stores; I have had the privilege of association with art connoisseurs and collectors, and the equal privilege of association with self-taught folk musicians of the Negro community; last, and probably not least, I have become the father of two boys. All these experiences have helped to fill out my exposition of semantic theory; I have added many examples drawn from daily life and controversy; many of my convictions have been strengthened through contact with problems in which the lack of semantic awareness among those involved has clearly been one of the sources of difficulty. The reader who has read *Language in Action* will find, I believe, that the present volume offers fewer generalizations in a form that leaves him asking, "Now that you've explained the principle, what do I do with it?"

The following are some of the changes which, I hope, make *Language in Thought and Action* a fuller, clearer, and more useful book than the earlier work. In the first place, the ethical assumptions underlying semantics have been made explicit rather than left implicit. Semantics is the study of human interaction through the mechanisms of linguistic communication. Consequent to the exchange of communications, co-operation sometimes results, and sometimes conflict. The basic ethical assumption of semantics, analogous to the medical assumption that health is preferable to illness, is that co-operation is preferable to conflict. I have tried to show why this assumption can (and must) be made, and have tried to unify the entire book around it as a central theme.

Secondly, a great deal of new material has been added under the heading of "Applications" at the end of each chapter. A book on semantics is not something simply to be read and put aside. Its principles, to be meaningful, must be tried out in one's own thinking and speaking and writing and behavior; they must be tested against one's own observation and experience. The "Applications" therefore have a double purpose: they offer a means whereby the reader may, in addition to reading *about* semantics, absorb the semanticist's point of view through the undertaking of actual semantic investigations and exercises; they also are a way of urging the reader not to take the writer's word for anything that is in this book.

In the present volume, some of the technical terms used in *Language in Action* have been abandoned; those which have been retained are, I hope, applied with greater consistency and defined more sharply than was formerly the case. Among the new materials added is a chapter offering the outlines of a semantic theory of literature—one which will contribute, I hope, to the uniting of psychological and literary approaches to the evaluation of literary art. In the discussion of the language of social criticism and social change, an attempt has been made to show (especially in Chapter 12, "The Society Behind the Symbols" and in Chapter 16, the discussion of social institutions and cultural lag) the degree to which knowledge of fields other than semantics is necessary to those who aspire to apply semantics to social problems. The uses of the "abstraction ladder" as a critical instrument for the examination and evaluation of writing and speaking (one's own or other people's) have been made considerably more explicit and, I trust, more useful. The interrelatedness of the various functions of language has also been stressed and, I hope, clarified. Additional stress has been given, too, to the use of semantics as an instrument of self-knowledge and self-criticism.

My deepest debt in this book is to the General Semantics ("non-Aristotelian system") of Alfred Korzybski. I have also drawn heavily upon the works of other contributors to semantics: especially Ogden and Richards, Leonard Bloomfield, Thurman Arnold, Jean Piaget, Charles Morris, Wendell Johnson, Susanne Langer, and Kenneth Burke. I am also deeply indebted to the writings of numerous psychologists and psychiatrists with one or another of the dynamic points of view which stem from Sigmund Freud: Karl Menninger, Karen Horney, Trigant Burrow, Carl R. Rogers, Franz Alexander, Thomas French, Rudolph Dreikurs, and many others. I have also found extremely helpful the writings of many cultural anthropologists: especially those of Benjamin Lee Whorf, Ruth Benedict, and Margaret Mead. In the past several years, semantic insight—i.e., insight into human symbolic behavior and into human interaction through symbolic mechanisms—has come from all sorts of disciplines: not only from linguistics, philosophy, psychology, and cultural anthropology, but also from attitude research and public opinion study, from new techniques in psychotherapy, from physiology and neurology, from mathematical biophysics and cybernetics. How are all these separate insights to be brought together and synthesized? This is a task which I cannot claim to have performed here, but I have examined the problem long enough to believe that it cannot be done without some set of broad and informing principles such as is to be found in the General Semantics of Korzybski.

Since anything approaching a full citation of sources would have made these pages unduly formidable in appearance, I have appended, in lieu of detailed documentation, a list of books (pp. 309-312) which I have found especially useful. However, none of the authors whose works I have profited by is to be held accountable for the errors or shortcomings of this book or for the liberties I have taken in the restatement, application, and modification of existing theories.

Many persons have made comments, raised questions, and offered suggestions which have helped to shape the present work. Professor Basil H. Pillard, who for many years has been applying semantics to the teaching of English and to student counseling at Antioch College, Yellow Springs, Ohio, has gone over the manuscript word by word; he has offered innumerable valuable suggestions and has supplied more than half of the "Applications." To him, and to his students who tried out many of the "Applications" as classroom exercises and offered criticisms of many chapters of the manuscript, I owe a profound debt of thanks. Professor James M. McCrimmon, of the Humanities Division of the University of Illinois, has also given extraordinarily practical and helpful suggestions which have influenced almost every chapter of this book.

S. I. H.

Chicago, Illinois

Contents

A Semantic Parable

Once upon a time (said the Professor), there were two small communities, spiritually as well as geographically situated at a considerable distance from each other. They had, however, these problems in common: Both were hard hit by a depression, so that in each of the towns there were about one hundred heads of families unemployed. There was, to be sure, enough food, enough clothing, enough materials for housing, but these families simply did not have money to procure these necessities.

The city fathers of A-town, the first community, were substantial businessmen, moderately well educated, good to their families, kindhearted, and sound-thinking. The unemployed tried hard, as unemployed people usually do, to find jobs; but the situation did not improve. The city fathers, as well as the unemployed themselves, had been brought up to believe that there is always enough work for everyone, if you only look for it hard enough. Comforting themselves with this doctrine, the city fathers could have shrugged their shoulders and turned their backs on the problem, except for the fact that they were genuinely kindhearted men. They could not bear to see the unemployed men and their wives and children starving. In order to prevent starvation, they felt that they had to provide these people with some means of sustenance. Their principles told them, nevertheless, that if people were given something for nothing, it would demoralize their character. Naturally this made the city fathers even more unhappy, because they were faced with the horrible choice of (1) letting the unemployed starve, or (2) destroying their moral character.

The solution they finally hit upon, after much debate and soul-searching, was this. They decided to give the unemployed families relief of fifty dollars a month; but to insure against the pauperization of the recipients, they decided that this fifty dollars was to be accompanied by a moral lesson, to wit: the obtaining of the assistance would be made so difficult, humiliating, and disagreeable that there would be no temptation for anyone to go through the process unless it was absolutely necessary; the moral disapproval of the community would be turned upon the recipients of the money at all times in such a way that they would try hard to get off relief and regain their self-respect. Some even proposed that people on relief be denied the vote, so that the moral lesson would be more deeply impressed upon them. Others suggested that their names be published at regular intervals in the newspapers, so that there would be a strong incentive to get off relief. The city fathers had enough faith in the goodness of human nature to expect that the recipients would be grateful, since they were getting something for nothing, something which they hadn't worked for.

When the plan was put into operation, however, the recipients of the relief checks proved to be an ungrateful, ugly bunch. They seemed to resent the cross-examinations and inspections at the hands of the relief investigators, who, they said, took advantage of a man's misery to snoop into every detail of his private life. In spite of uplifting editorials in A-town *Tribune* telling them how grateful they ought to be, the recipients of the relief refused to learn any moral lessons, declaring that they were "just as good as anybody else." When, for example, they permitted themselves the rare luxury of a movie or an evening of bingo, their neighbors looked at them sourly as if to say, "I work hard and pay my taxes just in order to support loafers like you in idleness and pleasure." This attitude, which was fairly characteristic of those members of the community who still had jobs, further embittered the relief recipients, so that they showed even less gratitude as time went on and were constantly on the lookout for insults, real or imaginary, from people who might think that they weren't as good as anybody else. A number of them took to moping all day long, to thinking that their lives had been failures; one or two even committed suicide. Others found that it was hard to look their wives and kiddies in the face, because they had failed to provide. They all found it difficult to maintain their club and fraternal relationships, since they could not help feeling that their fellow citizens despised them for having sunk so low. Their wives, too, were unhappy for the same reasons and gave up their social activities. Children whose parents were on relief felt inferior to classmates whose parents were not public charges. Some of these children developed inferiority complexes which affected not only their grades at school, but their careers after graduation. Several other relief recipients, finally, felt they could stand their loss of self-respect no longer and decided, after many efforts to gain honest jobs, to earn money by their own efforts, even if they had to go in for robbery. They did so and were caught and sent to the state penitentiary.

The depression, therefore, hit A-town very hard. The relief policy had averted starvation, no doubt, but suicide, personal quarrels, unhappy homes, the weakening of social organizations, the maladjustment of children, and, finally, crime, had resulted. The town was divided in two, the "haves" and the "have-nots," so that there was class hatred. People shook their heads sadly and declared that it all went to prove over again what they had known from the beginning, that giving people something for nothing inevitably demoralizes their character. The citizens of A-town gloomily waited for prosperity to return, with less and less hope as time went on.

The story of the other community, B-ville, was entirely different. B-ville was a relatively isolated town, too far out of the way to be reached by Rotary Club speakers and university extension services. One of the aldermen, however, who was something of an economist, explained to his fellow aldermen that unemployment, like sickness, accident, fire, tornado, or death, hits unexpectedly in modern society, irrespective of the victim's merits or deserts. He went on to say that B-ville's homes, parks, streets, industries, and everything else B-ville was proud of had been built in part by the work of these same people who were now unemployed. He then proposed to apply a principle of insurance: If the work these unemployed people had previously done for the community could be regarded as a form of premium paid to the community against a time of misfortune, payments now made to them to prevent their starvation could be regarded as insurance claims. He therefore proposed that all men of good repute who had worked in the community in whatever line of useful endeavor, whether as machinists, clerks, or bank managers, be regarded as citizen policyholders, having claims against the city in the case of unemployment for fifty dollars a month until such time as they might again be employed. Naturally, he had to talk very slowly and patiently, since the idea was entirely new to his fellow aldermen. But he described his plan as a "straight business proposition," and finally they were persuaded. They worked out the details as to the conditions under which citizens should be regarded as policyholders in the city's social insurance plan to everybody's satisfaction and decided to give checks for fifty dollars a month to the heads of each of B-ville's indigent families.

B-ville's claim adjusters, whose duty it was to investigate the claims of the citizen policyholders, had a much better time than A-town's relief investigators. While the latter had been resentfully regarded as snoopers, the former, having no moral lesson to teach but simply a business transaction to carry out, treated their clients with businesslike courtesy and got the same amount of information as the relief investigators with considerably less difficulty. There were no hard feelings. It further happened, fortunately, that news of B-ville's plans reached a liberal newspaper editor in the big city at the other end of the state. This writer described the plan in a leading feature story headed "B-VILLE LOOKS AHEAD. Great Adventure in Social Pioneering Launched by Upper Valley Community." As a result of this publicity, inquiries about the plan began to come to the city hall even before the first checks were mailed out. This led, naturally, to a considerable feeling of pride on the part of the aldermen, who, being boosters, felt that this was a wonderful opportunity to put B-ville on the map.

Accordingly, the aldermen decided that instead of simply mailing out the checks as they had originally intended, they would publicly present the first checks at a monster civic ceremony. They invited the governor of the state, who was glad to come to bolster his none-too-enthusiastic support in that locality, the president of the state university, the senator from their district, and other functionaries. They decorated the National Guard armory with flags and got out the American Legion Fife and Drum Corps, the Boy Scouts, and other civic organizations. At the big celebration, each family to receive a social insurance check was marched up to the platform to receive it, and the governor and the mayor shook hands with each of them as they came trooping up in their best clothes. Fine speeches were made; there was much cheering and shouting; pictures of the event showing the recipients of the checks shaking hands with the mayor, and the governor patting the heads of the children, were published not only in the local papers but also in several metropolitan picture sections.

Every recipient of these insurance checks had a feeling, therefore, that he had been personally honored, that he lived in a wonderful little town, and that he could face his unemployment with greater courage and assurance, since his community was back of him. The men and women found themselves being kidded in a friendly way by their acquaintances for having been "up there with the big shots," shaking hands with the governor, and so on. The children at school found themselves envied for having had their pictures in the papers. All in all, B-ville's unemployed did not commit suicide, were not haunted by a sense of failure, did not turn to crime, did not get personal maladjustments, did not develop class hatred, as the result of their fifty dollars a month. . . .

At the conclusion of the Professor's story, the discussion began:

"That just goes to show," said the Advertising Man, who was known among his friends as a realistic thinker, "what good promotional work can do. B-ville's city council had real advertising sense, and that civic ceremony was a masterpiece . . . made everyone happy . . . put over the scheme in a big way. Reminds me of the way we do things in our business: as soon as we called horse-mackerel tuna-fish, we developed a big market for it. I suppose if you called relief 'insurance,' you could actually get people to like it, couldn't you?"

"What do you mean, 'calling' it insurance?" asked the Social Worker. "B-ville's scheme wasn't relief at all. It *was* insurance. That's what all such payments should be. What gets me is the stupidity of A-town's city council and all people like them in not realizing that what they call 'relief' is simply the payment of just claims which those unemployed have on a community in a complex interdependent industrial society."

"Good grief, man! Do you realize what you're saying?" cried the

Advertising Man in surprise. "Are you implying that those people had any *right* to that money? All I said was that it's a good idea to *disguise* relief as insurance if it's going to make people any happier. But it's still relief, no matter what you *call* it. It's all right to kid the public along to reduce discontent, but we don't need to kid ourselves as well!"

"But they *do* have a right to that money! They're not getting something for nothing. It's insurance. They did something for the community, and that's their prem—"

"Say, are you crazy?"

"Who's crazy?"

"You're crazy. Relief is relief, isn't it? If you'd only call things by their right names . . ."

"But, confound it, insurance is insurance, isn't it?"

(Since the gentlemen are obviously losing their tempers, it will be best to leave them. The Professor has already sneaked out. When last heard of, not only had the quarrelers stopped speaking to each other, but so had their wives—and the Advertising Man was threatening to disinherit his son if he didn't break off his engagement with the Social Worker's daughter.)

This story has been told not to advance arguments in favor of "social insurance" or "relief" or for any other political and economic arrangement, but simply to show a fairly characteristic sample of language in action. Do the words we use make as much difference in our lives as the story of A-town and B-ville seems to indicate? We often talk about "choosing the right words to express our thoughts," as if thinking were a process entirely independent of the words we think in. But is thinking such an independent process? Do the words we utter arise as a result of the thoughts we have, or are the thoughts we have determined by the linguistic systems we happen to have been taught? The Advertising Man and the Social Worker seem to be agreed that the results of B-ville's program were good, so that we can assume that their notions of what is socially desirable are similar. Nevertheless, they *cannot agree.*

Alfred Korzybski, in his preface to *Science and Sanity* (which discusses many problems similar to those discussed in this book), asks the reader to imagine what the state of technology would be if all lubricants contained emery dust, the presence of which had never been detected. Machines would be short-lived and expensive; the machine age would be a dream of the distant future. If, however, someone were to discover the presence of the emery, we should at once know *in what direction to proceed* in order to release the potentialities of machine power.

Why do people disagree? It isn't a matter of education or intelligence, because quarreling, bitterness, conflict, and breakdown are just as common among the educated as the uneducated, among the clever as the stupid. Human relations are no better among the privileged than the underprivileged. Indeed, well-educated people are often the cleverest in proving that insurance is *really* insurance and that relief is *really* relief—and being well educated they often have such high principles that nothing will make them modify their position in the slightest. Are disagreements then the inevitable results of the nature of human problems and the nature of man? Possibly so—but if we give this answer, we are confessing to being licked before we have even started our investigations.

The student of language observes, however, that it is an extremely rare quarrel that does not involve some kind of *talking*. Almost invariably, before noses are punched or shooting begins, *words are exchanged*—sometimes only a few, sometimes millions. We shall, therefore, look for the "previously undetected emery dust" (or whatever it is that heats up and stops our intellectual machinery) in *language*—that is to say, *our linguistic habits* (how we talk and think and listen) and *our unconscious attitudes toward language*. If we are even partially successful in our search, we may get an inkling of the *direction in which to proceed* in order to release the now imperfectly realized potentialities of human co-operation.

P.S. Those who have concluded that the point of the story is that the Social Worker and the Advertising Man were "only arguing about different names for the same thing," are asked to reread the story and explain what they mean by (1) "only" and (2) "the same thing."

BOOK ONE

The Functions of Language

Ch'en K'ang asked Poyu [Confucius' only son], "Is there anything special that you were taught by your father?" Poyu replied, "No. One day my father was standing alone and I ran past the court, and he asked me, 'Have you learned poetry?' And I said, 'Not yet.' He said, 'If you don't study poetry, your language will not be polished.' So I went back and studied poetry. Another day he was standing alone, and I went past the court, and he said to me, 'Have you studied the ceremonies?' And I said, 'Not yet.' And he said, 'If you don't study the ceremonies, you have no guide for your conduct.' And I went back and studied the ceremonies. I was taught to study these two things." Ch'en K'ang came away quite pleased and said, "I asked him one question and learned three things. I learned what Confucius said about poetry. I learned what he said about ceremonies. And I learned that the Master taught his own son in exactly the same way as he taught his disciples.

Aphorisms of Confucius
Translated by Lin Yutang

1. Language and Survival

One cannot but wonder at this constantly recurring phrase "getting something for nothing," as if it were the peculiar and perverse ambition of disturbers of society. Except for our animal outfit, practically all we have is handed to us gratis. Can the most complacent reactionary flatter himself that he invented the art of writing or the printing press, or discovered his religious, economic, and moral convictions, or any of the devices which supply him with meat and raiment or any of the sources of such pleasure as he may derive from literature or the fine arts? In short, civilization is little else than getting something for nothing.
JAMES HARVEY ROBINSON

Whenever agreement or assent is arrived at in human affairs . . . this agreement is reached by linguistic processes, or else it is not reached.
BENJAMIN LEE WHORF

What Animals Shall We Imitate?

People in our culture who like to think of themselves as tough-minded and realistic, including influential political leaders and businessmen as well as go-getters and hustlers of smaller caliber, tend to take it for granted that human nature is "selfish" and that life is a struggle in which only the fittest may survive. According to this philosophy, the basic law by which man must live, in spite of his surface veneer of civilization, is the law of the jungle. The "fittest" are those who can bring to the struggle superior force, superior cunning, and superior ruthlessness.

The wide currency of this philosophy of the "survival of the fittest" enables people who act ruthlessly and selfishly, whether in personal rivalries, business competition, or international relations, to allay their consciences by telling themselves that they are only obeying a "law of nature." But a disinterested observer is entitled to ask whether the ruthlessness of the tiger, the cunning of the ape, and obedience to the "law of the jungle" are actually evidences of *human* fitness to survive. If human beings are to pick up pointers on behavior from the lower animals, are there not animals other than beasts of prey from which we might learn lessons in survival?

We might, for example, point to the rabbit or the deer and define fitness to survive as superior rapidity in running away from our enemies. We might point to the earthworm or the mole and define it as the ability to keep out of sight and out of the way. We might point to the oyster or the housefly and define it as the ability to propagate our kind faster than our enemies can eat us up. If we are looking to animals for models of behavior, there is also the pig, an animal which many human beings have tried to emulate since time immemorial. (It will be remembered that in the *Odyssey* Circe gave ingenious and practical encouragement to those who had inclinations in this direction.) In Aldous Huxley's *Brave New World*, we are given a picture of a world such as would be designed for us by those who would model human beings after the social ants. The world, under the management of a super-brain-trust, might be made as well-integrated, smooth, and efficient as an ant colony, and as Huxley shows, just about as meaningless. If we simply look to animals in order to define what we mean by "fitness to survive," there is no limit to the subhuman systems of behavior that can be devised: we may emulate lobsters, dogs, sparrows, parakeets, giraffes, skunks, or the parasitical worms, because they have all obviously survived in one way or another. We are still entitled to ask, however, if *human* survival does not revolve around a different kind of fitness from that exhibited by the lower animals.

Because of the wide prevalence of the dog-eat-dog "survival of the fittest" philosophy in our world (although the atomic bomb has awakened *some* people to the need for a change in philosophy), it is worth while to look into the present scientific standing of the phrase "survival of the fittest." Biologists today distinguish between two kinds of "struggle for survival." First, there is the *interspecific* struggle of different species of animals with each other, such as between wolves and deer, or between men and bacteria. Second, there is the *intraspecific* struggle among members of a single species, as when rats fight other rats, or men fight other men. There is a great deal of evidence in modern biology to show that those species which have developed elaborate means of intraspecific competition often unfit themselves for interspecific competition, so that such species are either already extinct or are threatened with extinction at any time. The peacock's tail, although useful in sexual competition against other peacocks, is only a hindrance in coping with the environment or competing against other species. The peacock could therefore be wiped out overnight by a sudden change in ecological balance. There is evidence, too, that strength and fierceness in fighting and killing other animals, whether in interspecific or intraspecific competition, have never been enough of themselves to guarantee the survival of a species. Many a mammoth reptile, equipped with magnificent offensive and defensive armaments, ceased to walk the earth millions of years ago. If we are going to talk about human survival, one of the first things to do, even if we grant that man must fight to live, is to distinguish between those qualities that are useful to men in fighting the environment and other species (for example, floods, weather, wild animals, bacteria, or grasshoppers) and those qualities (such as aggressiveness) that are useful in fighting other men.

The principle that if we don't hang together we shall all hang separately was discovered by nature long before it was put into words by man. Co-operation within a species (and sometimes with other species) is essential to the survival of most living creatures. Man, moreover, is the *talking* animal—and any theory of human survival that leaves this fact out of account is no more scientific than would be a theory of beaver survival that failed to consider the interesting uses a beaver makes of its teeth and flat tail. Let us see what talking—human communication—means.

Co-operation

When someone shouts at you, "look out!" and you jump just in time to avoid being hit by an automobile, you owe your escape from injury to the fundamental co-operative act by which most of the higher animals survive, namely, communication by means of noises. You did not see the car coming; nevertheless, someone did see it, and he made certain *noises to communicate* his alarm to you. In other words, although your nervous system did not record the danger, you were unharmed because another nervous system did record it. You had, for the time being, the advantage of someone else's nervous system in addition to your own.

Indeed, most of the time when we are listening to the noises people make or looking at the black marks on paper that stand for such noises, we are drawing upon the experiences of others in order to make up what we ourselves have missed. Now obviously the more an individual can make use of the nervous systems of others to supplement his own, the easier it is for him to survive. And, of course, the more individuals there are in a group accustomed to co-operating by making helpful noises at each other, the better it is for all—within the limits, naturally, of the group's talents for social organization. Birds and animals congregate with their own kind and make noises when they find food or become alarmed. In fact, gregariousness as an aid to self-defense and survival is forced upon animals as well as upon men by the necessity of uniting nervous systems even more than by the necessity of uniting physical strength. Societies, both animal and human, might almost be regarded as huge co-operative nervous systems.

While animals use only a few limited cries, however, human beings use extremely complicated systems of sputtering, hissing, gurgling, clucking, cooing noises called *language,* with which they express and report what goes on in their nervous systems. Language is, in addition to being more complicated, immeasurably more flexible than the animal cries from which it was developed—so flexible indeed that it can be used not only to report the tremendous variety of things that go on in the human nervous system, but *to report those reports.* That is, when an animal yelps, he may cause a second animal to yelp in imitation or alarm, but the second yelp is not *about* the first yelp. But when a man says, "I see a river," a second man can say, "He says he sees a river"—which is a statement about a statement. About this statement-about-a-statement further statements can be made—and about these, still more. *Language, in short, can be about language.* This is a fundamental way in which human noise-making systems differ from the cries of animals.

The Pooling of Knowledge

In addition to having developed language, man has also developed means of making, on clay tablets, bits of wood or stone, skins of animals, and paper, more or less permanent marks and scratches which *stand for* language. These marks enable him to communicate with people who are beyond the reach of his voice, both in space and in time. There is a long course of evolution from the marked trees that indicated Indian trails to the metropolitan daily newspaper, but they have this in common: They pass on what one individual has known to other individuals, for their convenience or, in the broadest sense, instruction. The Indians are dead, but many of their trails are still marked and can be followed to this day. Archimedes is dead, but we still have his reports on what he observed in his experiments in physics. Keats is dead, but he can still tell us how he felt on first reading Chapman's Homer. From our newspapers and radios we learn with great rapidity facts about the world we live in. From books and magazines we learn how hundreds of people whom we shall never be able to see have felt and thought. All this information is useful to us at one time or another in the solution of our own problems.

A human being, then, is never dependent on his own experience alone for his information. Even in a primitive culture he can make use of the experience of his neighbors, friends, and relatives, which they communicate to him by means of language. Therefore, instead of remaining helpless because of the limitations of his own experience and knowledge, instead of having to discover what others have already discovered, instead of exploring the false trails they explored and repeating their errors, he can *go on from where they left off.* Language, that is to say, makes progress possible.

Indeed, most of what we call the human characteristics of our species are expressed and developed through our ability to co-operate by means of our systems of making meaningful noises and meaningful scratches on paper. Even people who belong to backward cultures in which writing has not been invented are able to exchange information and to hand down from generation to generation considerable stores of traditional knowledge. There seems, however, to be a limit both to the trustworthiness and to the amount of knowledge that can be transmitted orally. But when writing is invented, a tremendous step forward is taken. The accuracy of reports can be checked and rechecked by successive generations of observers. The amount of knowledge accumulated ceases to be limited by people's ability to remember what has been told them. The result is that in any literate culture of a few centuries' standing, human beings accumulate vast stores of knowledge—far more than any individual in that culture can read in his lifetime, let alone remember. These stores of knowledge, which are being added to constantly, are made widely available to all who want them through such mechanical processes as printing and through such distributive agencies as the book trade, the newspaper and magazine trade, and library systems. The result is that all of us who can read any of the major European or Asiatic languages are potentially in touch with the intellectual resources of centuries of human endeavor in all parts of the civilized world.

A physician, for example, who does not know how to treat a patient suffering from a rare disease can look up the disease in the *Index Medicus,* which will send him in turn to medical journals published in all parts of the world. In these he may find records of similar cases as reported and described by a physician in Rotterdam, Holland, in 1873, by another physician in Bangkok, Siam, in 1909, and by still other physicians in Kansas City in 1924. With such records before him, he can better handle his own case. Again, if a person is worried about ethics, he is not limited to the advice of the pastor of the Elm Street Baptist Church; he may go to Confucius, Aristotle, Jesus, Spinoza, and many others whose reflections on ethical problems are on record. If one is worried about love, he can get advice not only from his mother or best friend, but from Sappho, Ovid, Propertius, Shakespeare, Havelock Ellis, or any of a thousand others who knew something about it and wrote down what they knew.

Language, that is to say, is the indispensable mechanism of human life—of life such as ours that is molded, guided, enriched, and made possible by the accumulation of the *past* experience of members of our own species. Dogs and cats and chimpanzees do not, so far as we can tell, increase their wisdom, their information, or their control over their environment from one generation to the next. But human beings do. The cultural accomplishments of the ages, the invention of cooking, of weapons, of writing, of printing, of methods of building, of games and amusements, of means of transportation, and the discoveries of all the arts and sciences come to us as *free gifts from the dead.* These gifts, which none of us has done anything to earn, offer us not only the opportunity for a richer life than our forebears enjoyed, but also the opportunity to add to the sum total of human achievement by our own contributions, however small.

To be able to read and write, therefore, is to learn to profit by and take part in the greatest of human achievements—that which makes all other achievements possible—namely, the pooling of our experiences in great co-operative stores of knowledge, available (except where special privilege, censorship, or suppression stand in the way) to all. From the warning cry of primitive man to the latest scientific monograph or radio newsflash, language is social. Cultural and intellectual co-operation is the great principle of *human* life.

This is by no means an easy principle to accept or to understand—except as a kind of pious truism that we should like, because we are well-meaning people, to believe. We live in a highly competitive society, each of us trying to outdo the other in wealth, in popularity or social prestige, in dress, in scholastic grades or golf scores. As we read our daily papers, there is always news of conflict rather than of co-operation—conflict between labor and management, between rival corporations or movie stars, between rival political parties and nations. Over us all hangs the perpetual fear of another war even more unthinkably horrible than the last. One is often tempted to say that conflict, rather than co-operation, is the great governing principle of human life.

But what such a philosophy overlooks is that, despite all the competition at the surface, there is a huge substratum of co-operation *taken for granted* that keeps the world going. The co-ordination of the efforts of engineers, actors, musicians, utilities companies, typists, program directors, advertising agencies, writers, and hundreds of others is required to put on a single radio program. Hundreds of thousands of persons co-operate in the production of motor cars, including suppliers and shippers of raw materials from different parts of the earth. Any organized business activity whatsoever is an elaborate act of co-operation, in which every individual worker contributes his share. A lockout or a strike is a *withdrawal of co-operation*—things are regarded as "back to normal" when co-operation is restored. We may indeed as individuals compete for jobs, but our function in the job, once we get it, is to contribute at the right time and place to that innumerable series of co-operative acts that eventually result in automobiles being manufactured, in cakes appearing in pastry shops, in department stores being able to serve their customers, in the trains and airlines running as scheduled. And what is important for our purposes here is that all this co-ordination of effort necessary for the functioning of society is *of necessity achieved by language or else it is not achieved at all.*

The Niagara of Words

And how does all this affect Mr. T. C. Mits?[1] From the moment he switches on an early morning news broadcast until he falls asleep at night over a novel or a magazine, he is, like all other people living in modern civilized conditions, swimming in words. Newspaper editors, politicians, salesmen, radio comedians, columnists, luncheon club speakers, and clergymen; colleagues at work, friends, relatives, wife and children; market reports, direct mail advertising, books, and billboards—all are assailing him with words all day long. And Mr. Mits himself is constantly contributing to that verbal Niagara every time he puts on an advertising campaign, delivers a speech, writes a letter, or even chats with his friends.

---

[1] Lillian and Hugh Lieber, of Long Island University, are responsible for christening this gentleman, *The Celebrated Man In The Street.* Mits' wife's name is, of course, Wits. See *The Education of T. C. Mits* and *Mits, Wits, and Logic.*

When things go wrong in Mr. Mits' life—when he is worried, perplexed, or nervous, when family, business, or national affairs are not going as he thinks they should, when he finds himself making blunder after blunder in personal or financial matters—he blames a number of things as responsible for his difficulties. Sometimes he blames the weather, sometimes his health or the state of his nerves, sometimes his glands, or, if the problem is a larger one, he may blame his environment, the economic system he lives under, a foreign nation, or the cultural pattern of his society. When he is pondering the difficulties of other people, he may attribute their troubles too to causes such as these, and he may add still another, namely, "human nature." (He doesn't blame his own "human nature" unless he is in a very bad way indeed.) It rarely, if ever, occurs to him to investigate, among other things, the nature and constituents of that daily verbal Niagara as a possible source of trouble.

Indeed, there are few occasions on which Mr. Mits thinks about language as such. He wonders from time to time about a grammatical point. Sometimes he feels an uneasiness about his own verbal accomplishments, so that he begins to wonder if he shouldn't take steps to "improve his vocabulary." Once in a while he is struck by the fact that some people (although he never includes himself among these) "twist the meanings of words," especially during the course of arguments, so that words are often "very tricky." Occasionally, too, he notices, usually with irritation, that words sometimes "mean different things to different people." This condition, he feels, would be cured if people would only consult their dictionaries oftener and learn the "true meanings" of words. He knows, however, that they will not—at least, not any oftener than he does, which is not very often—so that he puts this down as another instance of the weakness of human nature.

This, unfortunately, is about the limit of Mr. Mits' linguistic speculations. But in this respect Mr. Mits is representative not only of the general public, but also of many scientific workers, publicists, and writers. Like most people, he takes words as much for granted as the air he breathes, and gives them about as much thought. (After all, he has been talking ever since he can remember.) Mr. Mits' body automatically adjusts itself, within certain limits, to changes in climate or atmosphere, from cold to warm, from dry to moist, from fresh to foul; no conscious effort on his part is required to make these adjustments. Nevertheless, he is ready to acknowledge the effect that climate and air have upon his physical well-being, and he takes measures to protect himself from unhealthy air, either by getting away from it, or by installing air-conditioning systems to purify it. But Mr. Mits, like the rest of us, also adjusts himself automatically to changes in the verbal climate, from one type of discourse to another, from one set of terms to another, from the listening habits of one kind of social occasion to those of another kind of social occasion, without conscious effort. He has yet, however, to acknowledge the effect of his verbal climate on his mental health and well-being.

Nevertheless, Mr. Mits is profoundly involved in the words he absorbs daily and in the words he uses daily. Words in the newspaper make him pound his fist on the breakfast table. Words his superiors speak to him puff him out with pride, or send him scurrying to work harder. Words about himself, which he has overheard being spoken behind his back, worry him sick. Words which he spoke before a clergyman some years ago have tied him to one woman for life. Words written down on pieces of paper keep him at his job, or bring bills in his mail every month which keep him paying and paying. Words written down by other people, on the other hand, keep them paying him month after month. With words woven into almost every detail of his life, it seems amazing that Mr. Mits' thinking on the subject of language should be so limited.

Mr. Mits has also noticed that when large masses of people, for example under totalitarian regimes, are permitted by their governments to hear and read only carefully selected words, their conduct becomes so strange that he can only regard it as mad. Yet he has observed that some individuals who have the same educational attainments and the same access to varied sources of information that he has, are nevertheless just as mad. He listens to the views of some of his neighbors and he cannot help wondering, "How can they think such things? Don't they see the same things happening that I see? They must be crazy!" Does such madness, he asks, illustrate again the "inevitable frailty of human nature"? Mr. Mits, who, as an American, likes to regard all things as possible, does not like the conclusion that "nothing can be done about it," but often he can hardly see how he can escape it. Occasionally, timidly, Mr. Mits approaches one more possibility, "Maybe I'm crazy myself. Maybe we're all nuts!" Such a conclusion leads to so complete an impasse, however, that he quickly drops the notion.

One reason for Mr. Mits' failure to get any further in his thinking about language is that he believes, as most people do, that words are not really important; what is important is the "ideas" they stand for. But what is an "idea" if it is not the *verbalization* of a cerebral itch? This, however, is something that has rarely, if ever, occurred to Mr. Mits. The fact that the implications of one set of terms may lead inevitably into blind alleys while the implications of another set of terms may not; the fact that the historical or sentimental associations that some words have make calm discussion impossible so long as those words are employed; the fact that language has a multitude of different kinds of uses, and that great confusion arises from mistaking one kind of use for another; the fact that a person speaking a language of a structure entirely different from that of English, such as Japanese, Chinese, or Turkish, may not even think the same thoughts as an English-speaking person—these are unfamiliar notions to Mr. Mits, who has always assumed that the important thing is always to get one's "ideas" straight first, after which the words would take care of themselves.

Whether he realizes it or not, however, Mr. Mits is affected every hour of his life not only by the words he hears and uses, *but also by his unconscious assumptions about language.* If, for example, he likes the name "Albert" and would like to christen his child by that name but superstitiously avoids doing so because he once knew an "Albert" who committed suicide, he is operating, whether he realizes it or not, under certain assumptions about the relationship of language to reality. Such unconscious assumptions determine the effect that words have on him—which in turn determines the way he acts, whether wisely or foolishly. Words—the way he uses them and the way he takes them when spoken by others—largely shape his beliefs, his prejudices, his ideals, his aspirations. They constitute the moral and intellectual atmosphere in which he lives—in short, his *semantic environment*.

This book is devoted, then, to the study of the relationships between language, thought, and behavior. We shall examine language and people's linguistic habits as they reveal themselves in thinking (at least nine-tenths of which is talking to oneself), speaking, listening, reading, and writing. *It will be the basic assumption of this book that widespread intraspecific co-operation through the use of language is the fundamental mechanism of human survival. A parallel assumption will be that when the use of language results, as it so often does, in the creation or aggravation of disagreements and conflicts, there is something wrong with the speaker, the listener, or both.* Human "fitness to survive" means the ability to talk and write and listen and read in ways that increase the chances for you *and fellow-members of your species* to survive *together*.

Applications

Since one of the purposes of this book is to help the reader understand more clearly how language works and how this understanding can be applied to the practical situations of life, the reader will find at the end of each chapter a section entitled "Applications." Some of these are designed to enable the reader to test how clearly he has understood what the author is saying in the chapter; others suggest operations or activities by which the reader can experimentally test out some of the ideas set forth.

In those Applications where the reader is invited to analyze examples of language in action, it should be emphasized that there is seldom one— and only one—"right answer." The point is, rather, to become conscious of what is going on: what silent assumptions of the speaker or writer and of the listener or reader appear to be involved in a given example.

If the reader discusses his analyses or experiments with others who are reading this book, he should try to avoid hair-splitting and verbal free-for-alls. It is well to be able to give a clear account of one's reasons for reaching a certain result, but one can learn a great deal by listening carefully to what others did and what *their* reasons are for *their* conclusions.

The ideas in this book will be helpful in proportion as the reader puts them to the test of actual experience and decides for himself how valid and useful they are for his own thinking and living. The Applications throughout the book are simply starters in this direction, but it *is* important that what is read here be put to the test of experience.

We all tend to assume that what we have read without too much difficulty we have understood. This assumption is not, of course, always justified. The reader may find it interesting to check his own interpretative processes (and perhaps also the clarity of the writer's exposition) by going over the following list and indicating which statements *agree with,* which statements *disagree with,* and which statements *have no relation to* what has been said in this chapter.

1. Human beings should study the entire animal kingdom in order to find out which animals are most worth imitating.

2. Heathens believe in the law of the jungle; Christians do not.

3. The Battle of the Bulge is an example of *intraspecific* struggle.

4. Cockroach powder and DDT are weapons of *interspecific* struggle.

5. Intraspecific struggle must be replaced by co-operation if man is to survive as a species.

6. So far as we can observe, animals do not increase their store of knowledge from one generation to the next.

7. If you fall in love, you should read a good book.

8. Through language man is able to profit by the experience of the dead as well as the living members of his species.

9. There ought to be laws prohibiting strikes and lockouts.

10. Cultural and intellectual co-operation is the great principle of human life.

11. However, there is little prospect that human nature can be so altered as to make co-operation possible on a wide scale.

12. Because we are over-deluged with words, everybody should keep his mouth shut.

13. Man has little or no way of controlling his semantic environment.

14. Because language is so important people have got to learn to think more logically if they want to solve their problems.

15. Because language is so important, learning the correct definitions of words is basic to human survival.

16. Language, thought, and behavior are intimately related to each other.

17. When a discussion leads to increasing and deeper disagreement, there is something wrong with the language habits of one or more of the persons involved.

2. Symbols

This basic need, which certainly is obvious only in man, is the need of symbolization. The symbol-making function is one of man's primary activities, like eating, looking, or moving about. It is the fundamental process of the mind, and goes on all the time.
                                                    SUSANNE K. LANGER

Man's achievements rest upon the use of symbols.
                                                    ALFRED KORZYBSKI

The Symbolic Process

Animals struggle with each other for food or for leadership, but they do not, like human beings, struggle with each other for things that *stand for* food or leadership: such things as our paper symbols of wealth (money, bonds, titles), badges of rank to wear on our clothes, or low-number license plates, supposed by some people to stand for social precedence. For animals, the relationship in which one thing *stands for* something else does not appear to exist except in very rudimentary form.[1]

[1] One investigator, J. B. Wolfe, trained chimpanzees to put poker chips into an especially constructed vending machine ("chimpomat") which supplied grapes, bananas, and other food. The chimpanzees proved to be able to distinguish chips of different "values" (1 grape, 2 grapes, zero, and so on) and also proved to be willing to work for them if the rewards were fairly immediate. They tended, however, not to work as they accumulated more chips. Their "money system" was definitely limited to rudimentary and immediate transactions. See Robert M. Yerkes' *Chimpanzees: A Laboratory Colony* (Yale University Press, 1943).

Other examples of animals successfully learning to react meaningfully to things-that-stand-for-other-things can readily be offered, but as a general rule these animal reactions are extremely simple and limited when contrasted with human possibilities in this direction. For example, it appears likely that a chimpanzee might be taught to drive a simplified car, but there would be one thing wrong with its driving: its reactions are such that if a red light showed when it was half way across a street, it would stop in the middle of the crossing, while, if a green light showed when another car was stalled in its path, it would go ahead regardless of consequences. In other words, so far as such a chimpanzee would be concerned, the red light could hardly be said to *stand for* stop; it *is* stop.

The process by means of which human beings can arbitrarily make certain things *stand for* other things may be called the *symbolic process*. Whenever two or more human beings can communicate with each other, they can, by agreement, make anything stand for anything. For example, here are two symbols:

X   Y

We can agree to let X stand for buttons and Y stand for bows; then we can freely change our agreement and let X stand for the Chicago White Sox and Y for the Cincinnati Reds; or let X stand for Chaucer and Y for Shakespeare, X for the CIO and Y for the AFL. *We are, as human beings, uniquely free to manufacture and manipulate and assign values to our symbols as we please.* Indeed, we can go further by making symbols that stand for symbols. If necessary we can, for instance, let the symbol M stand for all the X's in the above example (buttons, White Sox, Chaucer, CIO) and let N stand for all the Y's (bows, Cincinnati Reds, Shakespeare, AFL). Then we can make another symbol, T, stand for M and N, which would be an instance of a symbol of symbols of symbols. This freedom to create symbols of *any* assigned value and to create *symbols that stand for symbols* is essential to what we call the symbolic process.

Everywhere we turn, we see the symbolic process at work. Feathers worn on the head or stripes on the sleeve can be made to stand for military leadership; cowrie shells or rings of brass or pieces of paper can stand for wealth; crossed sticks can stand for a set of religious beliefs; buttons, elks' teeth, ribbons, special styles of ornamental haircutting or tattooing, can stand for social affiliations. The symbolic process permeates human life at the most primitive as well as at the most civilized levels. Warriors, medicine men, policemen, doormen, telegraph boys, cardinals, and kings wear costumes that symbolize their occupations. Savages collect scalps, college students collect membership keys in honorary societies, to symbolize victories in their respective fields. There are few things that men do or want to do, possess or want to possess, that have not, in addition to their mechanical or biological value, a symbolic value.

All fashionable clothes, as Thorstein Veblen has pointed out in his *Theory of the Leisure Class* are highly symbolic: materials, cut, and ornament are dictated only to a slight degree by considerations of warmth, comfort, or practicability. The more we dress up in fine clothes, the more we restrict our freedom of action. But by means of delicate embroideries, easily soiled fabrics, starched shirts, high heels, long and pointed fingernails, and other such sacrifices of comfort, the wealthy classes manage to symbolize, among other things, the fact that they don't have to work for a living. The not-so-wealthy, on the other hand, by imitating these symbols of wealth, symbolize their conviction that, even if they do work for a living, they are just as good as anybody else. Again, we select our furniture to serve as visible symbols of our taste, wealth, and social position; we trade in perfectly good cars for later models, not always to get better transportation, but to give evidence to the community that we can afford such luxuries. We often choose our residences on the basis of a feeling that it "looks well" to have a "good address." We like to put expensive food on our tables, not always because it tastes better than cheap food, but because it tells our guests that we wish to do them honor.[2]

Such complicated and apparently unnecessary behavior leads philosophers, both amateur and professional, to ask over and over again, "Why can't human beings live simply and naturally?" Often the complexity of human life makes us look enviously at the relative simplicity of lives such as dogs and cats lead. But the symbolic process, which makes possible the absurdities of human conduct, also makes possible language and therefore all the human achievements dependent upon language. The fact that more things can go wrong with motorcars than with wheelbarrows is no reason for going back to wheelbarrows. Similarly, the fact that the symbolic process makes complicated follies possible is no reason for wanting to return to a cat-and-dog existence. A better solution is to understand the symbolic process so that instead of being its slaves we become, to some degree at least, its masters.

[2] The writer owns an eight-year-old car in good running condition. A friend of his, a repairman who knows the condition of the car, has been urging him to trade it in for a new model. "But why?" the writer asked. "The old car's in fine shape still." The repairman answered scornfully, "Yeah, but what the hell. All you've got is transportation." The writer is beginning to weaken.

Language as Symbolism

Of all forms of symbolism, language is the most highly developed, most subtle, and most complicated. It has been pointed out that human beings, by agreement, can make anything stand for anything. Now, human beings have agreed, in the course of centuries of mutual dependency, to let the various noises that they can produce with their lungs, throats, tongues, teeth, and lips systematically stand for specified happenings in their nervous systems. We call that system of agreements *language*. For example, we who speak English have been so trained that, when our nervous systems register the presence of a certain kind of animal, we may make the following noise: "There's a cat." Anyone hearing us expects to find that, by looking in the same direction, he will experience a similar event in his nervous system—one that will lead him to make an almost identical noise. Again, we have been so trained that when we are conscious of wanting food, we make the noise, "I'm hungry."

There is, as has been said, *no necessary connection between the symbol and that which is symbolized*. Just as men can wear yachting costumes without ever having been near a yacht, so they can make the noise, "I'm hungry," without being hungry. Furthermore, just as social rank can be symbolized by feathers in the hair, by tattooing on the breast, by gold ornaments on the watch chain, or by a thousand different devices according to the culture we live in, so the fact of being hungry can be symbolized by a thousand different noises according to the culture we live in: "J'ai faim," or "Es hungert mich," or "Ho appetito," or "Hara ga hetta," and so on.

However obvious these facts may appear at first glance, they are actually not so obvious as they seem except when we take special pains to think about the subject. Symbols and things symbolized are independent of each other; nevertheless, we all have a way of feeling as if, and sometimes acting as if, there were necessary connections. For example, there is the vague sense we all have that foreign languages are inherently absurd: foreigners have such funny names for things, and why can't they call things by their right names? This feeling exhibits itself most strongly in those English and American tourists who seem to believe that they can make the natives of any country understand English if they shout loud enough. Like the little boy who was reported to have said, "Pigs are called pigs because they are such dirty animals," they feel that the symbol is inherently connected in some way with the things symbolized. Then there are the people who feel that since snakes are "nasty, slimy creatures" (incidentally, snakes are *not* slimy), the word "snake" is a *nasty, slimy word*.

The Pitfalls of Drama

Naïveté regarding the symbolic process extends to symbols other than words, of course. In the case of drama (stage, movies, radio), there appear to be people in almost every audience who never quite fully realize that a play is a set of fictional, symbolic representations. An actor is one who *symbolizes* other people, real or imagined: Fredric March may, in a given play, enact the role of (symbolize) a drunkard. The fact that Mr. March can do so with extraordinary realism proves nothing about his drinking habits, if any. Nevertheless, there are movie-goers who, instead of admiring Mr. March's skill in acting, begin to feel sorry for Mrs. March who is, alas, married to such a heavy drinker! Lewis Stone, who often plays the part of a judge, often gets letters from fans asking for legal advice. James Cagney, who plays "tough guy" roles, is often challenged to fight by men who say to him, "Think you're tough, do you? Lemme show you!" It was said some years ago that when Edward G. Robinson, who plays gangster roles with extraordinary vividness, visited Chicago, local hoodlums telephoned him at his hotel to pay their professional respects.

One is reminded of the story of the actor, playing the part of a villain in a traveling theatrical troupe, who, at a particularly tense moment in the play, was shot by an overexcited cowpuncher in the audience. The cowpuncher of this story, however, is no more ridiculous than those thousands of people today, many of them adults, who write fan letters to a ventriloquist's dummy, or those goodhearted but impressionable people who send presents to the broadcasting station when two characters in a radio serial get married, or those astonishing patriots who rushed to recruiting offices to help defend the nation when, on October 30, 1938, the United States was "invaded" by an "army from Mars" in a radio dramatization.[3]

An extreme case of this kind is that of a woman who had a baby on the same day a fictitious baby was born to the heroine in her favorite soap-opera. She named her baby "Margaret" because the soap-opera "baby" was given that name. Some time later, the soap-opera "baby" "died." Thereupon the woman went into a state of inconsolable grief, being convinced that *her own baby* was dead. When her friends tried to convince her that *that* was her own baby, alive and howling right there beside her, she would not be consoled. "You can't fool me," she said. "Margaret is dead. I heard it on the radio." The woman was, of course, placed in a mental hospital—this was probably only one of many such misevaluations she was in the habit of making. Whatever else was wrong with her, one way of describing this particular misevaluation is to say that the words (in this case of the soap-opera) not only possessed for her the characteristics of reality, but *became a substitute reality completely shutting out the facts.*

The Word Is Not The Thing

The above, however, are only the more striking examples of confused attitudes toward words and symbols. There would be little point in mentioning them if we were *uniformly and permanently aware* of the independence of symbols from things symbolized, as all human beings, in the writer's opinion, *can be* and *should be.*[4]

[3] See Hadley Cantril's *The Invasion from Mars* (Princeton University Press, 1940); also John Houseman's "The Men from Mars," in *Harper's Magazine,* December 1948.

[4] Much of the make-believe activity of small children, even as young as two years, appears to arise from the spontaneous and joyous discovery of the symbolic process, involving clear distinctions between symbols and things symbolized and a pleasure in the independence and manipulability of symbols. A great deal of the natural wisdom of children is, however, snuffed out in the course of their education.

But we are not. Most of us have, in some area or other of our thinking, improper habits of evaluation. For this, society itself is often
to blame: most societies systematically encourage, concerning certain topics, the habitual confusion of symbols with things symbolized. For example, if a Japanese schoolhouse caught on fire, it used
to be obligatory in the days of emperor-worship to try to rescue
the emperor's *picture* (there was one in every schoolhouse), even
at the risk of one's life. (If you got burned to death, you were
posthumously ennobled.) In our society, we are encouraged to go
into debt in order that we may display, as symbols of prosperity,
shiny new automobiles. Strangely enough, the possession of shiny
automobiles even under these conditions makes their "owners" *feel*
prosperous. In all civilized societies (and probably in many primitive ones as well), the symbols of piety, of civic virtue, or of patriotism are often prized above actual piety, civic virtue, or patriotism.
In one way or another, we are all like the brilliant student who
cheats in his exams in order to make Phi Beta Kappa: it is so much
more important to have the symbol than the things it stands for.

The habitual confusion of symbols with things symbolized,
whether on the part of individuals or societies, is serious enough at
all levels of culture to provide a perennial human problem.[5] But
with the rise of modern communications systems, there arises with
peculiar urgency the problem of confusion of verbal symbols with
realities. We are constantly being talked at, by teachers, preachers,
salesmen, public relations counsels, governmental agencies, and
moving-picture sound tracks. The cries of the hawkers of soft
drinks, soap chips, and laxatives pursue us into our homes, thanks
to the radio—and in some houses the radio is never turned off from
morning to night. The mailman brings direct mail advertising. Billboards confront us on the highway, and we even take portable
radios with us to the seashore.

We live in an environment shaped and largely created by hitherto
unparalleled semantic influences: mass circulation newspapers and
magazines which are given to reflecting, in a shocking number of

[5] The charge against the Pharisees, it will be remembered, was that they were
obsessively concerned with the symbols of piety at the expense of an adequate concern with its spirit.

cases, the weird prejudices and obsessions of their publishers and owners; radio programs, both local and network, almost completely dominated by commercial motives; public relations counsels, who are simply highly paid craftsmen in the art of manipulating and reshaping our semantic environment in ways favorable to their clients. It is an exciting environment, but fraught with danger: it is only a slight exaggeration to say that Hitler conquered Austria by radio.

Citizens of a modern society need, therefore, more than ordinary "common sense"—which was recently defined by Stuart Chase as that which tells you that the world is flat. They need to be scientifically aware of the powers and limitations of symbols, especially words, if they are to guard against being driven into complete bewilderment by the complexity of their semantic environment. The first of the principles governing symbols is this: The symbol is NOT the thing symbolized; the word is NOT the thing; the map is NOT the territory it stands for.

Maps and Territories

There is a sense in which we all live in two worlds. First, we live in the world of happenings about us which we know at first hand. But this is an extremely small world, consisting only of that continuum of the things that we have actually seen, felt, or heard— the flow of events constantly passing before our senses. So far as this world of personal experience is concerned, Africa, South America, Asia, Washington, New York, or Los Angeles do not exist if we have never been to these places. Chiang Kai-shek is only a name if we have never seen him. When we ask ourselves how much we know at first hand, we discover that we know very little indeed.

Most of our knowledge, acquired from parents, friends, schools, newspapers, books, conversation, speeches, and radio, is received *verbally*. All our knowledge of history, for example, comes to us only in words. The only proof we have that the Battle of Waterloo ever took place is that we have had reports to that effect. These reports are not given us by people who saw it happen, but are based

on other reports: reports of reports of reports, which go back ultimately to the first-hand reports given by people who did see it happening. It is through reports, then, and through reports of reports,
that we receive most knowledge: about government, about what is
happening in China, about what picture is showing at the down-
town theater—in fact, about anything which we do not know
through direct experience.

Let us call this world that comes to us through words the *verbal
world,* as opposed to the world we know or are capable of knowing
through our own experience, which we shall call the *extensional
world.* (The reason for the choice of the word "extensional" will
become clear later.) The human being, like any other creature, begins
to make his acquaintance with the extensional world from infancy.
Unlike other creatures, however, he begins to receive, as soon as he
can learn to understand, reports, reports of reports, reports of reports
of reports. In addition he receives inferences made from reports,
inferences made from other inferences, and so on. By the time a
child is a few years old, has gone to school and to Sunday school,
and has made a few friends, he has accumulated a considerable
amount of second- and third-hand information about morals, geography, history, nature, people, games—all of which information together constitutes his verbal world.

Now this verbal world ought to stand in relation to the extensional world as a *map* does to the *territory* it is supposed to represent. If a child grows to adulthood with a verbal world in his head
which corresponds fairly closely to the extensional world that he
finds around him in his widening experience, he is in relatively
small danger of being shocked or hurt by what he finds, because
his verbal world has told him what, more or less, to expect. He is
prepared for life. If, however, he grows up with a false map in
his head—that is, with a head crammed with false knowledge and
superstition—he will constantly be running into trouble, wasting his
efforts, and acting like a fool. He will not be adjusted to the world
as it is; he may, if the lack of adjustment is serious, end up in a
mental hospital.

Some of the follies we commit because of false maps in our heads
are so commonplace that we do not even think of them as remark-

able. There are those who protect themselves from accidents by carrying a rabbit's foot in the pocket. Some refuse to sleep on the thirteenth floor of hotels—this is so common that most big hotels, even in the capitals of our scientific culture, skip "13" in numbering their floors. Some plan their lives on the basis of astrological predictions. Some play fifty-to-one shots on the basis of dream books. Some hope to make their teeth whiter by changing their brand of tooth paste. All such people are living in verbal worlds that bear little, if any, resemblance to the extensional world.

Now, no matter how beautiful a map may be, it is useless to a traveler unless it accurately shows the relationship of places to each other, the structure of the territory. If we draw, for example, a big dent in the outline of a lake for, let us say, artistic reasons, the map is worthless. But if we are just drawing maps for fun without paying any attention to the structure of the region, there is nothing in the world to prevent us from putting in all the extra curlicues and twists we want in the lakes, rivers, and roads. No harm will be done *unless someone tries to plan a trip by such a map.*

Similarly, by means of imaginary or false reports, or by false inferences from good reports, or by mere rhetorical exercises, we can manufacture at will, with language, "maps" which have no reference to the extensional world. Here again no harm will be done unless someone makes the mistake of regarding such "maps" as representing real territories.

We all inherit a great deal of useless knowledge, and a great deal of misinformation and error (maps that were formerly thought to be accurate), so that there is always a portion of what we have been told that must be discarded. But the cultural heritage of our civilization that is transmitted to us—our socially pooled knowledge, both scientific and humane—has been valued principally because we have believed that it gives us accurate maps of experience. The analogy of verbal worlds to maps is an important one and will be referred to frequently throughout this book. It should be noticed at this point, however, that there are two ways of getting false maps of the world into our heads: first, by having them given to us; second, by making them up for ourselves by misreading the true maps given to us.

Applications

The reader who wants to put to work the ideas that are presented in this book would do well to start keeping a scrapbook or a filing folder or a set of 5 x 7 filing cards. Start a collection of quotations, newspaper clippings, editorials, anecdotes, and so forth, that illustrate in one way or another the confusion of symbols with things symbolized. The ensuing chapters of this book will suggest other kinds of confusion to look for. Look for those instances in which people seem to think that there are *necessary* connections between symbols and things symbolized —between words and what words stand for.

After a few such examples are collected and studied, the reader will be able to recognize readily similar patterns of thought in his contemporaries and friends and, perhaps, even in himself.

I. The following examples of language in action, taken from a variety of sources, are examples of what one should be on the lookout for. The reader should try to state explicitly what silent, unconscious assumptions about the relation of words (maps) to things (territories) seem to be guiding the writer or speaker in each case.

1. The gates of the 1933 Century of Progress Exposition at Chicago were opened, through the use of the photoelectric cell, by the light of the star, Arcturus. It is reported that a woman, on being told this, remarked, "Isn't it wonderful how those scientists know the names of all those stars!"

> SAMPLE ANALYSIS: Apparently this woman, on the basis of an unconscious assumption that there are necessary connections between names and things, believes that scientists discover a star's name by observing it very carefully. Come to think of it, how *do* stars get their names? Obviously, every star that has a name was *given* its name by somebody at some time. Apparently in ancient times people named stars after gods and goddesses, and star-clusters on the basis of accidental resemblances to known objects, like the Dipper and the Scales. Query: Do scientists have any more systematic ways of naming stars today? Surely they must. Check and find out. *Webster's New International Dictionary* or the *Encyclopædia Britannica* will help.

2. (A child is being questioned.) "Could the sun have been called 'moon' and the moon 'sun'?—*No.*—Why not?—*Because the sun shines brighter than the moon.* . . . But if everyone had called the sun 'moon' and the moon 'sun,' would we have known it was wrong?—*Yes, because the sun is always bigger, it always stays like it is and so does the moon.* —Yes, but the sun isn't changed, only its name. Could it have been called . . . etc.?—*No . . . Because the moon rises in the evening, and the sun in the day.*" —JEAN PIAGET, *The Child's Conception of the World*

3. The City Council of Cambridge, Massachusetts, unanimously passed a resolution (December 1939) making it illegal "to possess, harbor, sequester, introduce or transport, within the city limits, any book, map, magazine, newspaper, pamphlet, handbill or circular containing the words Lenin or Leningrad."

4. "State Senator John McNaboe of New York bitterly opposed a bill for the control of syphilis in May, 1937, because 'the innocence of children might be corrupted by a widespread use of the term. . . . This particular word creates a shudder in every decent woman and decent man.'" —STUART CHASE, *The Tyranny of Words*

5. A picture in the magazine *Life* (October 28, 1940), shows the backs of a sailor's hands, with the letters "H-O-L-D F-A-S-T" tattooed on the fingers. The caption explains, "This tattoo was supposed to keep sailors from falling off yardarm."

6. "New York (AP)—A man is facing death on a first-degree murder conviction by a General Sessions court jury in a fatal shooting growing out of what he called an insult to his dog. Testimony at the trial showed Christopher Maikish, 40, shot Vincent Conlon, a war veteran, last September in a restaurant.

"Witnesses said the trouble started when Conlon suggested Maikish take a half-eaten hamburger sandwich home to his dog. Maikish replied the dog would not eat hamburger and Conlon called the animal, a pure bred Doberman pinscher, a 'fussy mutt.' Because there was no recommendation of mercy, a sentence of death in the electric chair is mandatory." —Chicago *Daily News,* January 22, 1948

7. ". . . the Ukrainian delegate charged Greece had 'anti-democratic' motives in wanting to demilitarize the Bulgarian border. Philip Dragoumis, Greek undersecretary of foreign affairs, tartly replied, 'Democracy is a Greek word and Greece knows better than anyone else how to interpret it.'" —Unidentified newspaper clipping

8. "The naive attitude towards language may be illustrated by an experiment that was conducted with a group of high-school seniors. They were asked to explain why a dog is called a dog. Here are some of the curious and revealing answers: 'A dog is called a dog, I think, because when it was first seen it got its name because it was an easy word to pronounce.' 'The same reason that God is called God.' 'I think they called a dog a dog because they didn't have anything else to call it.' 'A dog is called dog for the simple reason that prehistoric man saw a strange animal running around and the sounds that came out of his mouth at that time resembled a dog. Hence a dog is called a dog.' 'I think a dog is called a dog because the name dog is given to the lowest form of animal. I mean a dog doesn't care where or how he does his dirt.' "

—CHARLES I. GLICKSBERG, in *ETC.: A Review of General Semantics*

9. "If you spell it backwards, it spells Nature's!"
—Patent medicine advertisement

II. Select a word which has a strong emotional charge (negative or positive), such as "spider," "gun," "math," or "Mexican," and describe the feelings which are associated with the term. Where did they come from? To what extent are these feelings based on reactions to the "map" and to what extent on an actual acquaintance with the "territory"?

III. Look around for some other examples, like the mother of Margaret referred to in this chapter, where someone is in danger of substituting fictitious maps for reality.

IV. Take an orange or an apple that bears no special distinguishing marks. Write a description of it in a couple of hundred words. Put your orange or apple in with a dozen or so similar oranges or apples, give the description to a friend and see if he can readily pick the one described from the others. Then let him write a description of another one and try to pick out the one he has described.

V. What makes a map a "good" map or a "bad" one, anyway? If an outline map of the United States had the following cities arranged in this fashion (the left standing for the west):

St. Louis   Washington   San Francisco

people would say it was an incorrect map. What would be the result of trying to follow such a map? What needs to be done to make it a correct map? Something more is involved than just putting the names

in the "right places." How do we know what the "right places" are?
The map is certainly *not* the territory but aren't there some similarities
between a correct map and the territory it stands for? Try to put into
words some of these similarities and see how well they apply to words
and the things that words stand for.

For further discussion see Alfred Korzybski, *Science and Sanity*
(Science Press, 1933), p. 750, or Wendell Johnson, *People in Quandaries*
(Harper, 1946), pp. 131-33.

VI. "A newspaper gives the reader the impression of being closer to
life than a book, and he is likely to confuse what he has read in it with
actual experiences he has not had.

"'You should have seen Charlie White,' a middle-aged bore may say
to me in a bar. '*He* had a left hook.'

"I too know that White had a left hook, because I read about it so
often, but it is no more or less likely that the fellow talking saw him
than that I saw Ty Cobb, about whose base-running I talk with the
same knowing ease. I don't think I ever did see Cobb, personally, but I
do know I saw Hans Wagner and Christy Mathewson in a game between the Pirates and Giants when I was small, and I can't remember
what either of them looked like on that particular day or what he did.
What I *know* about them, like what I know about Cobb, is simply the
cumulative product of newspaper stories and newspaper photographs,
and in that way I know as much about Cobb as I do about either.

"In the same way, the first President I actually saw was Warren
Gamaliel Harding, but he is a paler memory to me than the first Roosevelt, or Taft or Wilson. And it is incredible to me even now that I
never saw Franklin D. Roosevelt, who was nearly as much of a personal experience as my own father."

—A. J. LIEBLING, *The Wayward Pressman*

How much of what Mr. Liebling "knows" is "map-knowledge" and
how much is "territory-knowledge"? Recall some similar experiences
from your own reading and background.

3. The Language of Reports

To put it briefly, in human speech, different sounds have different meanings. To study this co-ordination of certain sounds with certain meanings is to study language. This co-ordination makes it possible for man to interact with great precision. When we tell someone, for instance, the address of a house he has never seen, we are doing something which no animal can do.
LEONARD BLOOMFIELD

Vague and insignificant forms of speech, and abuse of language, have so long passed for mysteries of science; and hard or misapplied words with little or no meaning have, by prescription, such a right to be mistaken for deep learning and height of speculation, that it will not be easy to persuade either those who speak or those who hear them, that they are but the covers of ignorance and hindrance of true knowledge. JOHN LOCKE

For the purposes of the interchange of information, the basic symbolic act is the *report* of what we have seen, heard, or felt: "There is a ditch on each side of the road." "You can get those at Smith's hardware store for $2.75." "There aren't any fish on that side of the lake, but there are on this side." Then there are reports of reports: "The longest waterfall in the world is Victoria Falls in Rhodesia." "The Battle of Hastings took place in 1066." "The papers say that there was a big smash-up on Highway 41 near Evansville." Reports adhere to the following rules: first, they are *capable of verification;* second, they *exclude,* as far as possible, *inferences* and *judgments.* (These terms will be defined later.)

Verifiability

Reports are verifiable. We may not always be able to verify them ourselves, since we cannot track down the evidence for every piece of history we know, nor can we all go to Evansville to see the remains of the smash-up before they are cleared away. But if we are roughly agreed on the names of things, on what constitutes a "foot," "yard," "bushel," and so on, and on how to measure time, there is relatively little danger of our misunderstanding each other. Even in a world such as we have today, in which everybody seems to be quarreling with everybody else, *we still to a surprising degree trust each other's reports*. We ask directions of total strangers when we are traveling. We follow directions on road signs without being suspicious of the people who put them up. We read books of information about science, mathematics, automotive engineering, travel, geography, the history of costume, and other such factual matters, and we usually assume that the author is doing his best to tell us as truly as he can what he knows. And we are safe in so assuming most of the time. With the emphasis that is being given today to the discussion of biased newspapers, propagandists, and the general untrustworthiness of many of the communications we receive, we are likely to forget that we still have an enormous amount of reliable information available and that deliberate misinformation, except in warfare, still is more the exception than the rule. The desire for self-preservation that compelled men to evolve means for the exchange of information also compels them to regard the giving of false information as profoundly reprehensible.

At its highest development, the language of reports is the language of science. By "highest development" we mean greatest general usefulness. Presbyterian and Catholic, workingman and capitalist, German and Englishman, *agree* on the meanings of such symbols as $2 \times 2 = 4$, $100°$ C., HNO_3, 3:35 A.M., 1940 A.D., 5000 *r.p.m.*, 1000 *kilowatts, pulex irritans,* and so on. But how, it may be asked, can there be agreement about even this much among people who are at each other's throats about practically everything else: political philosophies, ethical ideas, religious beliefs, and the survival of my business *versus* the survival of yours? The answer is that circumstances *compel men to agree,* whether they wish to or not. If, for example, there were a dozen different religious sects in the United States, each insisting on its own way of naming the time of the day and the days of the year, the mere necessity of having a dozen different calendars, a dozen different kinds of watches, and a dozen sets of schedules for business hours, trains, and radio programs, to say nothing of the effort that would be required for translating terms from one nomenclature to another, would make life as we know it impossible.[1]

The language of reports, then, including the more accurate reports of science, is "map" language, and because it gives us reasonably accurate representations of the "territory," it enables us to get work done. Such language may often be what is commonly termed "dull" or "uninteresting" reading: one does not usually read logarithmic tables or telephone directories for entertainment. But we could not get along without it. There are numberless occasions in the talking and writing we do in everyday life that *require that we state things in such a way that everybody will agree with our formulation.*

---

[1] According to information supplied by the Association of American Railroads, "Before 1883 there were nearly 100 different time zones in the United States. It wasn't until November 18 of that year that . . . a system of standard time was adopted here and in Canada. Before then there was nothing but local or 'solar' time. . . . The Pennsylvania Railroad in the East used Philadelphia time, which was five minutes slower than New York time and five minutes faster than Baltimore time. The Baltimore & Ohio used Baltimore time for trains running out of Baltimore, Columbus time for Ohio, Vincennes (Indiana) time for those going out of Cincinnati. . . . When it was noon in Chicago, it was 12:31 in Pittsburgh; 12:24 in Cleveland; 12:17 in Toledo; 12:13 in Cincinnati; 12:09 in Louisville; 12:07 in Indianapolis; 11:50 in St. Louis; 11:48 in Dubuque; 11:39 in St. Paul, and 11:27 in Omaha. There were 27 local time zones in Michigan alone. . . . A person traveling from Eastport, Maine, to San Francisco, if he wanted always to have the right railroad time and get off at the right place, had to twist the hands of his watch 20 times en route." Chicago *Daily News,* September 29, 1948.

Inferences

The reader will find that practice in writing reports is a quick means of increasing his linguistic awareness. It is an exercise which will constantly provide him with his own examples of the principles of language and interpretation under discussion. The reports should be about first-hand experience—scenes the reader has witnessed himself, meetings and social events he has taken part in, people he knows well. They should be of such a nature that they can be verified and agreed upon. For the purpose of this exercise, inferences will be excluded.

Not that inferences are not important—we rely in everyday life and in science as much on *inferences* as on reports—in some areas of thought, for example, geology, paleontology, and nuclear physics, reports are the foundations, but inferences (and inferences upon inferences) are the main body of the science. An inference, as we shall use the term, is *a statement about the unknown made on the basis of the known.* We may *infer* from the handsomeness of a woman's clothes her wealth or social position; we may *infer* from the character of the ruins the origin of the fire that destroyed the building; we may *infer* from a man's calloused hands the nature of his occupation; we may *infer* from a senator's vote on an armaments bill his attitude toward Russia; we may *infer* from the structure of the land the path of a prehistoric glacier; we may *infer* from a halo on an unexposed photographic plate that it has been in the vicinity of radioactive materials; we may *infer* from the noise an engine makes the condition of its connecting rods. Inferences may be carelessly or carefully made. They may be made on the basis of a great background of previous experience with the subject-matter, or no experience at all. For example, the inferences a good mechanic can make about the internal condition of a motor by listening to it are often startlingly accurate, while the inferences made by an amateur (if he tries to make any) may be entirely wrong. But the common characteristic of inferences is that they are statements about matters which are not directly known, made on the basis of what has been observed.

The avoidance of inferences in our suggested practice in report-writing requires that we make no guesses as to what is going on in other people's minds. When we say, "He was angry," we are not reporting; we are making an inference from such observable facts as the following: "He pounded his fist on the table; he swore; he threw the telephone directory at his stenographer." In this particular example, the inference appears to be fairly safe; nevertheless, it is important to remember, especially for the purposes of training oneself, that it is an inference. Such expressions as "He thought a lot of himself," "He was scared of girls," "He has an inferiority complex," made on the basis of casual social observation, and "What Russia really wants to do is to establish a world communist dictatorship," made on the basis of casual newspaper reading, are highly inferential. One should keep in mind their inferential character and, in our suggested exercises, should substitute for them such statements as "He rarely spoke to subordinates in the plant," "I saw him at a party, and he never danced except when one of the girls asked him to," "He wouldn't apply for the scholarship although I believe he could have won it easily," and "The Russian delegation to the United Nations has asked for A, B, and C. Last year they voted against M and N, and voted for X and Y. On the basis of facts such as these, the newspaper I read makes the inference that what Russia really wants is to establish a world communist dictatorship. I tend to agree."

Judgments

In our suggested writing exercise, judgments are also to be excluded. By judgments, we shall mean *all expressions of the writer's approval or disapproval of the occurrences, persons, or objects he is describing*. For example, a report cannot say, "It was a wonderful car," but must say something like this: "It has been driven 50,000 miles and has never required any repairs." Again statements like "Jack lied to us" must be suppressed in favor of the more verifiable statement, "Jack told us he didn't have the keys to his car with him. However, when he pulled a handkerchief out of his pocket a few minutes later, a bunch of car keys fell out." Also a report may not say, "The senator was stubborn, defiant, and unco-operative," or "The senator courageously stood by his principles"; it must say instead, "The senator's vote was the only one against the bill."

Many people regard statements like the following as statements of "fact": "Jack *lied* to us," "Jerry is a *thief*," "Tommy is *clever*." As ordinarily employed, however, the word "lied" involves first an inference (that Jack knew otherwise and deliberately misstated the facts) and secondly a judgment (that the speaker disapproves of what he has inferred that Jack did). In the other two instances, we may substitute such expressions as, "Jerry was convicted of theft and served two years at Waupun," and "Tommy plays the violin, leads his class in school, and is captain of the debating team." After all, to say of a man that he is a "thief" is to say in effect, "He has stolen *and will steal again*"—which is more of a prediction than a report. Even to say, "He has stolen," is to make an inference (and simultaneously to pass a judgment) on an act about which there may be difference of opinion among those who have examined the evidence upon which the conviction was obtained. But to say that he was "convicted of theft" is to make a statement capable of being agreed upon through verification in court and prison records.

Scientific verifiability rests upon the external observation of facts, not upon the heaping up of judgments. If one person says, "Peter is a deadbeat," and another says, "I think so too," the statement has not been verified. In court cases, considerable trouble is sometimes caused by witnesses who cannot distinguish their judgments from the facts upon which those judgments are based. Cross-examinations under these circumstances go something like this:

WITNESS: That dirty double-crosser Jacobs ratted on me.
DEFENSE ATTORNEY: Your honor, I object.
JUDGE: Objection sustained. (Witness's remark is stricken from the record.) Now, try to tell the court exactly what happened.
WITNESS: He double-crossed me, the dirty, lying rat!
DEFENSE ATTORNEY: Your honor, I object!
JUDGE: Objection sustained. (Witness's remark is again stricken from the record.) Will the witness try to stick to the facts.

WITNESS: But I'm telling you the facts, your honor. He did double-cross me.

This can continue indefinitely unless the cross-examiner exercises some ingenuity in order to get at the facts behind the judgment. To the witness it is a "fact" that he was "double-crossed." Often hours of patient questioning are required before the factual bases of the judgment are revealed.

Many words, of course, simultaneously convey a report and a judgment on the fact reported, as will be discussed more fully in a later chapter. For the purposes of a report as here defined, these should be avoided. Instead of "sneaked in," one might say "entered quietly"; instead of "politicians," "congressmen," or "aldermen," or "candidates for office"; instead of "bureaucrat," "public official"; instead of "tramp," "homeless unemployed"; instead of "dictatorial set-up," "centralized authority"; instead of "crackpots," "holders of uncommon views." A newspaper reporter, for example, is not permitted to write, "A crowd of suckers came to listen to Senator Smith last evening in that rickety firetrap and ex-dive that disfigures the south edge of town." Instead he says, "Between seventy-five and a hundred people heard an address last evening by Senator Smith at the Evergreen Gardens near the South Side city limits."

Snarl-Words and Purr-Words

Throughout this book, it is important to remember that we are considering language not as an isolated phenomenon, but language in action—language in the full context of the nonlinguistic events which are its setting. The making of noises with the vocal organs is a muscular activity, and like other muscular activities, often involuntary. Our responses to powerful stimuli, such as to something that makes us very angry, are a complex of muscular and physiological events: the contracting of fighting muscles, the increase of blood pressure, change in body chemistry, clutching one's hair, and so on, *and* the making of noises, such as growls and snarls. We are a little too dignified, perhaps, to growl like dogs, but we do the next best thing and substitute series of words, such as "You dirty double-crosser!" "The filthy scum!" Similarly, if we are pleasurably agitated, we may, instead of purring or wagging the tail, say things like "She's the sweetest girl in all the world!"

Speeches such as these are, as direct expressions of approval or disapproval, judgments in their simplest form. They may be said to be human equivalents of snarling and purring. "She's the sweetest girl in all the world" is not a statement about the girl; it is a purr. This seems to be a fairly obvious fact; nevertheless, it is surprising how often, when such a statement is made, both the speaker and the hearer feel that something has been said about the girl. This error is especially common in the interpretation of utterances of orators and editorialists in some of their more excited denunciations of "Reds," "greedy monopolists," "Wall Street," "radicals," "foreign ideologies," and in their more fulsome dithyrambs about "our way of life." Constantly, because of the impressive sound of the words, the elaborate structure of the sentences, and the appearance of intellectual progression, we get the feeling that something is being said about something. On closer examination, however, we discover that these utterances merely say, "What I hate ('Reds,' 'Wall Street,' or whatever) I hate very, very much," and "What I like ('our way of life') I like very, very much." We may call such utterances "snarl-words" and "purr-words." They are not reports describing conditions in the extensional world in any way.

To call these judgments "snarl-words" and "purr-words" does not mean that we should simply shrug them off. It means that we should be careful to *allocate the meaning correctly*—placing such a statement as "She's the sweetest girl in the world" as a revelation of the speaker's state of mind, and not as a revelation of facts about the girl. If the "snarl-words" about "Reds," or "greedy monopolists" are accompanied by verifiable reports (which would also mean that we have previously agreed as to who, specifically, is meant by the terms "Reds" or "greedy monopolists"), we might find reason to be just as disturbed as the speaker. If the "purr-words" about the sweetest girl in the world are accompanied by verifiable reports about her appearance, manners, skill in cooking, and so on, we might find reason to admire her too. But "snarl-words" and "purr-words" as such, unaccompanied by reports, offer nothing further to discuss, except possibly the question, "Why do you feel as you do?"

It is usually fruitless to debate such questions as "Was President Roosevelt a great statesman or merely a skillful politician?" "Is the music of Wagner the greatest music of all time or is it merely hysterical screeching?" "Which is the finer sport, tennis or baseball?" "Could Joe Louis in his prime have licked Bob Fitzsimmons in his prime?" To take sides on such issues of conflicting judgments is to reduce oneself to the same level of stubborn imbecility as one's opponents. But to ask questions of the form, "Why do you like (or dislike) Roosevelt (or Wagner, or tennis, or Joe Louis)?" is to learn something about one's friends and neighbors. After listening to their opinions and their reasons for them, we may leave the discussion slightly wiser, slightly better informed, and perhaps slightly less one-sided than we were before the discussion began.

How Judgments Stop Thought

A judgment ("He is a fine boy," "It was a beautiful service," "Baseball is a healthful sport," "She is an awful bore") is a conclusion, summing up a large number of previously observed facts. The reader is probably familiar with the fact that students almost always have difficulty in writing themes of the required length because their ideas give out after a paragraph or two. The reason for this is that those early paragraphs contain so many judgments that there is little left to be said. When the conclusions are carefully excluded, however, and observed facts are given instead, there is never any trouble about the length of papers; in fact, they tend to become too long, since inexperienced writers, when told to give facts, often give far more than are necessary, because they lack discrimination between the important and the trivial.

Still another consequence of judgments early in the course of a written exercise—and this applies also to hasty judgments in everyday thought—is the temporary blindness they induce. When, for example, an essay starts with the words, "He was a real Wall Street executive," or "She was a typical cute little co-ed," if we continue writing at all, we must make all our later statements consistent with those judgments. The result is that all the individual characteristics of this particular "executive" or this particular "co-ed" are lost sight of entirely; and the rest of the essay is likely to deal not with observed facts, but with the writer's private notion (based on previously read stories, movies, pictures, and so forth) of what "Wall Street executives" or "typical co-eds" look like. The premature judgment, that is, often prevents us from seeing what is directly in front of us. Even if the writer feels sure at the beginning of a written exercise that the man he is describing is a "loafer" or that the scene he is describing is a "beautiful residential suburb," he will conscientiously keep such notions out of his head, lest his vision be obstructed.

Slanting

In the course of writing reports of personal experiences, it will be found that in spite of all endeavors to keep judgments out, some will creep in. An account of a man, for example, may go like this: "He had apparently not shaved for several days, and his face and hands were covered with grime. His shoes were torn, and his coat, which was several sizes too small for him, was spotted with dried clay." Now, in spite of the fact that no judgment has been stated, a very obvious one is implied. Let us contrast this with another description of the same man. "Although his face was bearded and neglected, his eyes were clear, and he looked straight ahead as he walked rapidly down the road. He looked very tall; perhaps the fact that his coat was too small for him emphasized that impression. He was carrying a book under his left arm, and a small terrier ran at his heels." In this example, the impression about the same man is considerably changed, simply by the inclusion of new details and the subordination of unfavorable ones. Even if explicit judgments are kept out of one's writing, implied judgments will get in.

How, then, can we ever give an impartial report? The answer is, of course, that we cannot attain complete impartiality while we use the language of everyday life. Even with the very impersonal language of science, the task is sometimes difficult. Nevertheless, we can, by being aware of the favorable or unfavorable feelings that certain words and facts can arouse, attain enough impartiality for practical purposes. Such awareness enables us to balance the implied favorable and unfavorable judgments against each other. To learn to do this, it is a good idea to write two essays at a time on the same subject, both strict reports, to be read side by side: the first to contain facts and details likely to prejudice the reader in favor of the subject, the second to contain those likely to prejudice the reader against it. For example:

FOR	AGAINST
He had white teeth.	His teeth were uneven.
His eyes were blue, his hair blond and abundant.	He rarely looked people straight in the eye.
He had on a clean blue shirt.	His shirt was frayed at the cuffs.
He often helped his wife with the dishes.	He rarely got through drying dishes without breaking a few.
His pastor spoke very highly of him.	His grocer said he was always slow about paying his bills.

Slanting Both Ways at Once

This process of selecting details favorable or unfavorable to the subject being described may be termed slanting. Slanting gives no explicit judgments, but it differs from reporting in that it deliberately makes certain judgments inescapable. The writer striving for impartiality will, therefore, take care to slant both for and against his subject, trying as conscientiously as he can to keep the balance even. The next stage of the exercise, then, should be to rewrite the parallel essays into a single coherent essay in which details on both sides are included.

His teeth were white, but uneven; his eyes were blue, his hair blond and abundant. He did not often look people straight in the eye. His shirt was slightly frayed at the cuffs, but it was clean. He frequently helped his wife with the dishes, but he broke many of them. Opinion about him in the community was divided. His grocer said he was slow about paying his bills, but his pastor spoke very highly of him.

This example is, of course, oversimplified and admittedly not very graceful. But practice in writing such essays will first of all help to prevent one from slipping unconsciously from observable facts to judgments; that is, from "He was a member of the Ku Klux Klan" to "the dirty scoundrel!" Next, it will reveal how little we really want to be impartial anyway, especially about our best friends, our parents, our alma mater, our own children, our country, the company we work for, the product we sell, our competitor's product, or anything else in which our interests are deeply involved. Finally, we will discover that, even if we have no wish to be impartial, we write more clearly, more forcefully, and more convincingly by this process of sticking as close as possible to observable facts. There will be, as someone once remarked, more horsepower and less exhaust.

A few weeks of practice in writing reports, slanted reports, and reports slanted both ways will improve powers of observation, as well as ability to recognize soundness of observation in the writings of others. A sharpened sense for the distinction between facts and judgments, facts and inferences, will reduce susceptibility to the flurries of frenzied public opinion which certain people find it to their interest to arouse. Alarming judgments and inferences can be made to appear inevitable by means of skillfully slanted reports. A reader who is aware of the technique of slanting, however, is relatively difficult to stampede by such methods. He knows too well that there may be other relevant facts which have been left out.

Discovering One's Bias

Here, however, a caution is necessary. When a newspaper tells a story in a way that we dislike, leaving out facts we think important and playing up unimportant facts in ways that we think unfair, we are often tempted to say, "Look how they've slanted the story! What a dirty trick!" In making such a statement we are, of course, making an inference about the newspaper's editors. We are assuming that what seems important or unimportant to us seems equally important or unimportant to them, and on the basis of that assumption we are inferring that the editors "deliberately" gave the story a misleading emphasis. Is this necessarily the case? Can the reader, as an outsider, say whether a story assumes a given form because the editors "deliberately slanted it that way" or because that was the way the events appeared to them?

The point is that, by the process of selection and abstraction imposed on us by our own interests and background, experience comes to all of us (including newspaper editors) already "slanted." If you happen to be pro-CIO, pro-Catholic, and a midget-auto racing fan, your ideas of what is important or unimportant will of necessity be different from those of a man who happens to be indifferent to all three of your favorite interests. If, then, some newspapers often seem to side with the big businessman on public issues, the reason is less a matter of "deliberate" slanting than the fact that publishers are often, in enterprises as large as modern urban newspapers, big businessmen themselves, accustomed both in work and in social life to associating with other big businessmen. Nevertheless, the best newspapers, whether owned by "big businessmen" or not, often do try to tell us as accurately as possible what is going on in the world, because they are run by newspapermen who conceive it to be part of their professional responsibility to present fairly the conflicting points of view in controversial issues. Such newspapermen are *reporters* indeed.

But to get back to our exercises—the importance of trying to "slant both ways" lies not in the hope of achieving a godlike impartiality in one's thinking and writing—which is manifestly an impossible goal. It lies in discovering what poor reporters most of us really are—in other words, how little we see of the world since we of necessity see it from our own point of view. To discover one's own biases is the beginning of wisdom.

If one man says, "Co-operatives will be the salvation of America," and another replies, "Co-operatives are un-American," they might as well stop talking right there. If, however, one says, "Co-operatives seem to me, *from where I sit,* to offer a solution to our problems," and the other says, *"From where I sit,* they look like a pretty vicious institution," the possibility of further communication between the two remains. "Whenever agreement or assent is arrived at in human affairs . . . this agreement is reached by linguistic processes, or else it is not reached." To be aware of one's own "slant" and to be able to make allowances for it is to remain capable of continuing those linguistic processes that may eventually lead to agreement.

Applications

I. Here are a number of statements which the reader may attempt to classify as judgments, inferences, or reports. Since the distinctions are not always clear-cut, a one-word answer will not ordinarily be adequate. Note that we are concerned here with the nature of the statements, not their truth or falsity; for example, the statement, "Water freezes at 10° Centigrade," is, although inaccurate, a report.

1. She goes to church only in order to show off her clothes.

   SAMPLE ANALYSIS: In usual circumstances under which such a statement would be made, this would be an *inference,* since people ordinarily would not admit that they go to church for that reason. A *judgment* is also strongly implied, since it is assumed that one ought to have better reasons.

2. There is something essentially unclean about eating meat and fish.

3. Cary Grant has lots of personality.

4. "Rough-grained Split Leather Brief Case; artificial leather gussets. 3 position lock with key. 16 x 11 in. Color: black or brown. Shpg. wt. 2 lbs. Price, $4.86."　　　　　—Sears, Roebuck and Company Catalog

5. 　　　　　"Commuter—one who spends his life
   　　　　　In riding to and from his wife;
   　　　　　A man who shaves and takes a train
   　　　　　And then rides back to shave again."
   　　　　　　　　—E. B. WHITE

6. To commit murder is wrong under all circumstances.

7. The Russian people do not want war.

8. He is a typical bureaucrat.

9. An intelligent man makes his own opportunities.

10. The senator's support of the bill was a move to catch the veteran vote.

11. "This is the eve of the meeting in Philadelphia of the traitors, tatter-demalions, political degenerates and imbeciles and the leaven of gullible innocents who have adopted Henry Wallace as a composite fool and mahatma for the campaign of 1948. To the Communists, he is a fool. To the few earnest fools in his following, he is a Guru. They are holding a convention according to the regular American political forms, but with some variations, to nominate as their candidate for President the candidate of Josef Stalin."

—WESTBROOK PEGLER, in his column of July 22, 1948

12. "Was there really a pressing national emergency? Harry Truman said there was. But who was talking—the President or the politician? Harry Truman's call for a special session of Congress was made at a political convention; it would be judged largely on its political motives and for its political effect. Harry Truman, who, like all Presidents, occupies a dual position as head of the Government and leader of a political party, had used his powers as President to further his party's fortune.

"The maneuver was almost unprecedented. Not since 1856 had a President called back Congress in an election year. It was a daring stroke of political chicanery. . . ."   —Time, July 26, 1948

13.   "That time of year thou may'st in me behold
When yellow leaves, or few, or none do hang
Upon those boughs that shake against the cold,
Bare ruined choirs where late the sweet birds sang."

—WILLIAM SHAKESPEARE

14. "And Adam lived an hundred and thirty years, and begat a son in his likeness, after his image; and called his name Seth: And the days of Adam after he had begotten Seth were eight hundred years: and he begat sons and daughters: And all the days that Adam lived were nine hundred and thirty years: and he died."   —Genesis 5:3-5

II. In addition to trying such exercises in report writing and the exclusion of judgments and inferences as are suggested in this chapter, the reader might try writing (a) reports heavily slanted *against* persons or organizations he *likes,* and (b) reports heavily slanted *in favor of* persons or organizations he *dislikes*. For example, imagine that your luncheon club or fraternity or lodge is a subversive organization and report all the facts about its activities and members upon which unfavorable inferences could be made; or imagine that one of your most disagreeable neighbors has been offered a job two thousand miles away and write a factual letter of recommendation to help him get the job. Such exercises are a necessary preliminary to "slanting both ways at once," which is obviously an impossible task for anyone who sees things in only one way.

III. "Harry Thompson visited Russia in 1935"; "Rex Davis is a millionaire"; "Betty Armstrong does not believe in God." Accepting these three statements as true, write several hundred words of unfounded inferences, and inferences upon inferences, about these people. Of course, you don't know who Harry Thompson, Rex Davis, and Betty Armstrong are, but don't let that stop you. Just go ahead and make inferences.

IV. Selecting a subject about which you are almost completely uninformed, such as "Whither Modern Youth?" "The Evils of Bureaucracy," "The CIO: a Threat to the American Way," "The National Association of Manufacturers: a Threat to Democracy," "The Future of Women," "Let's Cut Out the Fads and Frills in Education," or "The South: Yesterday and Today," write a one-thousand-word essay consisting solely of sweeping generalizations, broad judgments, and unfounded inferences. Use plenty of "loaded" words. Knock off five points (out of a possible 100) for each verifiable fact used. If you can consistently score 95 or better on all these and other such topics, and your grammar and spelling are plausible, quit your present job. Fame and fortune are within your grasp.

4. Contexts

[*On being asked to define New Orleans jazz*]: *"Man, when you got to ask what it is, you'll never get to know."*

LOUIS ARMSTRONG

Dictionary definitions frequently offer verbal substitutes for an unknown term which only conceal a lack of real understanding. Thus a person might look up a foreign word and be quite satisfied with the meaning "bullfinch" without the slightest ability to identify or describe this bird. Understanding does not come through dealings with words alone, but rather with the things for which they stand. Dictionary definitions permit us to hide from ourselves and others the extent of our ignorance.

H. R. HUSE *

How Dictionaries Are Made

It is an almost universal belief that every word has a correct meaning, that we learn these meanings principally from teachers and grammarians (except that most of the time we don't bother to, so that we ordinarily speak "sloppy English"), and that dictionaries and grammars are the supreme authority in matters of meaning and usage. Few people ask by what authority the writers of dictionaries and grammars say what they say. The docility with which most people bow down to the dictionary is amazing, and the person who says, "Well, the dictionary is wrong!" is looked upon as out of his mind.

Let us see how dictionaries are made and how the editors arrive at definitions. What follows applies, incidentally, only to those dictionary offices where first-hand, original research goes on—not those in which editors simply copy existing dictionaries. The task of

---

* From *The Illiteracy of the Literate* by H. R. Huse, copyright, 1933, by D. Appleton-Century Company, Inc. Reprinted by permission of Appleton-Century-Crofts, Inc.

writing a dictionary begins with the reading of vast amounts of the literature of the period or subject that it is intended to cover. As the editors read, they copy on cards every interesting or rare word, every unusual or peculiar occurrence of a common word, a large number of common words in their ordinary uses, and also the sentences in which each of these words appears, thus:

---

pail

The dairy *pails* bring home increase of milk
Keats, *Endymion*
I, 44-45

That is to say, the context of each word is collected, along with the word itself. For a really big job of dictionary writing, such as the *Oxford English Dictionary* (usually bound in about twenty-five volumes), millions of such cards are collected, and the task of editing occupies decades. As the cards are collected, they are alphabetized and sorted. When the sorting is completed, there will be for each word anywhere from two to three to several hundred illustrative quotations, each on its card.

To define a word, then, the dictionary editor places before him the stack of cards illustrating that word; each of the cards represents an actual use of the word by a writer of some literary or historical importance. He reads the cards carefully, discards some, rereads the rest, and divides up the stack according to what he thinks are the several senses of the word. Finally, he writes his definitions, following the hard-and-fast rule that each definition *must* be based on what the quotations in front of him reveal about the meaning of the word. The editor cannot be influenced by what *he* thinks a given word *ought* to mean. He must work according to the cards, or not at all.

The writing of a dictionary, therefore, is not a task of setting up authoritative statements about the "true meanings" of words, but a task of *recording,* to the best of one's ability, what various words *have meant* to authors in the distant or immediate past. *The writer of a dictionary is a historian, not a lawgiver.* If, for example, we had been writing a dictionary in 1890, or even as late as 1919, we could have said that the word "broadcast" means "to scatter" (seed and so on) but we could not have decreed that from 1921 on, the commonest meaning of the word should become "to disseminate audible messages, etc., by wireless telephony." To regard the dictionary as an "authority," therefore, is to credit the dictionary writer with gifts of prophecy which neither he nor anyone else possesses. In choosing our words when we speak or write, we can be *guided* by the historical record afforded us by the dictionary, but we cannot be *bound* by it, because new situations, new experiences, new inventions, new feelings, are always compelling us to give new uses to old words. Looking under a "hood," we should ordinarily have found, five hundred years ago, a monk; today, we find a motorcar engine.

Verbal and Physical Contexts

The way in which the dictionary writer arrives at his definitions is merely the systematization of the way in which we all learn the meanings of words, beginning at infancy, and continuing for the rest of our lives. Let us say that we have never heard the word "oboe" before, and we overhear a conversation in which the following sentences occur:

He used to be the best *oboe* player in town. . . . Whenever they came to that *oboe* part in the third movement, he used to get very excited. . . . I saw him one day at the music shop, buying a new reed for his *oboe*. . . . He never liked to play the clarinet after he started playing the *oboe*. . . . He said it wasn't much fun, because it was too easy.

Although the word may be unfamiliar, its meaning becomes clear to us as we listen. After hearing the first sentence, we know that an "oboe" is "played," so that it must be either a game or a musical instrument. With the second sentence the possibility of its being a game is eliminated. With each succeeding sentence the possibilities as to what an "oboe" may be are narrowed down until we get a fairly clear idea of what is meant. This is how we learn by *verbal context.*

But even independently of this, we learn by physical and social context. Let us say that we are playing golf and that we have hit the ball in a certain way with certain unfortunate results, so that our companion says to us, "That's a bad *slice.*" He repeats this remark every time our ball fails to go straight. If we are reasonably bright, we learn in a very short time to say, when it happens again, "That's a bad slice." On one occasion, however, our friend says to us, "That's not a *slice* this time; that's a *hook.*" In this case we consider what has happened, and we wonder what is different about the last stroke from those previous. As soon as we make the distinction, we have added still another word to our vocabulary. The result is that after nine holes of golf, we can use both these words accurately—and perhaps several others as well, such as "divot," "number-five iron," "approach shot," *without ever having been told what they mean.* Indeed, we may play golf for years without ever being able to give a dictionary definition of "to slice": "To strike (the ball) so that the face of the club draws inward across the face of the ball, causing it to curve toward the right in flight (with a right-handed player)" (*Webster's New International Dictionary*). But even without being able to give such a definition, we should still be able to use the word accurately whenever the occasion demanded.

We learn the meanings of practically all our words (which are, it will be remembered, merely complicated noises), not from dictionaries, not from definitions, but from hearing these noises as they accompany actual situations in life and learning to associate certain noises with certain situations. Even as dogs learn to recognize "words," as for example by hearing "biscuit" at the same time as an actual biscuit is held before their noses, so do we all learn to interpret language by being aware of the happenings that accompany the noises people make at us—by being aware, in short, of contexts.

The definitions given by little children in school show clearly how they associate words with situations; they almost always define in terms of physical and social contexts: "Punishment is when you have been bad and they put you in a closet and don't let you have any supper." "Newspapers are what the paper boy brings and you wrap up the garbage with it." These are good definitions. The main reason that they cannot be used in dictionaries is that they are too specific; it would be impossible to list the myriads of situations in which every word has been used. For this reason, dictionaries give definitions on a high level of abstraction; that is, with particular references left out for the sake of conciseness. This is another reason why it is a great mistake to regard a dictionary definition as telling us all about a word.

Extensional and Intensional Meaning

From this point on, it will be necessary to employ some special terms in talking about meaning: *extensional meaning,* which will also be referred to as *denotation,* and *intensional meaning*—note the *s*—which will also be referred to as connotation. Briefly explained, the extensional meaning of an utterance is that which it *points to* or denotes in the extensional world, referred to in Chapter 2 above. That is to say, the extensional meaning is something that *cannot be expressed in words,* because it is that which words stand for. An easy way to remember this is to put your hand over your mouth and point whenever you are asked to give an extensional meaning.

The *intensional meaning* of a word or expression, on the other hand, is that which is *suggested* (connoted) inside one's head. Roughly speaking, whenever we express the meaning of words by uttering more words, we are giving intensional meaning, or connotations. To remember this, put your hand over your eyes and let the words spin around in your head.

Utterances may have, of course, both extensional and intensional meaning. If they have no intensional meaning at all—that is, if they start no notions whatever spinning about in our heads—they are meaningless noises, like foreign languages that we do not understand. On the other hand, it is possible for utterances to have no extensional meaning at all, in spite of the fact that they may start many notions spinning about in our heads. The statement, "Angels watch over my bed at night," is one that has intensional but no extensional meaning. This does not mean that there are no angels watching over my bed at night. When we say that the statement has no extensional meaning, we are merely saying that we cannot see, touch, photograph, or in any scientific manner detect the presence of angels. The result is that, if an argument begins on the subject whether or not angels watch over my bed, *there is no way of ending the argument to the satisfaction of all disputants,* the Christians and the non-Christians, the pious and the agnostic, the mystical and the scientific. Therefore, whether we believe in angels or not, knowing in advance that any argument on the subject will be both endless and futile, we can avoid getting into fights about it.

When, on the other hand, statements have extensional content, as when we say, "This room is fifteen feet long," arguments can come to a close. No matter how many guesses there are about the length of the room, all discussion ceases when someone produces a tape measure. This, then, is the important difference between extensional and intensional meanings: namely, when utterances have extensional meanings, discussion can be ended and agreement reached; when utterances have intensional meanings only and no extensional meanings, arguments may, and often do, go on indefinitely. Such arguments can result only in irreconcilable conflict.

Among individuals, they may result in the breaking up of friendships; in society, they often split organizations into bitterly opposed groups; among nations they may aggravate existing tensions so seriously as to become real obstacles to the peaceful settling of disputes.

Arguments of this kind may be termed "non-sense arguments," because they are based on utterances about which no sense data can be collected. Needless to say, there are occasions when the hyphen may be omitted—that depends on one's feelings toward the particular argument under consideration. The reader is requested to provide his own examples of "non-sense arguments." Even the foregoing example of the angels may give offense to some people, in spite of the fact that no attempt is made to deny or affirm the existence of angels. He can imagine, therefore, the uproar that might result from giving a number of examples from theology, politics, law, economics, literary criticism, and other fields in which it is not customary to distinguish clearly sense from non-sense.

The "One Word, One Meaning" Fallacy

Everyone, of course, who has ever given any thought to the meanings of words has noticed that they are always shifting and changing in meaning. Usually, people regard this as a misfortune, because it "leads to sloppy thinking" and "mental confusion." To remedy this condition, they are likely to suggest that we should all agree on "one meaning" for each word and use it only with that meaning. Thereupon it will occur to them that we simply cannot make people agree in this way, even if we could set up an ironclad dictatorship under a committee of lexicographers who would place censors in every newspaper office and microphones in every home. The situation, therefore, appears hopeless.

Such an impasse is avoided when we start with a new premise altogether—one of the premises upon which modern linguistic thought is based: namely, that *no word ever has exactly the same meaning twice.* The extent to which this premise fits the facts can be demonstrated in a number of ways. First, if we accept the proposition that the contexts of an utterance determine its meaning, it becomes apparent that since no two contexts are ever *exactly* the same, no two meanings can ever be exactly the same. How can we "fix the meaning" even for so common an expression as "to believe in" when it can be used in such sentences as the following:

I believe in you (I have confidence in you).
I believe in democracy (I accept the principles implied by the term democracy).
I believe in Santa Claus (It is my opinion that Santa Claus exists).

Secondly, we can take, for example, a word of "simple" meaning like "kettle." But when John says "kettle," its intensional meanings to him are the common characteristics of all the kettles John remembers. When Peter says "kettle," however, its intensional meanings to him are the common characteristics of all the kettles he remembers. *No matter how small or how negligible the differences may be between John's "kettle" and Peter's "kettle," there is some difference.*

Finally, let us examine utterances in terms of extensional meanings. If John, Peter, Harold, and George each say "my typewriter," we would have to point to four different typewriters to get the extensional meaning in each case: John's new Underwood, Peter's old Corona, Harold's L. C. Smith, and the undenotable intended "typewriter" that George plans some day to buy: "My typewriter, when I buy one, will be a noiseless." Also, if John says "my typewriter" today, and again "my typewriter" tomorrow, the extensional meaning is different in the two cases, because the typewriter is not exactly the same from one day to the next (nor from one minute to the next): slow processes of wear, change, and decay are going on constantly. Although we can say, then, that the differences in the meanings of a word on one occasion, on another occasion a minute later, and on still another occasion another minute later, are negligible, we cannot say that the meanings are *exactly* the same.

To say dogmatically that we know what a word means *in advance of its utterance* is nonsense. All we can know in advance is *approximately* what it will mean. After the utterance, we interpret what has been said in the light of both verbal and physical contexts, and act according to our interpretation. An examination of the verbal context of an utterance, as well as the examination of the utterance itself, directs us to the intensional meanings; an examination of the physical context directs us to the extensional meanings. When John says to James, "Bring me that book, will you?" James looks in the direction of John's pointed finger (physical context) and sees a desk with several books on it (physical context); he thinks back over their previous conversation (verbal context) and knows which of those books is being referred to.

Interpretation *must* be based, therefore, on the totality of contexts. If it were otherwise, we should not be able to account for the fact that even if we fail to use the right (customary) words in some situations, people can very frequently understand us. For example:

> A: Gosh, look at that second baseman go!
> B (looking): You mean the shortstop?
> A: Yes, that's what I mean.

> A: There must be something wrong with the oil line; the engine has started to balk.
> B: Don't you mean "gas line"?
> A: Yes—didn't I say gas line?

Contexts sometimes indicate so clearly what we mean that often we do not even have to say what we mean in order to be understood.

The Ignoring of Contexts

It is clear, then, that the ignoring of contexts in any act of interpretation is at best a stupid practice. At its worst, it can be a vicious practice. A common example is the sensational newspaper story in which a few words by a public personage are torn out of their context and made the basis of a completely misleading account. There is the incident of an Armistice Day speaker, a university teacher, who declared before a high-school assembly that the Gettysburg Address was "a powerful piece of propaganda." The context clearly revealed that "propaganda" was being used according to its dictionary meanings rather than according to its popular meanings;

it also revealed that the speaker was a very great admirer of Lincoln's. However, the local newspaper, completely ignoring the context, presented the account in such a way as to convey the impression that the speaker had called Lincoln a liar. On this basis, the newspaper began a campaign against the instructor. The speaker remonstrated with the editor of the newspaper, who replied, in effect, "I don't care what else you said. You said the Gettysburg Address was propaganda, didn't you?" This appeared to the editor complete proof that Lincoln had been maligned and that the speaker deserved to be discharged from his position at the university. Similar practices may be found in advertisements. A reviewer may be quoted on the jacket of a book as having said, "A brilliant work," while reading of the context may reveal that what he really said was, "It just falls short of being a brilliant work." There are some people who will always be able to find a defense for such a practice in saying, "But he did use the words, 'a brilliant work,' didn't he?"

People in the course of argument very frequently complain about words meaning different things to different people. Instead of complaining, they should accept it as a matter of course. It would be startling indeed if the word "justice," for example, were to have the same meaning to the nine justices of the United States Supreme Court; we should get nothing but unanimous decisions. It would be even more startling if "justice" meant the same to President Truman as to Joseph Stalin. If we can get deeply into our consciousness the principle that no word ever has the same meaning twice, we will develop the habit of automatically examining contexts, and this enables us to understand better what others are saying. As it is, however, we are all too likely, when a word sounds familiar, to assume that we understand it even when we don't. In this way we read into people's remarks meanings that were never intended. Then we waste energy in angrily accusing people of "intellectual dishonesty" or "abuse of words," when their only sin is that they use words in ways unlike our own, as they can hardly help doing, especially if their background has been widely different from ours. There are cases of intellectual dishonesty and the abuse of words, of course, but they do not always occur in the places where people think they do.

In the study of history or of cultures other than our own, contexts take on special importance. To say, "There was no running water or electricity in the house," does not condemn an English house in 1570, but says a great deal against a house in Chicago in 1949. Again, if we wish to understand the Constitution of the United States, it is not enough, as our historians now tell us, merely to look up all the words in the dictionary and to read the interpretations written by Supreme Court justices. We must see the Constitution in its historical context: the conditions of life, the current ideas, the fashionable prejudices, and the probable interests of the people who drafted the Constitution. After all, the words "The United States of America" stood for quite a different-sized nation and a different culture in 1790 from what they stand for today. When it comes to very big subjects, the range of contexts to be examined, verbal, social, and historical, may become very large indeed.

The Interaction of Words

All this is not to say, however, that the reader might just as well throw away his dictionary, since contexts are so important. Any word in a sentence—any sentence in a paragraph, any paragraph in a larger unit—whose meaning is revealed by its context, is itself part of the context of the rest of the text. To look up a word in a dictionary, therefore, frequently explains not only the word itself, but the rest of the sentence, paragraph, conversation, or essay in which it is found. All words within a given context interact upon one another.

Realizing, then, that a dictionary is a historical work, we should understand the dictionary thus: "The word *mother* has most frequently been used in the past among English-speaking people to indicate a female parent." From this we can safely infer, "If that is how it has been used, that is what it *probably* means in the sentence I am trying to understand." This is what we normally do, of course; after we look up a word in the dictionary, we re-examine the context to see if the definition fits. If the context reads, "Mother began to form in the bottle," one may have to look at the dictionary more carefully.

A dictionary definition, therefore, is an invaluable guide to interpretation. Words do not have a single "correct meaning"; they apply to *groups* of similar situations, which might be called *areas of meaning*. It is for definition in terms of areas of meaning that a dictionary is useful. In each use of any word, we examine the particular context and the extensional events denoted (if possible) to discover the *point* intended within the area of meaning.

Applications

I. If you were compiling a dictionary and had before you only the following quotations, what definition would you write for the word "shrdlu"? Don't just try to find a one-word synonym but write out a ten to twenty word definition.

1. He was exceptionally skillful with a shrdlu.
2. He says he needs a shrdlu to shape the beams.
3. I saw Mr. Jenkins yesterday buying a new handle for his shrdlu.
4. The steel head of Jenkins' shrdlu was badly chipped.
5. Don't bother with a saw or an ax; a shrdlu will do the job faster and better.

From the following quotations make up a definition in less than twenty words of "wanky."

1. He seems to be perpetually wanky.
2. Some people feel most wanky in the early morning but I get that way just before supper.
3. If you want to get over that wanky feeling, take Johnson's Homogenized Yeast Tablets.
4. Everybody feels more or less wanky on a hot, humid day.
5. . . . the wanky, wanky bluebell
   That droops upon its stem . . .
6. I am not cross, just wanky.

II. Two new terms—*extensional* and *intensional*—were introduced in this chapter and will be used frequently in the rest of this book. Some readers assume from the sound and the spelling that *extensional* comes from "extension" in the sense of "prolonging, stretching out" and that *intensional* comes from "intention" meaning "purpose or design." Those who are inclined to make such incorrect assumptions would do well to read again pages 54-58, asking, "What do these terms mean in this particular context?"

III. There are a number of words which, depending on their contexts, denote sometimes "the act of" and sometimes "the results of." For example, compare the word "building" in the following sentences:

a. The building of the stadium took three years.

b. The building which was completed in 1897 still stands.

In sentence *a* "building" refers to the "act of building," "the building process"; in sentence *b* it refers to a "finished building." Using the following words, compose parallel sentences in which the context makes clear a similar shift in meaning.

entertainment	creation
invention	destruction
knowledge	

IV. Which of the following in the contexts in which they are likely to occur are non-sense questions and which not? Can you tell why?

1. Is democracy a failure?

SAMPLE ANALYSIS: Unless there is reasonable agreement as to the extensional meaning of "democracy" and "failure," a discussion of this question is not likely to be fruitful. It might be broken up into smaller questions such as these: "Assuming that democracy is a success if 60 or more per cent of those able to vote in presidential elections do vote, what was the percentage of voters in the elections of 1940, 1944, 1948 . . . ?" "Assuming that democracy may be said to be reasonably successful if intelligent but underprivileged children are given the opportunity to finish their schooling, what percentage of fourth grade children with I.Q.'s of over 125 finish high school?" If, however, we talk chiefly in terms of intensional meanings of the terms "democracy" and "failure," disagreement and ill-feeling are likely to result. In many contexts where such a question is brought up for discussion, it would seem to be a non-sense question.)

2. Did Abraham Lincoln write the Gettysburg Address?
3. Why was I born?
4. Is Eisenhower a greater general than Napoleon?
5. Does Frank Sinatra earn more money than Bing Crosby?
6. Should women work after marriage?
7. What is the meaning of life?

8. Are whites more intelligent than Negroes?

9. Where do flies go in the wintertime?

10. Am I the first girl you ever kissed?

11. Will the position of the stars on March 29 be such as to augur a successful business trip if I start out on that date? My birthday is November 6.

12. Is the universe expanding?

13. "DEAR DOROTHY DIX: How can a wife tell when her husband loves her? I have been married ten years and my husband and I quarrel constantly. He beats me and swears at me, and then tells how much he loves me and cries over it all. Now I would like to leave him and go back to my folks, but he won't let me go. Says he can't bear to be separated from me. Please tell me what to do. Do you think he really loves me? —UNHAPPY WIFE." —Chicago *Sun-Times*, December 15, 1948

Read Wendell Johnson's discussion of non-sense questions in his book, *People in Quandaries* (Harper, 1946), pp. 289-92.

V. Keep a record of some arguments you overhear in the next twenty-four hours with these questions in mind:

1. What is the question at issue?

2. Is it a non-sense question or could it be answered by observation of the disputed facts?

3. To what extent do the participants reach agreement? If the argument ends in disagreement, can you think of any procedures that might have helped to bring about agreement?

VI. If you think you are clear about the "one word, one meaning" fallacy discussed in this chapter, try your hand at this problem:

"Some years ago, being with a camping party in the mountains, I returned from a solitary ramble to find everyone engaged in a ferocious metaphysical dispute. The corpus of the dispute was a squirrel—a live squirrel supposed to be clinging to one side of a tree-trunk; while over against the tree's opposite side a human being was imagined to stand. This human witness tries to get sight of the squirrel by moving rapidly around the tree, but no matter how fast he goes, the squirrel moves as fast in the opposite direction and always keeps the tree between himself and the man, so that never a glimpse of him is caught. The resultant metaphysical problem now is this: *Does the man go around the squirrel, or not?* He goes round the tree, sure enough, and the squirrel is on the tree; but does he go round the squirrel? In the unlimited leisure of the wilderness discussion had been worn threadbare. Everyone had taken sides, and was obstinate; and the numbers on both sides were even. Each side, when I appeared, therefore appealed to me to make it a majority. Mindful of the scholastic adage that whenever you meet a contradiction you must make a distinction, I immediately sought and found one, as follows. . . ."

—WILLIAM JAMES

Make a distinction that would help end the argument and show clearly the source of the dispute. Note also the different meanings of the word "opposite" in this passage.

VII. In any good standard dictionary, words are defined in terms of areas of meaning and, for most words, there are many *different* areas of meaning. See if you can provide contexts (in this case, sentences) that will make clear the different areas of meaning of the following words:

frame	open
strike	pink
cut	point

EXAMPLE: *pool.*

The brook formed a *pool* at the bend.

He lay in a *pool* of blood.

Let's go to the *pool* for a swim!

The wheat *pool* succeeded in sustaining the price of wheat.

He had the winning team in our baseball *pool.*

The balls clicked sharply on the *pool* table.

At the present time, it is not possible to *pool* the research findings of scientists all over the world.

VIII. Sit in a chair and say the words, "my chair," pointing to the object. Now, after moving to another chair, say again "my chair" and point to the object. Is the extensional meaning of the words still the same? Is the intensional meaning of the words still the same?

Take a sheet of paper and write your name half a dozen times. There are now before you six examples of the extensional meaning of the words "my signature." Compare them carefully. Are the extensional meanings in any two cases the same? Would they be the same if they were printed?

Take a piece of chewing gum from its wrapper and examine it carefully. Chew it for a time, then examine it again. Has the intensional meaning of "this chewing gum" been altered? How has the extensional meaning been affected?

5. The Language of Social Cohesion

> Two little dogs sat by the fire
> Over a fender of coal dust;
> Said one little dog to the other little dog,
> "If you don't talk, why, I must."
>
> MOTHER GOOSE

> *Are words in Phatic Communion* ["a type of speech in which *ties of union are created by a mere exchange of words"*] *used primarily to convey meaning, the meaning which is symbolically theirs? Certainly not! They fulfil a social function and that is their principal aim, but they are neither the result of intellectual reflection, nor do they necessarily arouse reflection in the listener.*
>
> BRONISLAW MALINOWSKI

Noises as Expression

What above all complicates the problems of interpretation is the fact that informative uses of language are intimately fused with older and deeper functions of language, so that only a small proportion of utterances in everyday life can be described as purely informative. We have every reason to believe that the ability to use language for strictly informative purposes was developed relatively late in the course of linguistic evolution. Long before we developed language as we now know it, we probably made, like the lower animals, all sorts of cries, expressive of such internal conditions as hunger, fear, loneliness, triumph, and sexual desire. We can recognize a variety of such noises and the conditions of which they are symptoms in our domestic animals. Gradually such noises seem to have become more and more differentiated, consciousness expanded.

Grunts and gibberings became language. Therefore, although we have developed language in which accurate reports may be given, we almost universally tend to *express* our internal condition *first,* then to follow up with a report if necessary: "Ow! (expression) My tooth hurts" (report). Many utterances are, as we have seen with regard to "snarl-words" and "purr-words," vocal equivalents of expressive gestures, such as crying in pain, baring the teeth in anger, nuzzling to express friendliness, dancing with delight, and so on. When words are used as vocal equivalents of expressive gestures, we shall say that language is being used in *presymbolic* ways. These presymbolic uses of language coexist with our symbolic systems, and the talking we do in everyday life is a thorough blending of symbolic and presymbolic.

Indeed, the presymbolic factors in everyday language are always most apparent in expressions of strong feeling of any kind. If we carelessly step off a curb when a car is coming, it doesn't much matter whether someone yells, "Look out!" or "Kiwotsuke!" or "Hey!" or "Prends garde!" or simply utters a scream, so long as whatever noise is made is uttered loudly enough to alarm us. It is the fear expressed in the *loudness* and *tone* of the cry that conveys the necessary sensations, and not the words. Similarly, commands given sharply and angrily usually produce quicker results than the same commands uttered tonelessly. The quality of the voice itself, that is to say, has a power of expressing feelings that is almost independent of the symbols used. We can say, "I hope you'll come to see us again," in a way that clearly indicates that we hope the visitor never comes back. Or again, if a young lady with whom we are strolling says, "The moon is bright tonight," we are able to tell by the tone whether she is making a meteorological observation or indicating that she wants to be kissed.

Very small infants understand the love, the warmth, or the irritation in a mother's voice long before they are able to understand her words. Most children retain this sensitivity to presymbolic factors in language. Some adults retain and refine this sensitivity as they grow older; they are the people credited with "intuition" or "unusual tact." Their talent lies in their skill in interpreting tones of voice, facial expressions, and other symptoms of the internal condition of the speaker: they listen not only to *what* is said, but to *how* it is said. On the other hand, people who have spent much of their lives in the study of *written* symbols (scientists, intellectuals, book-keepers) tend to be relatively deaf to everything but the surface sense of the words. If a lady wants a person of this kind to kiss her, she usually has to tell him so in so many words.

Noise for Noise's Sake

Sometimes we talk simply for the sake of hearing ourselves talk; that is, for the same reason that we play golf or dance. The activity gives us a pleasant sense of being alive. Children prattling, adults singing in the bathtub, are alike enjoying the sound of their voices. Sometimes large groups make noises together, as in group singing, group recitation, or group chanting, for similar presymbolic reasons. In all this, the significance of the words used is almost completely irrelevant. We may, for example, chant the most lugubrious words about a desire to be carried back to a childhood home in old Virginny, when in actuality we have never been there and haven't the slightest intention of going.

What we call social conversation is again largely presymbolic in character. When we are at a tea or dinner party, for example, we all have to talk—about anything: the weather, the performance of the Chicago White Sox, Thomas Mann's latest book, or Ingrid Bergman's last picture. It is typical of these conversations that, except among very good friends, few of the remarks made on these subjects are ever important enough to be worth making for their informative value. Nevertheless, it is regarded as rude to remain silent. Indeed, in such matters as greetings and farewells—"Good morning"—"Lovely day"—"And how's your family these days?"—"It was a pleasure meeting you"—"Do look us up the next time you're in town"—it is regarded as a social error not to say these things even if we do not mean them. There are numberless daily situations in which we talk simply because it would be impolite not to. Every social group has its own form of this kind of talking—"the art of conversation," "small talk," or the mutual kidding that

Americans love so much. From these social practices it is possible to state, as a general principle, that *the prevention of silence is itself an important function of speech,* and that it is completely impossible for us in society to talk only when we "have something to say."

This presymbolic talk for talk's sake is, like the cries of animals, a form of activity. We talk together about nothing at all and thereby establish friendships. The purpose of the talk is not the communication of information, as the symbols used would seem to imply ("I see the Dodgers are out in the lead again"), but the establishment of communion. Human beings have many ways of establishing communion among themselves: breaking bread together, playing games together, working together. But talking together is the most easily arranged of all these forms of collective activity. The *togetherness* of the talking, then, is the most important element in social conversation; the subject matter is only secondary.

There is a principle at work, therefore, in the selection of subject matter. Since the purpose of this kind of talk is the establishment of communion, *we are careful to select subjects about which agreement is immediately possible.* Consider, for example, what happens when two strangers feel the necessity or the desire to talk to each other:

"Nice day, isn't it?"

"It certainly is." (Agreement on one point has been established. It is safe to proceed.)

"Altogether, it's been a fine summer."

"Indeed it has. We had a nice spring, too." (Agreement on two points having been established, the second party invites agreement on a third point.)

"Yes, it was a lovely spring." (Third agreement reached.)

The togetherness, therefore, is not merely in the talking itself, but in the opinions expressed. Having agreed on the weather, we go on to further agreements—that it is nice farming country around here, that it certainly is scandalous how prices are going up, that New York is certainly an interesting place to visit but it would be awful to have to live there, and so on. *With each new agreement, no matter how commonplace or how obvious, the fear and sus-*

picion of the stranger wears away, and the possibility of friendship enlarges. When further conversation reveals that we have friends or political views or artistic tastes or hobbies in common, a friend is made, and genuine communication and co-operation can begin.

The Value of Unoriginal Remarks

An incident in the writer's own experience illustrates how necessary it sometimes is to give people the opportunity to agree. Early in 1942, a few weeks after the beginning of the war and at a time when rumors of Japanese spies were still widely current, he had to wait two or three hours in a small railroad station in a strange city. He became aware as time went on that the other people waiting in the station were staring at him suspiciously and feeling uneasy about his presence. One couple with a small child was staring with special uneasiness and whispering to each other. The writer therefore took occasion to remark to the husband that it was too bad that the train should be late on so cold a night. He agreed. The writer went on to remark that it must be especially difficult to travel with a small child in winter when train schedules were so uncertain. Again the husband agreed. The writer then asked the child's age and remarked that the child looked very big and strong for his age. Again agreement—this time with a slight smile. The tension was relaxing.

After two or three more exchanges, the man asked, "I hope you don't mind my bringing it up, but you're Japanese, aren't you? Do you think the Japs have any chance of winning this war?"

"Well," the writer replied, "your guess is as good as mine. I don't know any more than I read in the papers. (This was true.) But the way I figure it, I don't see how the Japanese, with their lack of coal and steel and oil and their limited industrial capacity, can ever beat a powerfully industrialized nation like the United States."

The writer's remark was admittedly neither original nor well-informed. Hundreds of radio commentators and editorial writers were saying exactly the same thing during those weeks. But because they were, the remark *sounded familiar* and was *on the right side,* so that it was easy to agree with. The man agreed at once, with what seemed like genuine relief. How much the wall of suspicion had broken down was indicated in his next question, "Say, I hope your folks aren't over there while the war is going on."

"Yes, they are. My father and mother and two young sisters are over there."

"Do you ever hear from them?"

"How can I?"

"Do you mean you won't be able to see them or hear from them till after the war is over?" Both he and his wife looked troubled and sympathetic.

There was more to the conversation, but the result was that within ten minutes after it had begun they had invited the writer to visit them in their city and have dinner with them in their home. And the other people in the station, seeing the writer in conversation with people who *didn't* look suspicious, ceased to pay any attention to him and went back to reading their papers and staring at the ceiling.[1]

Maintenance of Communication Lines

Such presymbolic uses of language not only establish new lines of communication, but keep old lines open. Old friends like to talk even when they have nothing especially to say to each other. In the same way that long-distance telephone operators, ship radio officers, and army signal corps outposts chatter with each other even when there are no official messages to communicate, so do people who live in the same household or work in the same office continue to talk to each other even when there is nothing much to say. The purpose in both cases seems to be partly to relieve tedium, but partly, and more importantly, to keep the lines of communication open.

[1] Perhaps it should be added that the writer was by no means *consciously* applying the principles of this chapter during the incident. This account is the result of later reflection. He was simply groping, as anyone else might do, for a way to relieve his own loneliness and discomfort in the situation.

Hence the situation between many a married couple:

WIFE: Wilbur, why don't you talk to me?

HUSBAND (interrupted in his reading of Schopenhauer or *The Racing Form*): What's that?

WIFE: Why don't you talk to me?

HUSBAND: But there isn't anything to say.

WIFE: You don't love me.

HUSBAND (thoroughly interrupted, and somewhat annoyed): Oh, don't be silly. You know I do. (Suddenly consumed by a passion for logic.) Do I run around with other women? Don't I turn my paycheck over to you? Don't I work my head off for you and the kids?

WIFE (way out on a logical limb, but still not satisfied): But still I wish you'd say something.

HUSBAND: Why?

WIFE: Well, because.

Of course, in a way the husband is right. His actions are an extensional demonstration of his love. They speak louder than words. But, in a different way, the wife is right. How does one know that the lines of communication are still open unless one keeps them at work? When a radio engineer says into a microphone, "One . . . two . . . three . . . four . . . testing . . ." he isn't saying anything much. But it is nevertheless important at times that he say it.

Presymbolic Language in Ritual

Sermons, political caucuses, conventions, "pep rallies," and other ceremonial gatherings illustrate the fact that all groups—religious, political, patriotic, scientific, and occupational—like to gather together at intervals for the purpose of sharing certain accustomed activities, wearing special costumes (vestments in religious organizations, regalia in lodges, uniforms in patriotic societies, and so on), eating together (banquets), displaying the flags, ribbons, or emblems of their group, and marching in processions. Among these ritual activities is always included a number of speeches, either traditionally worded or specially composed for the occasion, whose principal function is *not* to give the audience information it did not have before, *not* to create new ways of feeling, but something else altogether.

What this something else is, we shall analyze more fully in Chapter 7 on "The Language of Social Control." We can analyze now, however, one aspect of language as it appears in ritual speeches. Let us look at what happens at a "pep rally" such as precedes college football games. The members of "our team" are "introduced" to a crowd that already knows them. Called upon to make speeches, the players mutter a few incoherent and often ungrammatical remarks, which are received with wild applause. The leaders of the rally make fantastic promises about the mayhem to be performed on the opposing team the next day. The crowd utters "cheers," which normally consist of animalistic noises arranged in extremely primitive rhythms. *No one comes out any wiser or better informed than he was before he went in.*

To some extent religious ceremonies are equally puzzling at first glance. The priest or clergyman in charge utters set speeches, *often in a language incomprehensible to the congregation* (Hebrew in orthodox Jewish synagogues, Latin in the Roman Catholic Church, Sanskrit in Chinese and Japanese temples), with the result that, as often as not, no information whatsoever is communicated to those present.

If we approach these linguistic events from a detached point of view, and if also we examine our own reactions when we enter into the spirit of such occasions, we cannot help observing that, whatever the words used in ritual utterance may signify, we often do not think very much about their signification during the course of the ritual. Most of us, for example, have often repeated the Lord's Prayer or sung "The Star-Spangled Banner" without thinking about the words at all. As children we are taught to repeat such sets of words before we can understand them, and many of us continue to say them for the rest of our lives without bothering about their signification. Only the superficial, however, will dismiss these facts as "simply showing what fools human beings are." We cannot regard such utterances as "meaningless," because they have a genuine effect upon us. We may come out of church, for example, with no clear memory of what the sermon was about, but with a sense never-theless that the service has somehow "done us good."

What is the "good" that is done us in ritual utterances? It is the *reaffirmation of social cohesion:* the Christian feels closer to his fellow-Christians, the Elk feels more united with his brother Elks, the American feels more American and the Frenchman more French, as the result of these rituals. Societies are held together by such bonds of common reactions to sets of linguistic stimuli.

Ritualistic utterances, therefore, whether made up of words that have symbolic significance at other times, of words in foreign or obsolete tongues, or of meaningless syllables, may be regarded as consisting in large part of presymbolic uses of language: that is, *accustomed sets of noises* which convey no information, but to which feelings (often group feelings) are attached. Such utterances rarely make sense to anyone not a member of the group. The abra-cadabra of a lodge meeting is absurd to anyone not a member of the lodge. When language becomes ritual, that is to say, its effect becomes to a considerable extent independent of whatever signifi-cations the words once possessed.

Advice to the Literal-Minded

Presymbolic uses of language have this characteristic in common: their functions can be performed, if necessary, without the use of grammatically and syntactically articulated symbolic words. They can even be performed without recognizable speech at all. Group feeling may be established, for example, among animals by collec-tive barking or howling, and among human beings by college cheers, community singing, and such collective noise-making activi-ties. Indications of friendliness such as we give when we say "Good morning" or "Nice day, isn't it?" can be given by smiles, gestures, or, as among animals, by nuzzling or sniffing. Frowning, laughing, smiling, jumping up and down, can satisfy a large number of needs for expression, without the use of verbal symbols. But the use of verbal symbols is more customary among human beings, so that instead of expressing our feelings by knocking a man down, we often verbally blast him to perdition; instead of forming social groups by huddling together like puppies, we write constitutions and bylaws and invent rituals for the vocal expression of our cohesion.

To understand the presymbolic elements that enter into our everyday language is extremely important. We cannot restrict our speech to the giving and asking of factual information; we cannot confine ourselves strictly to statements that are literally true, or we should often be unable to say even "Pleased to meet you" when the occasion demanded. The intellectually persnickety often tell us that we ought to "say what we mean" and "mean what we say," and "talk only when we have something to talk about." These are, of course, impossible prescriptions.

Ignorance of the existence of these presymbolic uses of language is not so common among uneducated people (who often perceive such things intuitively) as it is among the educated. The educated often listen to the chatter at teas and receptions and conclude from the triviality of the conversation that all the guests (except themselves) are fools. They may discover that people often come away from church services without any clear memory of the sermon and conclude that churchgoers are either fools or hypocrites. They may hear political oratory and wonder "how anybody can believe such rot," and sometimes conclude therefrom that people in general are so unintelligent that it would be impossible for democracy to be made to work. Almost all such gloomy conclusions about the stupidity or hypocrisy of our friends and neighbors are unjustifiable on such evidence, because they usually come from applying the standards of symbolic language to linguistic events that are either partly or wholly presymbolic in character.

One further illustration may make this clearer. Let us suppose that we are on the roadside struggling with a flat tire. A not-very-bright-looking but friendly youth comes up and asks, "Got a flat tire?" If we insist upon interpreting his words literally, we will regard this as an extremely silly question and our answer may be, "Can't you see I have, you dumb ox?" If we pay no attention to what the words say, however, and understand his meaning, we will return his gesture of friendly interest by showing equal friendliness, and in a short while he may be helping us to change the tire.[2] In a similar way, many situations in life as well as in literature demand that we pay no attention to what the words say, since the meaning may often be a great deal more intelligent and intelligible than the surface *sense* of the words themselves. It is probable that a great deal of our pessimism about the world, about humanity, and about democracy may be due in part to the fact that unconsciously we apply the standards of symbolic language to presymbolic utterances.

Applications

I. Try, with a group of friends, the following game. Set aside, during an afternoon gathering or an evening party, a period during which the rules are that no one is permitted to say anything except the word "Urglu" (to be uttered with any variations of pitch or tone necessary to convey different meanings) and that anyone using ordinary language during that period is to be fined. Notice what *can* and *cannot* be communicated by the use of such a single nonsense-word, accompanied by whatever gestures or facial expressions seem necessary. (Incidental query: Why is it that party-games, although often interesting when played, sound so silly when described?)

II. At the next meeting of a club or committee where group discussion is expected, notice the occasions when presymbolic language is used. At what points of the meeting does it seem to help the group along? Are there times when it seems to stall the meeting?

[2] Dr. Karl Menninger, in *Love Against Hate* (Harcourt, Brace, 1942), comments on this passage and offers the following translation of "Got a flat tire?" in terms of its psychological meaning: "Hello—I see you are in trouble. I'm a stranger to you but I might be your friend now that I have a chance to be if I had any assurance that my friendship would be welcomed. Are you approachable? Are you a decent fellow? Would you appreciate it if I helped you? I would like to do so but I don't want to be rebuffed. This is what my voice sounds like. What does your voice sound like?" Why does not the youth simply say directly, "I would be glad to help you"? Dr. Menninger explains: "But people are too timid and mutually distrustful to be so direct. *They want to hear one another's voices. People need assurance that others are just like themselves.*" (Italics added.)

Or observe the ways in which an effective chairman at a banquet, an orator at a Farm Bureau or Grange picnic, or a popular master of ceremonies at a night club operates. Don't be too "objective" about this sort of exercise—don't sit there deadpan and detached, like an ethnologist from a different civilization taking notes on native customs. Enter rather into the spirit of the occasion, observing your own reactions as well as the reactions of others to the meaningfully meaningless utterances that are made. The detached approach may be taken on the following day, when you are writing down your observations, with the speeches, the audience reactions, and your own reactions as objects of study.

III. Keep track some day of the number of times a meeting of friends is begun with remarks about the weather. Why does the weather make such an easy opening? Is it true that women are more likely than men to greet each other with complimentary remarks about each other's appearance—"What a lovely new hat!" "Where *did* you get that bracelet?" "How well you look in that coat." Query: *Do men have special patterns of their own in greeting other men?*

It is the writer's impression that small children usually have not developed these presymbolic means of getting rapport with others. Observe with special care how children and adults who are strangers to each other get conversation started, if at all.

IV. Note the differences in forms of presymbolic usage in different classes of society, in different ethnic groups, in different countries. If the reader is well acquainted with more than one social class, or more than one nationality group, he might compare and contrast the different usages among the groups with which he is familiar. In the United States, there appear to the writer to be marked differences in the style and amount of presymbolic discourse between the general American middle-class culture and the cultures of immigrant groups who retain some of their Old World habits (Scandinavian farmers of the Midwest, Pennsylvania Dutch, Jews of the New York garment district, Italians, Poles, Germans of the Chicago northwest side, and so forth). There are also occupational and class differences: social usages among theatrical people, truckdrivers, women's clubs, artists and writers in urban Bohemias, and naval officers provide some sharp contrasts. An especially graceful ceremoniousness is to be found often in gatherings of American lower middle-class Negroes.

V. Try to live a whole day without any presymbolic uses of language, restricting yourself solely to (a) specific statements of fact which contribute to the hearer's information; (b) specific requests for needed information or services. This exercise is recommended only to those whose devotion to science and the experimental method is greater than their desire to keep their friends.

6. The Double Task of Language

Tens of thousands of years have elapsed since we shed our tails, but we are still communicating with a medium developed to meet the needs of arboreal man. . . . We may smile at the linguistic illusions of primitive man, but may we forget that the verbal machinery on which we so readily rely, and with which our metaphysicians still profess to probe the Nature of Existence, was set up by him, and may be responsible for other illusions hardly less gross and not more easily eradicable?

OGDEN AND RICHARDS

Connotations

Report language, as we have seen, is *instrumental* in character—that is, instrumental in getting work done; but, as we have seen, language is also used for the direct *expression* of the feelings of the speaker. Considering language from the point of view of the *hearer*, we can say that report language *informs* us but that these expressive uses of language (for example, judgments and what we have called presymbolic functions) *affect* us—that is, affect our feelings. When language is affective, it has the character of a kind of force.[1] A spoken insult, for example, provokes a return insult, just as a blow provokes a return blow; a loud and peremptory command compels,

---

[1] Such terms as "emotional" and "emotive" which imply misleading distinctions between the "emotional appeals" and "intellectual appeals" of language, should be carefully avoided. In any case, "emotional" applies too specifically to strong feelings. The word "affective," however, in such an expression as the "affective uses of language," describes not only the way in which language can arouse strong feelings, but also the way in which it arouses extremely subtle, sometimes unconscious, responses. "Affective" has the further advantage of introducing no inconvenient distinctions between "physical" and "mental" responses.

just as a push compels; talking and shouting are as much a display of energy as the pounding of the chest. And the first of the affective elements in speech, as we have seen, is the tone of voice, its loudness or softness, its pleasantness or unpleasantness, its variations during the course of the utterance in volume and intonation.

Another affective element in language is rhythm. *Rhythm* is the name we give to the effect produced by the repetition of auditory (or kinesthetic) stimuli at fairly regular intervals. From the boom-boom of a childish drum to the subtle nuances of cultivated poetry and music, there is a continuous development and refinement of man's responsiveness to rhythm. To produce rhythm is to arouse attention and interest; so affective is rhythm, indeed, that it catches our attention even when we do not want our attention distracted. *Rhyme* and *alliteration* are, of course, ways of emphasizing rhythm in language, through repetition of similar sounds at regular intervals. Political-slogan writers and advertisers therefore have a special fondness for rhyme and alliteration: "Tippecanoe and Tyler Too," "Rum, Romanism, and Rebellion," "Keep Cool with Coolidge," "Order from Horder," "Better Buy Buick"—totally absurd slogans so far as informative value is concerned, but by virtue of their sound capable of setting up small rhythmic echoes in one's head that make such phrases annoyingly difficult to forget.

In addition to tone of voice and rhythm, another extremely important affective element in language is the aura of feelings, pleasant or unpleasant, that surrounds practically all words. It will be recalled that in Chapter 4, a distinction was made between denotations (or extensional meaning) pointing to things, and connotations (or intensional meaning) "ideas," "notions," "concepts," and feelings suggested in the mind. These connotations can be divided into two kinds, the *informative* and the *affective*.

Informative Connotations

The informative connotations of a word are its socially agreed upon, "impersonal" meanings, *insofar as meanings can be given at all by additional words.* For example, if we talk about a "pig," we cannot readily give the extensional meaning (denotation) of the word unless there happens to be an actual pig around for us to point at; but we can give the informative connotations: "mammalian domestic quadruped of the kind generally raised by farmers to be made into pork, bacon, ham, lard . . ."—which are connotations upon which everybody can agree. Sometimes, however, the informative connotations of words used in everyday life differ so much from place to place and from individual to individual that a special substitute terminology with more fixed informative connotations has to be used when special accuracy is desired. The scientific names for plants and animals are an example of terminology with such carefully established informative connotations.

Affective Connotations

The affective connotations of a word, on the other hand, are the aura of personal feelings it arouses, as, for example, "pig": "Ugh! Dirty, evil-smelling creatures, wallowing in filthy sties," and so on. While there is no necessary agreement about these feelings—some people like pigs and others don't—it is the existence of these feelings that enables us to use words, under certain circumstances, *for their affective connotations alone,* without regard to their informative connotations. That is to say, when we are strongly moved, we express our feelings by uttering words with the affective connotations appropriate to our feelings, without paying any attention to the informative connotations they may have. We angrily call people "reptiles," "wolves," "old bears," "skunks," or lovingly call them "honey," "sugar," "duck," and "apple dumpling." Indeed, all verbal expressions of feeling make use to some extent of the affective connotations of words.

All words have, according to the uses to which they are put, some affective character. There are many words that exist more for their affective value than for their informative value; for example, we can refer to "that man" as "that gentleman," "that individual," "that person," "that gent," "that guy," "that hombre," "that bird," or "that bozo"—and while the person referred to may be the same in all these cases, each of these terms reveals a difference in our feelings toward him. Dealers in knickknacks frequently write "Gyfte Shoppe" over the door, hoping that such a spelling carries, even if their merchandise does not, the flavor of antiquity. Affective connotations suggestive of England and Scotland are often sought in the choice of brand names for men's suits and overcoats: "Glenmoor," "Regent Park," "Bond Street." Sellers of perfume choose names for their products that suggest France—"Mon Désir," "Indiscret," "Evening in Paris"—and expensive brands always come in "flacons," never in bottles. Consider, too, the differences among the following expressions:

> I have the honor to inform Your Excellency . . .
> This is to advise you . . .
> I should like to tell you, sir . . .
> I'm telling you, Mister . . .
> Cheez, boss, git a load of dis . . .

The parallel columns below also illustrate how affective connotations can be changed while extensional meanings remain the same.

Finest quality filet mignon.	First-class piece of dead cow.
Cubs trounce Giants 5-3.	Score: Cubs 5, Giants 3.
McCormick Bill steam-rollered through Senate.	Senate passes McCormick Bill over strong opposition.
She has her husband under her thumb.	She is deeply interested in her husband's affairs.
French armies in rapid retreat!	The retirement of the French forces to previously prepared positions in the rear was accomplished briskly and efficiently.
The governor appeared to be gravely concerned and said that a statement would be issued in a few days after careful examination of the facts.	The governor was on the spot.

The story is told that, during the Boer War, the Boers were described in the British press as "sneaking and skulking behind rocks and bushes." The British forces, when they finally learned from the

Boers how to employ tactics suitable to veldt warfare, were described as "cleverly taking advantage of cover."

A Note on Verbal Taboo

The affective connotations of some words provide obstacles, sometimes serious obstacles, to communication. In some circles of society, for example, it is "impolite" to speak of eating. A maid answering the telephone has to say, "Mr. Jones is at dinner," and not, "Mr. Jones is eating dinner." The same hesitation about referring too baldly to eating is shown in the economical use made of the French and Japanese words meaning "to eat," *manger* and *taberu;* a similar delicacy exists in many other languages. Again, when creditors send bills, they practically never mention "money," although that is what they are writing about. There are all sorts of circumlocutions: "We would appreciate your early attention to this matter." "May we look forward to an immediate remittance?" Furthermore, we ask movie ushers and filling-station attendants where the "lounge" or "rest room" is, although we usually have no intention of lounging or resting; indeed, it is impossible in polite society to state, without having to resort to a medical vocabulary, what a "rest room" is for. The word "dead" likewise is used as little as possible by many people, who substitute such expressions as "gone west," "passed away," "gone to his reward," and "departed." In every language there is a long list of such carefully avoided words whose affective connotations are so unpleasant or so undesirable that people cannot say them, even when they are needed.

Words having to do with physiology and sex—and words even vaguely suggesting physiological and sexual matters—have, especially in American culture, remarkable affective connotations. Ladies of the last century could not bring themselves to say "breast" or "leg"—not even of chicken—so that the terms "white meat" and "dark meat" were substituted. It was thought inelegant to speak of "going to bed," and "to retire" was used instead. In rural America there are many euphemisms for the word "bull"; among them are "he cow," "cow critter," "male cow," "gentleman cow." There are numerous and complicated verbal taboos in radio. Scientists and physicians asked to speak on the radio have been known to cancel their speeches in despair when they discovered that ordinary physiological terms, such as "stomach" and "bowels," are forbidden on some stations. Indeed, there are some words, well known to all of us, whose affective connotations are so powerful that if they were printed here, even for the purposes of scientific analysis, this book would be excluded from all public schools and libraries, and anyone placing a copy of it in the United States mails would be subject to Federal prosecution!

For reasons such as these, the first steps in sex education, whether among adults or in schools, are usually entirely linguistic. To most of the general public, the nontechnical vocabulary of sex is unusable and the technical vocabulary is unknown. Hence, prior to instruction, an affectively neutral vocabulary of sex has to be established.

The stronger verbal taboos have, however, a genuine social value. When we are extremely angry and we feel the need of expressing our anger in violence, the uttering of these forbidden words provides us with a relatively harmless verbal substitute for going berserk and smashing furniture; that is, they act as a kind of safety valve in our moments of crisis.

Why some words should have such powerful affective connotations while others *with the same informative connotations* should not is difficult to explain fully. Some of our verbal taboos, especially the religious ones, obviously originate in our earlier belief in word-magic; the names of gods, for example, were often regarded as too holy to be spoken. But all taboos cannot be explained in terms of word-magic. According to some psychologists, our verbal taboos on sex and physiology are probably due to the fact that we all have certain feelings of which we are so ashamed that we do not like to admit even to ourselves that we have them. We therefore resent words which remind us of those feelings, and get angry at the utterer of such words. Such an explanation would confirm the fairly common observation that some of the fanatics who object most strenuously to "dirty" books and plays do so not because their minds are especially pure, but because they are especially morbid.

Race and Words

The fact that some words arouse both informative and affective connotations simultaneously gives a special complexity to discussions involving religious, racial, national, and political groups. To many people, the word "communist" means simultaneously "one who believes in communism" (informative connotations) *and* "one who ought to be thrown in jail, run out of the country . . ." (affective connotations). Words applying to occupations of which one disapproves ("pickpocket," "racketeer"), like those applying to believers in philosophies of which one may disapprove ("atheist," "heretic," "Trotskyite," "Holy Roller"), likewise often communicate simultaneously a fact and a judgment on the fact.

In the western and southwestern parts of the United States, there are strong prejudices against Mexicans, both immigrant and American-born. The strength of this prejudice is indirectly revealed by the fact that polite people and newspapers have stopped using the word "Mexican" altogether, using the expression "Spanish-speaking person" instead. "Mexican" has been used with contemptuous connotations for so long that it has become, in the opinion of many people in the region, unsuitable for polite conversation. In some circles, the word is reserved for lower-class Mexicans, while the "politer" term is used for the upper class.

On subjects about which strong prejudices exist, we are compelled to talk in roundabout terms if we wish to avoid arousing the prejudices. Hence we have not only such terms as "Spanish-speaking persons," but also, in other contexts, "asocial types" instead of "criminals," "juvenile delinquents" and "problem children" instead of "little criminals," "segregees" [2] instead of "disloyal Japs," "exceptional (or atypical) children" instead of "backward (or stupid) kids," and so on.

[2] This term was used for Japanese-Americans who were "segregated" in Tule Lake Camp (California) during World War II. In addition to the avowed Japanese sympathizers, these included persons who had asked to be returned to Japan after the war (often for family reasons), those who felt disillusioned with America as a result of wartime experiences, and the minor children of all these groups.

These verbal stratagems are necessitated by the existence of strong affective connotations as well as by the often misleading implications of their blunter alternatives; they are not merely a matter of giving things fancy names in order to fool people, as the simple-minded often believe. Because the old names are "loaded," they dictate traditional patterns of behavior towards those to whom they are applied. When everybody "knew" what to do about "little criminals," they threw them in jail. Once in jail, "little criminals" showed a marked tendency to grow up into big criminals. When thoughtful people began to observe such facts, they started thinking out the problem all over again, using such terms as "juvenile delinquents" this time. It is significant that most people do not know for sure what to do about "juvenile delinquents." This is a hopeful sign. It may mean that they will continue to think until they reach better solutions than traditional moral indignation about "little criminals" has supplied. Similarly, it is possible that many who had dismissed Mexicans as "just Mexicans" may begin to think twice about their reactions when they are compelled by social usage to call them "Spanish-speaking Americans."

The meaning of words, as we have observed, changes from speaker to speaker and from context to context. In the case of "Japs" and "niggers," these words, although often used both as a designation and an insult, are sometimes used with no intent to offend. In some classes of society and in some geographical areas, there are people who know no other words for Japanese, and in other areas there are people who know no other words for Negroes. Ignorance of regional and class differences of dialect often results in feelings needlessly hurt. Those who believe that the meaning of a word is *in the word* often fail to understand this simple point of differences in usage. For example, an elderly Japanese woman of the writer's acquaintance living *in Chicago,* where the word "Jap" is often used simply to denote Japanese, always feels deeply insulted by the word, because *in California,* where she formerly lived, it was more often used with contemptuous connotations than not. She was therefore upset even by headlines over news stories praising the Japanese, such as "Jap-American War Heroes Return." "They're still calling us 'Japs,' " she would say. "Whenever I hear that word I feel dirty all over."

The word "nigger" has a similar effect on most Negroes. A distinguished Negro sociologist tells of an incident in his adolescence when he was hitchhiking far from home in regions where Negroes are hardly ever seen. He was befriended by an extremely kindly white couple who fed him and gave him a place to sleep in their home. However, they kept calling him "little nigger"—a fact which upset him profoundly even while he was grateful for their kindness. He finally got up courage to ask the man not to call him by that "insulting term."

"Who's insultin' you, son?" said the man.

"You are, sir—that name you're always calling me."

"What name?"

"Uh . . . you know."

"I ain't callin' you no names, son."

"I mean your calling me 'nigger.' "

"Well, what's insultin' about that? You are a nigger, ain't you?"

As the sociologist says now in telling the story, "I couldn't think of an answer then, and I'm not sure I can now."

In case the sociologist reads this book, we are happy to provide him with an answer, although it may be twenty-five years late. He might have said to his benefactor, "Sir, in the part of the country I come from, white people who treat colored people with respect call them 'Negroes,' while those who wish to show their contempt of colored people call them 'niggers.' I hope the latter is not your intention." And the man might have replied, had he been kindly in thought as he was in deed, "Well, you don't say! Sorry I hurt your feelings, son, but I didn't know." And that would have been that.

Negroes, having for a long time been victims of unfair persecution because of race, are often even more sensitive about racial appellations than the Japanese woman previously mentioned. It need hardly be said that Negroes suffer from the confusion of informative and affective connotations just as often as white people—or Japanese. Such Negroes, and those white sympathizers with the Negro cause who are equally naïve in linguistic matters, tend to feel that the entire colored "race" is vilified whenever and wherever the word "nigger" occurs. They bristle even when it occurs in such expressions as "niggertoe" (the name of an herb; also a dialect term for Brazil nut), "niggerhead" (a type of chewing tobacco), "niggerfish" (a kind of fish found in West Indian and Floridan waters)—and even the word "niggardly" (of Scandinavian origin, unrelated, of course, to "Negro") has to be avoided before some audiences.

Such easily offended people sometimes send delegations to visit dictionary offices to demand that the word "nigger" be excluded from future editions, being unaware that dictionaries, as has already been said (Chapter 4), perform a historical, rather than legislative, function. (They will probably come to bother the publishers of this book, too.) To try to reduce racial discrimination by getting dictionaries to stop including the word "nigger" is like trying to cut down the birth rate by shutting down the office of the county register of births. When racial discrimination against Negroes is done away with, the word will either disappear or else lose its present connotations. By losing its present connotations, we mean (1) that people who need to insult their fellow men will have found more interesting grounds on which to base their insults, and (2) that people who are called "niggers" will no longer fly off the handle any more than a person from New England does at being called a "Yankee."

One other curious fact needs to be recorded concerning the words used regarding race, religion, political heresy, economic dissent, and other such hotly debated issues. Every reader is acquainted with certain people who, according to their own flattering descriptions of themselves, "believe in being frank" and like to "call a spade a spade." By "calling a spade a spade" (the expression itself is a relic of the "right name" superstition discussed in Chapter 2), they usually mean calling anything or anyone by the term which has the strongest and most disagreeable affective connotations. Why people should pin medals on themselves for "candor" for performing this nasty feat has often puzzled the writer. Sometimes it is necessary to violate verbal taboos as an aid to clearer thinking, but more often "calling a spade a spade" is to provide our minds with a greased runway down which we may slide back into old *and discredited* patterns of evaluation and behavior.

Everyday Uses of Language

The language of everyday life, then, differs from "reports" such as those discussed in Chapter 3. As in reports, we have to be accurate in choosing words that have the informative connotations we want; otherwise the reader or hearer will not know what we are talking about. But in addition, we have to give those words the affective connotations we want in order that he will be interested or moved by what we are saying, and feel towards things the way we do. This double task confronts us in almost all ordinary conversation, oratory, persuasive writing, and literature. Much of this task, however, is performed intuitively; without being aware of it, we choose the tone of voice, the rhythms, and the affective connotations appropriate to our utterance. Over the informative connotations of our utterances we exercise somewhat more conscious control. Improvement in our ability to understand language, as well as in our ability to use it, depends, therefore, not only upon sharpening our sense for the informative connotations of words, but *also upon the sharpening of our insight into the affective elements in language through social experience, through contact with many kinds of people in many kinds of situations, and through literary study.*

The following, finally, are some of the things that can happen in any speech event:

1. The informative connotations may be inadequate or misleading, but the affective connotations may be sufficiently well directed so that we are able to interpret correctly. For example, when someone says, "Imagine who I saw today! Old What's-his-name—oh, you know who I mean—Whoosis, that old buzzard that lives on, oh—what's the name of that street!" there are means, certainly not clearly informative, by which we manage to understand who is being referred to.

2. The informative connotations may be correct enough and the extensional meanings clear, but the affective connotations may be inappropriate, misleading, or ludicrous. This happens frequently

when people try to write elegantly: "Jim ate so many bags of *Arachis hypogaea,* commonly known as peanuts, at the ball game today that he was unable to do justice to his evening repast."

3. Both informative and affective connotations may "sound all right," but there may be no "territory" corresponding to the "map." For example: "He lived for many years in the beautiful hill country just south of Chicago." There is no hill country just south of Chicago.

4. Both informative and affective connotations may be used *consciously* to create "maps" of "territories" that do not exist. There are many reasons why we should wish on occasion to do so. Of these, only two need be mentioned now. First we may wish to give pleasure:

> Yet mark'd I where the bolt of Cupid fell:
> It fell upon a little western flower,
> Before milk-white, now purple with love's wound,
> And maidens call it, Love-in-idleness.
> Fetch me that flower; the herb I show'd thee once:
> The juice of it on sleeping eyelids laid
> Will make or man or woman madly dote
> Upon the next live creature that it sees.
>   —*A Midsummer Night's Dream*

A second reason is to enable us to plan for the future. For example, we can say, "Let us suppose there is a bridge at the foot of this street; then the heavy traffic on High Street would be partly diverted over the new bridge; shopping would be less concentrated on High Street. . . ." Having visualized the condition that would result, we can recommend or oppose the bridge according to whether or not we like the probable results. The relationship of present words to future events is a subject we must leave for the next chapter.

Applications

I. The relative absence of information and the deluge of affective connotations in advertising is notorious. Nevertheless, it is revealing to analyze closely specimens like the following, separating the informative connotations (those which convey verifiable information on which agreement can readily be reached) from the affective connotations (those which express attitudes and judgments open to differences of opinion) into two parallel columns for contrast:

1. "You'll enjoy *different* tomato juice made from *aristocrat* tomatoes."

—Advertisement

SAMPLE ANALYSIS:

Affective Connotations	*Informative Connotations*
Because you have cultivated and discriminating tastes, you will prefer tomato juice made from superior, exclusive tomatoes to tomato juice made from common, ordinary tomatoes. A person with average tastes might not notice the difference but, since you appreciate the finer things of life, you will.	Tomato juice is made from tomatoes.

2. "The kingdoms of Nature have released some of their mighty secrets to Madame Helena Rubinstein and her chemists, as she created her wondrous new extra-rich 'Pasteurized' Night Cream. Appropriate for the atomic age of stupendous discoveries by scientists, this new formula comprises the newest scientific ingredients cleverly precision-blended in balanced perfection. In addition to the chemical ingredients, fresh fruits and vegetables have yielded their beneficent properties in a new way for the fair skins of women.

"One of the ingredients which Mme. Rubinstein discovered in the fruit kingdom acts as an emulsifier to make your skin absorb your night cream more quickly. This rarely used vegetable oil homogenizes with other ingredients to keep this cream always at its highest possible beautifying level. Imagine what this means to your complexion!

"You realize how important penetration is in your night cream. Mme. Rubinstein has infused her new 'Pasteurized' Night Cream with special agents that induce the rich, balming emollients to penetrate more effectively. . . . This cleansing cream is the only one that texturizes as it cleanses, to awaken fresh new beauty on contact with your skin!"   —Publicity release, quoted in *The New Yorker*

3. "Because Wombat has so long since occupied a place entirely apart from other motor cars, the announcement of a new Wombat has become a significant automotive event. . . . But no Wombat announcement has ever been as significant as the one which appears on these

pages. For, this year, Wombat presents its *creative masterpiece*—a wholly new V-type eight-cylinder engine—which is, beyond all doubt, the highest development yet attained in automotive power plants. . . . Drawing on the experience gained in thirty-five years of pioneering with V-type power, Wombat has produced a sensational engine—one eminently befitting the world's foremost producer of fine motor cars. . . . This great power plant has been twelve years in the building—for basic development work started in 1936. It has many unusual qualities which set it apart from all other creations of its kind. It provides an amazing increase in power—yet affords an increase in gasoline economy of approximately twenty per cent. And the manner of its performance actually challenges the imagination. It is liquid smooth; it is quick and eager beyond all experience; yet the power application is so effortless that the driver is scarcely aware of the engine's existence. The car seems almost to move by automatic propulsion. . . . Even experienced Wombat owners must put aside all previous conceptions of performance when they drive the 1949 Wombat, with this amazing new engine. It is a revelation—from silken start to silken stop. . . ." —Advertisement

4.   "Use Plenty of Genuine* Ice"

* " 'Genuine' ice is the pure, crystal-clear, taste-free, slow-melting, hard-frozen kind supplied *exclusively* by your local Ice Company. Call on them for *genuine* ice for every cooling need."

                                —National Association of Ice Industries

5. "Softly . . . softly . . . softly you move to the crib to make certain that all is well with the most precious thing in your life, the most wonderful baby in all the world. Softly, too, the smooth Ocean Brand Sheets welcome you when you return to your own bed. And softly these Ocean Brand Sheets meet your budget requirements. For these are the famous Ocean Combed Percales, latest products of Ocean Brand craftsmanship."   —Advertisement

6. "Something new—Hooper's feeding vitamins to tires. Hooper Vitamized Rubber puts you miles ahead. . . . Feeding a rubber vitamin to tires is one reason why Hoopers go on and on—delivering an extra dividend in money-saving mileage. The Hooper method of making Vitamized Rubber is your guarantee of an extra resilient, extra tough, extra long-wearing tire. See us today—see why you'll be miles ahead with Hoopers. . . . Remember . . . quality comes first with Hooper."

                                                —Advertisement

II. Bertrand Russell, on a British Broadcasting Company radio program called the Brains Trust, gave the following "conjugation" of an "irregular verb":

I am firm.
You are obstinate.
He is a pig-headed fool.

The New Statesman and Nation, quoting the above as a model, offered prizes to readers who sent in the best "irregular verbs" of this kind. Here are some of the entries, as published in the June 5, 1948, issue:

I am sparkling. You are unusually talkative. He is drunk.

I am righteously indignant. You are annoyed. He is making a fuss about nothing.

I am fastidious. You are fussy. He is an old woman.

I am a creative writer. You have a journalistic flair. He is a prosperous hack.

I am beautiful. You have quite good features. She isn't bad-looking, if you like that type.

I day dream. You are an escapist. He ought to see a psychiatrist.

I have about me something of the subtle, haunting, mysterious fragrance of the Orient. You rather overdo it, dear. She stinks.

"Conjugate," in a similar way, the following statements:

1. I am slender.
2. I am a trifle overweight.
3. I don't dance very well.
4. Naturally I use a little make-up.
5. I collect rare, old objects of art.
6. I don't like to play bridge with people who are too serious about it.
7. I don't claim to know all the answers.
8. I believe in old-fashioned, laissez-faire liberalism.
9. I need plenty of sleep.
10. I'm just an old-fashioned girl.
11. I don't care much about theories; I'm the practical type.
12. I believe in being frank.
13. I rarely find time to read books.

III. It is important to be able to sort out of any utterance *the information given* from *the speaker's feeling toward that information.* In order to sharpen one's perception in this respect, it is instructive sometimes to rewrite articles one reads, *using the same information given in the original and reversing the judgments.* For example, the following is a review by Rolfe Humphries of a book, *The Frieda Lawrence Collection of D. H. Lawrence Manuscripts: A Descriptive Bibliography,* by E. W. Tedlock, Jr. (University of New Mexico Press, 1948), as published in *The Nation,* June 26, 1948:

> This is a remarkable bibliography. Not only does it examine, with the cool painstaking labor of scholarship, the 193 manuscripts in Mrs. Lawrence's collection—and nine others thrown in for good measure—but also, it is informed with warmth, a growing sympathy, admiration, understanding of its subject, never forgetting that that subject was a man, never seeking to claim him as a literary property, as so often tends to be the case when scholars figure they have learned more facts about somebody than anybody else. There is enough material in Professor Tedlock's book to fascinate those with an appetite for such items as that the paper measures eight and a half by ten and five-eighths inches, or that the pages are incorrectly numbered; there is also material for those who want to study how an artist improved, corrected, extended, his initial attempts; beyond all that, the book is interesting to any who care about Lawrence, so that, as Frieda Lawrence says in a brief foreword, the love and truth in him may rouse the love and truth in others. Professor Tedlock's study is a valuable help, and readable.

Now let us suppose for the purpose of our exercise the existence of a different reviewer, one who dislikes the works of Lawrence, dislikes those who admire Lawrence, and has a low opinion of painstaking literary scholarship. Such a reviewer, using the same facts, might write his review in somewhat the following way:

> This bibliography examines, with the appalling industriousness of the professional pedant, the 193 manuscripts in Mrs. Lawrence's collection—and nine others thrown in for good measure. Professor Tedlock goes completely overboard for his subject. Like other worshipers at the Lawrence shrine, he is almost as much preoccupied with Lawrence the man as with his works—so much so, indeed, that it is surprising he does not take Lawrence over as a literary property, as so often tends to be the case when scholars figure they have learned more facts about somebody than anybody else. There is enough material in Professor Tedlock's book to fascinate those with an appetite for such items as that the paper measures eight and a half by ten and five-eighths inches, or that

the pages are incorrectly numbered; there is also material for those who, not content with the study of finished works, want to pry into the processes by which an artist improved, corrected, and extended his initial attempts; beyond all that, the book is interesting to any who, in this day and age, still insist on caring about Lawrence, so that what Frieda Lawrence calls, in a brief foreword, the "love" and "truth" in him may arouse a similar "love" and "truth" in others. To these followers of the Lawrence cult, Professor Tedlock's study is no doubt a valuable help. The style is readable.

No criticism of Mr. Humphries' review (or of Professor Tedlock's book or of D. H. Lawrence) is implied, of course, by this "revision." The task of the book reviewer is twofold: to report facts about the book under discussion *and* to express some of his feelings about the book and its subject. Mr. Humphries has, in a brief review, done something of both tasks—a good deal more of the former than the latter.

However, a critical reader should be able to read either Mr. Humphries' review or the "revision" above and derive the basic information that both reviews convey: that Professor Tedlock's book is painstakingly detailed in its examination of the Lawrence manuscripts, that it has a warm attitude toward Lawrence the man as well as toward his works, that it is likely to be useful to admirers of Lawrence, and so forth. In order to develop one's capacity to get at such basic information regardless of how the author happens to feel about that information, it is suggested that the reader try "revisions" of this kind. Book reviews are especially interesting to revise in this way. Some reviewers will be found to say little about the book and a great deal about their own tastes. Others write almost pure news stories, with little expression of their own likes or dislikes. "Interpretive reporting" of the kind found in *Time* and in many signed news-features in large newspapers—stories that not only tell what happened but also communicate an attitude toward the events or persons involved—is also interesting to revise in the manner suggested.

Try revising the following item from *Time* magazine (January 24, 1949), using the same basic information but with warm approval of Mr. Beck's undertaking:

Man of Peace

Ever since he got around aging Dan Tobin and became the real ruler of the Teamsters Union, Seattle's tough, pale-eyed Dave Beck has been remolding the A.F.L.'s biggest labor group to suit his fancy. Last week in Manhattan, Beck announced what he proposed to do with his juggernaut when he gets it well-streamlined. He was going to start a coast-to-coast organizing roundup that would make other labor-recruiting drives look like ballet tryouts.

Teamsters in all United States cities will simultaneously set out to double the union's membership from 1,000,000 to 2,000,000. They will go after new members in the automotive trades, bakeries, the beverage industry, building and construction, canneries, dairies, the taxicab and short-haul bus fields, general hauling, sales drivers, the produce field, warehouses and drive-away and truck-away enterprises.

With the air of a man about to pluck a ripe plum, Beck also made a soft-voiced announcement of his plans for New York City. The teamsters, he said, would concentrate on department store warehousemen but would also claim jurisdiction over the big city's brewery workers.

Beck added blandly that he was a "man of peace" and had no desire to revert to the "law of the jungle." He did not expect that other unions would "infringe on our jurisdiction." But he said, "if a union that should stick to clerks tries to get our warehousemen (a remark directed at the powerful C.I.O. Amalgamated Clothing Workers), we'll step in and organize the whole store to protect ourselves."

7. The Language of Social Control

The effect of a parade of sonorous phrases upon human conduct has never been adequately studied.

THURMAN W. ARNOLD

Making Things Happen

The most interesting and perhaps least understood of the relations between words and things is the relation between words and future events. When we say, for example, "Come here!" we are not describing the extensional world about us, nor are we merely expressing our feelings; we are trying to *make something happen*. What we call "commands," "pleas," "requests," and "orders" are the simplest ways we have of making things happen by means of words. There are, however, more roundabout ways. When we say, for example, "Our candidate is a great American," we are of course making an enthusiastic purr about him, but we may also be influencing other people to vote for him. Again, when we say, "Our war against the enemy is God's war. God wills that we must triumph," we are saying something that is incapable of scientific verification; nevertheless, it may influence others to help in the prosecution of the war. Or if we merely state as a fact, "Milk contains vitamins," we may be influencing others to buy milk.

Consider, too, such a statement as "I'll meet you tomorrow at two o'clock in front of the Palace Theater." Such a statement about *future* events can only be made, it will be observed, in a system in which symbols are independent of things symbolized. The future, like the recorded past, is a specifically human dimension. To a dog, the expression "hamburger *tomorrow*" is meaningless—he will look at you expectantly, hoping for the extensional meaning of the word "hamburger" to be produced *now*. Squirrels, to be sure, store food for "next winter," but the fact that they store food regardless of whether or not their needs are adequately provided for demonstrates that such behavior (usually called "instinctive") is governed neither by symbols nor by other interpreted stimuli. Human beings are unique in their ability to react meaningfully to such expressions as "next Saturday," "on our next wedding anniversary," "twenty years after date I promise to pay," "some day, perhaps five hundred years from now." That is to say, maps can be made, in spite of the fact that the territories they stand for are not yet an actuality. Guiding ourselves by means of such maps of territories-to-be, we can impose a certain predictability upon future events.

With words, therefore, we influence and to an enormous extent *control future events*. It is for this reason that writers write; preachers preach; employers, parents, and teachers scold; propagandists send out news releases; statesmen give addresses. All of them, for various reasons, are trying to influence our conduct—sometimes for our good, sometimes for their own. These attempts to control, direct, or influence the future actions of fellow human beings with words may be termed *directive uses of language*.

Now it is obvious that if directive language is going to direct, it cannot be dull or uninteresting. If it is to influence our conduct, it *must* make use of every affective element in language: dramatic variations in tone of voice, rhyme and rhythm, purring and snarling, words with strong affective connotations, endless repetition. If meaningless noises will move the audience, meaningless noises must be made; if facts move them, facts must be given; if noble ideals move them, we must make our proposals appear noble; if they will respond only to fear, we must scare them stiff.

The nature of the affective means used in directive language is limited, of course, by the nature of our aims. If we are trying to direct people to be more kindly toward each other, we obviously do not want to arouse feelings of cruelty or hate. If we are trying to direct people to think and act more intelligently, we obviously should not use subrational appeals. If we are trying to direct people to lead better lives, we use affective appeals that arouse their finest feelings. Included among directive utterances, therefore, are many of the greatest and most treasured works of literature: the Christian and Buddhist scriptures, the writings of Confucius, Milton's *Areopagitica,* and Lincoln's Gettysburg Address.

There are, however, occasions when it is felt that language is not sufficiently affective by itself to produce the results wanted. We supplement directive language, therefore, by *nonverbal affective appeals* of many kinds. We supplement the words "Come here" by gesturing with our hands. Advertisers are not content with saying in words how beautiful their products will make us; they supplement their words by the use of colored inks and by pictures. Newspapers were not content with saying that the New Deal was a "menace"; they supplied political cartoons depicting New Dealers as criminally insane people placing sticks of dynamite under magnificent buildings labeled "American way of life." The affective appeal of sermons and religious exhortations may be supplemented by costumes, incense, processions, choir music, and church bells. A political candidate seeking office reinforces his speech-making with a considerable array of nonverbal affective appeals: brass bands, flags, parades, picnics, barbecues, and free cigars.[1]

Now, if we want people to do certain things and are indifferent

---

[1] The following are excerpts from reports of the Republican National Convention of 1948: "There on the stage a gigantic photograph of the candidate, tinted somewhat too vividly, gazed steadily out over the throngs. Around the balcony hung other photographs: the Dewey family playing with their Great Dane; the Deweys at the circus; Dewey on the farm. Dewey infantrymen passed out soft drinks and small favors to gawking visitors and gave every 200th visitor a door prize. William Horne, a Philadelphia bank employee, was clocked in as the 45,000th visitor and got a sterling silver carving aid." (*Time,* July 5, 1948.) "Over loudspeakers of the Bellevue-Stratford came a constant stream of official exhortations against undue crowding at the entrance to the Dewey headquarters. The warnings were part of the game, but they were also justified. Why wouldn't the Dewey headquarters be jammed when prizes—from chewing gum and pocket combs to silk lingerie and dresses—were being doled out with the largess of a radio quiz show? At one point the Dewey people even staged a fashion show, complete with eight bathing beauties. A bewildered foreign newspaperman asked a fellow-reporter, 'How can I explain to France what this has to do with electing a President?' . . . The Stassen managers appeared to be saving up their circus talent for Convention Hall, where it turned out to be considerable, ranging from an Indian chief in full regalia to a shapely girl in sailor pants who did a nautical rumba on the rostrum." (*The Nation,* July 3, 1948.)

as to *why they do them,* then no affective appeals are excluded. Some political candidates want us to vote for them regardless of our reasons for doing so. Therefore, if we hate the rich, they will snarl at the rich for us; if we dislike strikers, they will snarl at the strikers; if we like clambakes, they will throw clambakes; if the majority of us like hillbilly music, they may say nothing about the problems of government, but travel among their constituencies with hillbilly bands. Again, many business firms want us to buy their products regardless of our reasons for doing so; therefore if delusions and fantasies will lead us to buy their products, they will seek to produce delusions and fantasies; if we want to be popular with the other sex, they will promise us popularity; if we like pretty girls in bathing suits, they will associate pretty girls in bathing suits with their products, whether they are selling shaving cream, automobiles, summer resorts, ice cream cones, house paint, or hardware. Only the law keeps them from presenting pretty girls without bathing suits. The records of the Federal Trade Commission, as well as the advertising pages of any big-circulation magazine, show that some advertisers will stop at practically nothing.

The Promises of Directive Language

Aside from the affective elements, verbal and nonverbal, accompanying directive utterances that are intended simply to attract attention or to create pleasant sensations—that is, repetition, beauty of language, the pretty colors in advertisements, brass bands in political parades, girl pictures, and so on—*practically all directive utterances say something about the future.* They are "maps," either explicitly or by implication, of *"territories" that are to be.* They direct us to do certain things with the stated or implied promise that if we do these things, certain consequences will follow: "If you adhere to the Bill of Rights, your civil rights too will be protected." "If you vote for me, I will have your taxes reduced." "Live according to these religious principles, and you will have peace in your soul." "Read this magazine, and you will keep up with important current events." "Take Lewis's Licorice Liver Pills and enjoy that glorious feeling that goes with regularity." Needless to say, some of these promises are kept, and some are not. Indeed, we encounter promises daily that are obviously incapable of being kept.

There is no sense in objecting as some people do to advertising and political propaganda—the only kind of directives they worry about—on the ground that they are based on "emotional appeals." Unless directive language has affective power of some kind, it is useless. We do not object to campaigns that tell us, "Give to the Community Chest and enable poor children to enjoy better care," although that is an "emotional appeal." Nor do we resent being reminded of our love of home, friends, and nation when people issue moral or patriotic directives at us. The important question to be asked of any directive utterance is, "Will things happen as promised if I do as I am directed? If I accept your philosophy, shall I achieve peace of mind? If I vote for you, will my taxes be reduced? If I use Lifeguard Soap, will my boy friend come back to me?"

We rightly object to advertisers who make false or misleading claims and to politicians who ignore their promises, although it must be admitted that, in the case of politicians, they are sometimes compelled to make promises that later circumstances prevent them from keeping. Life being as uncertain and as unpredictable as it is, we are constantly trying to find out what is going to happen next, so that we may prepare ourselves. Directive utterances undertake to tell us how we can bring about certain desirable events and how we can avoid undesirable events. If we can rely upon what they tell us about the future, the uncertainties of life are reduced. When, however, directive utterances are of such a character that things do *not* happen as predicted—when, after we have done as we were told, the peace in the soul has not been found, the taxes have not been reduced, the boy friend has not returned, there is disappointment. Such disappointments may be trivial or grave; in any event, they are so common that we do not even bother to complain about some of them. They are all serious in their implications, nevertheless. *Each of them serves, in greater or less degree, to break down that mutual trust that makes co-operation possible and knits people together into a society.*

Every one of us, therefore, who utters directive language, with

Semantic Reactions – Evaluation

Semantic Self Regulation – Feedback

Guided Miss

Retraining of Habits.

Semantic Environment.

To what extent did I distinguish
between fact and inferences, judgments
gives.

Did I remember to index my feelings

Semantic Self Regulation Chart

List of did I questions.

What
Goal

How
mille

its concomitant promises, stated or implied, is morally obliged to be as certain as he can, since there is no absolute certainty, that he is arousing no false expectations. Politicians promising the immediate abolition of poverty, national advertisers suggesting that tottering marriages can be restored to bliss by a change in the brand of laundry soap used in the family, newspapers threatening the collapse of the nation if the party they favor is not elected—all such utterers of nonsense are, for the reasons stated, menaces to the social order. It does not matter much whether such misleading directives are uttered in ignorance and error or with conscious intent to deceive, because the disappointments they cause are all similarly destructive of mutual trust among human beings.

The Foundations of Society

However, preaching, no matter how noble, and propaganda, no matter how persuasive, do not create society. We can, if we wish, ignore such directives. We come now to directive utterances that we cannot ignore if we wish to remain organized in our social groups.

What we call society is a vast network of mutual agreements. We agree to refrain from murdering our fellow citizens, and they in turn agree to refrain from murdering us; we agree to drive on the right-hand side of the road, and others agree to do the same; we agree to deliver specified goods, and others agree to pay us for them; we agree to observe the rules of an organization, and the organization agrees to let us enjoy its privileges. This complicated network of agreements, into which almost every detail of our lives is woven and upon which most of our expectations in life are based, consists essentially of *statements about future events which we are supposed, with our own efforts, to bring about.* Without such agreements, there would be no such thing as society. All of us would be huddling in miserable and lonely caves, not daring to trust anyone. With such agreements, and a will on the part of the vast majority of people to live by them, behavior begins to fall into relatively predictable patterns; co-operation becomes possible; peace and freedom are established.

Therefore, in order that we shall continue to exist as human beings, we *must* impose patterns of behavior on each other. We must make citizens conform to social and civic customs; we must make husbands dutiful to their wives; we must make soldiers courageous, judges just, priests pious, and teachers solicitous for the welfare of their pupils. In early stages of culture the principal means of imposing patterns of behavior was, of course, physical coercion. But such control can also be exercised, as human beings must have discovered extremely early in history, by *words*—that is, by directive language. Therefore, directives about matters which society as a whole regards as essential to its own safety are made especially powerful, so that no individual in that society will fail to be impressed with a sense of his obligations. To make doubly sure, the words are further reinforced by the assurance that punishment, possibly including torture and death, will be visited upon those who fail to heed them.

Directives with Collective Sanction

These directive utterances with collective sanction, which try to impose patterns of behavior upon the individual in the interests of the whole group, are among the most interesting of linguistic events. Not only are they usually accompanied by ritual; they are usually the central purpose of ritual. There is probably no kind of utterance that we take more seriously, that affects our lives more deeply, that we quarrel about more bitterly. Constitutions of nations and of organizations, legal contracts, and oaths of office are utterances of this kind; in marriage vows, confirmation exercises, induction ceremonies, and initiations, they are the essential constituent. Those terrifying verbal jungles called laws are simply the systematization of such directives, accumulated and codified through the centuries. In its laws, society makes its mightiest collective effort to impose predictability upon human behavior.

Directive utterances made under collective sanction may exhibit any or all of the following features:

1. Such language is almost always phrased in words that have affective connotations, so that people will be appropriately impressed and awed. Archaic and obsolete vocabulary or stilted phraseology quite unlike the language of everyday life is employed. For example: "Wilt thou, John, take this woman for thy lawful wedded wife?" "This lease, made this tenth day of July, A.D. One Thousand Nine Hundred and Forty-nine, between Samuel Smith, hereinafter called the Lessor, and Jeremiah Johnson, hereinafter called Lessee, WITNESSETH, that Lessor, in consideration of covenants and agreements hereinafter contained and made on the part of the Lessee, hereby leases to Lessee for a private dwelling, the premises known and described as follows, to wit . . ."

2. Such directive utterances are often accompanied by appeals to supernatural powers, who are called upon to help us carry out the vows, or to punish us if we fail to carry them out. An oath, for example, ends with the words, "So help me God." Prayers, incantations, and invocations accompany the utterance of important vows in practically all cultures, from the most primitive to the most civilized. These further serve, of course, to impress our vows on our minds.

3. If God does not punish us for failing to carry out our agreements, it is made clear either by statement or implication that our fellow men will. For example, we all realize that we can be imprisoned for desertion, nonsupport, or bigamy; sued for "breach of contract"; "unfrocked" for activities contrary to priestly vows; "cashiered" for "conduct unbecoming an officer"; "impeached" for "betrayal of public trust"; hanged for "treason."

4. The formal and public utterance of the vows may be preceded by preliminary disciplines of various kinds: courses of training in the meaning of the vows one is undertaking; fasting and self-mortification, as before entering the priesthood; initiation ceremonies involving physical torture, as before being inducted into the warrior status among primitive peoples or membership in college fraternities.

5. The utterance of the directive language may be accompanied

by other activities or gestures, all calculated to impress the occasion on the mind. For example, everybody in a courtroom stands up when a judge is about to open a court; huge processions and extraordinary costumes accompany coronation ceremonies; academic gowns are worn for commencement exercises; for many weddings, an organist and a soprano are procured and special clothes are worn.

6. The uttering of the vows may be immediately followed by feasts, dancing, and other joyous manifestations. Again the purpose seems to be to reinforce still further the effect of the vows. For example, there are wedding parties and receptions, graduation dances, banquets for the induction of officers, and, even in the most modest social circles, some form of "celebration" when a member of the family enters into a compact with society. In primitive cultures, initiation ceremonies for chieftains may be followed by feasting and dancing that last for several days or weeks.

7. In cases where the first utterance of the vows is not made a special ceremonial occasion, the effect on the memory is usually achieved by frequent repetition. The flag ritual ("I pledge allegiance to the flag of the United States . . .") is repeated daily in some schools. Mottoes, which are briefly stated general directives, are repeated frequently; sometimes they are stamped on dishes, sometimes engraved on a warrior's sword, sometimes inscribed in prominent places such as gates, walls, and doorways, where people can see them and be reminded of their duties.

The common feature of all these activities that accompany directive utterances, as well as of the affective elements in the language of directive utterances, is the deep effect they have on the memory. Every kind of sensory impression from the severe pain of initiation rites to the pleasures of banqueting, music, splendid clothing, and ornamental surroundings may be employed; every emotion from the fear of divine punishment to pride in being made the object of special public attention may be aroused. This is done in order that the individual who enters into his compact with society—that is, the individual who utters the "map" of the not-yet-existent "territory" —shall never forget to try to bring that "territory" into existence.

For these reasons, such occasions as when a cadet receives his commission, when a Jewish boy has his *bar mizvah,* when a priest takes his vows, when a policeman receives his badge, when a foreign-born citizen is sworn in as a citizen of the United States, or when a president takes his oath of office—these are events one never forgets. Even if, later on, a person realizes that he has not fulfilled his vows, he cannot shake off the feeling that he should have done so. All of us, of course, use and respond to these ritual directives. The phrases and speeches to which we respond reveal our deepest religious, patriotic, social, professional, and political allegiances more accurately than do the citizenship papers or membership cards that we may carry in our pockets or the badges that we may wear on our coats. A man who has changed his religion after reaching adulthood will, on hearing the ritual he was accustomed to hearing in childhood, often feel an urge to return to his earlier form of worship. In such ways, then, do human beings use words to reach out into the future and control each other's conduct.

It should be remarked that many of our social directives and many of the rituals with which they are accompanied are antiquated and somewhat insulting to adult minds. Rituals that originated in times when people had to be scared into good behavior are unnecessary to people who already have a sense of social responsibility. For example, a five-minute marriage ceremony performed at the city hall for an adult, responsible couple may "take" much better than a full-dress church ceremony performed for an infantile couple. In spite of the fact that the strength of social directives obviously lies in the willingness, the maturity, and the intelligence of the people to whom the directives are addressed, there is still a widespread tendency to rely upon the efficacy of ceremonies as such. This tendency is due, of course, to a lingering belief in word-magic, the notion that, by *saying* things repeatedly or in specified ceremonial ways, we can cast a spell over the future and force events to turn out the way we said they would—"There'll always be an England!" An interesting manifestation of this superstitious attitude towards words and rituals is to be found among some educators and some members of school boards who are faced with the problem of "educating students for democracy." Instead of increasing the time allotted for the factual study of democratic institutions, enlarging the opportunities for the day-to-day exercise of democratic practices, and thereby trying to develop the political insight and maturity of their students, such educators content themselves by staging bigger and better flag-saluting ceremonies and trebling the occasions for singing "God Bless America." If, because of such "educational" activities, the word "democracy" finally becomes a meaningless noise to some students, the result is hardly to be wondered at.

What Are "Rights"?

What, extensionally, is the meaning of the word "my" in such expressions as "my real estate," "my book," "my automobile"? Certainly the word "my" describes no characteristics of the objects named. A check changes hands and "your" automobile becomes "mine" but no change results in the automobile. What has changed?

The change is, of course, in *our social agreements covering our behavior* toward the automobile. Formerly, when it was "yours," you felt free to use it as you liked, while I did not. Now that it is "mine," I use it freely and you may not. The meaning of "yours" and "mine" lies not in the external world, but in *how we intend to act.* And when society as a whole recognizes my "right of ownership" (by issuing me, for example, a certificate of title), it agrees to protect me in my intentions to use the automobile and to frustrate, by police action if necessary, the intentions of those who may wish to use it without my permission. Society makes this agreement with me in return for my obeying its laws and paying my share of the expenses of government.

Are not, then, all assertions of ownership and statements about "rights" directives? Cannot, "This is *mine,*" be translated, "I am going to use this object; you keep your hands off"? Cannot, "Every child has a *right* to an education," be translated, *"Give* every child an education"? And is not the difference between "moral rights" and "legal rights" the difference between agreements which people believe *ought* to be made, and those which, through collective, legislative sanction, *have been* made?

Directives and Disillusionment

A few cautions may be added before we leave the subject of directive language. First, it should be remembered that, since words cannot "say all" about anything, the promises implied in directive language are never more than "outline maps" of "territories-to-be." The future will fill in those outlines, often in unexpected ways. Sometimes the future will bear no relation to our "maps" at all, in spite of all our endeavors to bring about the promised events. We swear always to be good citizens, always to do our duty, and so on, but we never quite succeed in being good citizens *every* day of our lives or in performing *all* our duties. A realization that directives cannot *fully* impose any pattern on the future saves us from having impossible expectations and therefore from suffering needless disappointments.

Secondly, one should distinguish between directive and informative utterances, which often look alike. Such statements as "A Boy Scout is clean and chivalrous and brave" or "Policemen are defenders of the weak" *set up goals* and do not necessarily describe the present situation. This is extremely important, because all too often people understand such definitions as being descriptive and are thereupon shocked, horrified, and disillusioned upon encountering a Boy Scout who is not chivalrous or a policeman who is a bully. They decide that they are "through with the Boy Scouts" or "disgusted with all policemen," which, of course, is nonsense.

A third source of disappointment and disillusionment arising from the improper understanding of directives arises from reading into directives things that were not said. A common instance is provided by advertisements of the antiseptics and patent medicines which people buy under the impression that they will prevent or cure colds. Because of rulings of the Federal Trade Commission, the writers of these advertisements carefully avoid saying that their preparations will prevent or cure anything. Instead, they say that they "help reduce the severity of the infection," "help relieve the symptoms of a cold," or "help guard against sniffling and other discomforts." If after reading these advertisements you feel that prevention or cure of colds has been promised, you are exactly the kind of sucker they are looking for.

Another way of reading into directives things that were not said is by believing promises to be more specific and concrete than they really are. When, for example, a candidate for political office promises to "help the farmer," and you vote for him, and then you discover that he helps the *cotton* farmer without helping the *potato* farmer (and you grow potatoes)—you cannot exactly accuse him of having broken his promise. Or, if another candidate promises to "protect union labor," and you vote for him, and he helps to pass legislation that infuriates the officials of your union (he calls it "legislation to protect union members from their own racketeering leadership")—again you cannot exactly accuse him of having broken his promise, since his action may well have been sincerely in accord with his notion of "helping union labor."

Politicians are often accused of breaking their promises. No doubt many of them do. But it must be remarked that they often do not promise as much as their constituents think they do. The platforms of the major parties are almost always at high levels of abstraction ("they mean all things to all men," as the cynical say), but they are often understood by voters to be more specific and concrete (i.e., at lower levels of abstraction) than they are. If one is "disillusioned" by the acts of a politician, sometimes the politician is to blame, but sometimes the voter is to blame for having had the illusion to start with—or, as we shall say, for having *confused different levels of abstraction*. What is meant by this expression will be more fully explained in ensuing chapters.

Applications

I. The following statements, in the contexts in which they are usually found, are directives. Which of these directives have collective sanction and which have not? What rewards (if any) are promised to those who follow the directives, and what punishments (if any) are threatened to those who do not? What is the likelihood, in each case, of the consequences following as promised?

1. And remember, ladies and gentlemen of the radio audience, whenever you say "Blotto Coffee" to your grocer, you are saying "thank you" to us.

> SAMPLE ANALYSIS: This is directive language since it attempts to influence the future behavior of the listener. Happily we are free to disregard this directive since it is in the interests of a business concern and, therefore, does not have collective sanction. There is an implied promise that if the listener will show his gratitude by purchasing Blotto Coffee, the manufacturer will continue to provide him with programs such as precede this announcement. If enough people obey this directive, the likelihood of this promise being kept is quite great. Better switch to tea.

2. "When first hooked a fish is strong and quick. The wise angler always gives his quarry a little time to get the edge and speed out of his runs. As soon as the first run or two are over, the maximum safe tackle strain can be applied whenever the fish stops running. A running or leaping fish should be played on a very light drag. The harder and faster a fish runs or leaps the sooner he will tire. This activity will tire a fish quicker than any strain the angler can put on him. Encourage your fish to run whenever possible but never let him rest. Big trout and salmon, difficult fish on any tackle, can be brought in as quickly on light tackle as on heavier gear if they are kept moving."
> —LEE WULFF, *Handbook of Freshwater Fishing*

3. "We hold these truths to be self-evident, that all men are created equal, that they are endowed by their Creator with certain inalienable Rights, that among these are life, liberty and the pursuit of happiness."
> —The Declaration of Independence

4. No Trespassing.

5. " 'No great stretch of the imagination is required to foresee that if nothing is done to check the growth in concentration, either the giant corporations will ultimately take over the country, or the government will be impelled to step in and impose some form of direct regulation in the public interest.' Thus declares the Federal Trade Commission, in a well-documented warning which shows the nearly fantastic rate at which independent firms are being currently 'merged' into the trusts.

"In either event, collectivism will have triumphed over free enterprise and the theory of competition will have been relegated to the limbo of well-intentioned but ineffective ideals."
> —*The Co-operative Builder,* August 12, 1948

6. "The French House, under the direction and control of the Department, provides a fine opportunity to gain fluency in the spoken language. French and bi-lingual members of the staff live at the House and help in directing conversation. Residence in the House is open to women, and both men and women may come there for meals. The House is not run for financial profit and prices are kept as low as possible.

"The Department strongly urges students of French to room or board at the House so as to take full advantage of the unusual opportunity for speaking the language in everyday situations and hearing it spoken at a normal conversational tempo.

"Applications for room reservations should be made early."

—Catalog of the University of Wisconsin

7. "THE HUMBLE WRINKLE BECOMES A WARTIME HERO. Outcast of former days, today the wrinkle in a piece of laundrywork is a symbol of our striving towards victory. Modestly, unassumingly, it says, 'I am here because so many laundry workers are in war plants—because so many more people patronize the laundry these busy days—because so many wartime restrictions surround me. But I'm really harmless. I don't hurt the appearance of laundrywork enough to talk about—and I certainly don't interfere with its usefulness. Not only that, but it's still, and always will be, completely sterilized to protect health!'

"To the wrinkle, our customers reply, 'We understand. Hats off to you in your moment of glory!'—NORTH CHICAGO LAUNDRY."

—Advertisement

8. *The New Colossus: Inscription for the Statue of Liberty*

Not like the brazen giant of Greek fame,
With conquering limbs astride from land to land
Here at our sea-washed sunset gates shall stand
A mighty woman with a torch, whose fame
Is the imprisoned lightning, and her name
Mother of Exiles. From her beaconhand
Glows world-wide welcome; her mild eyes command
The air-bridged harbour that twin cities frame.
"Keep, ancient lands, your storied pomp," cries she
With silent lips. "Give me your tired, your poor,
Your huddled masses yearning to breathe free.
The wretched refuse of your teeming shore,
Send these, the homeless, the tempest-tost to me,
I lift my lamp beside the golden door!"

—EMMA LAZARUS

II. Study the following statements in relation to the contexts in which they are likely to be found. Which are used principally as directives? Are there any which could hardly ever be used for directive purposes?

1. He is un-American.

   SAMPLE ANALYSIS: Ordinarily this statement is used as a strong judgment—a "snarl-word"—expressing the speaker's dislike of another person's opinions. Such a judgment ordinarily has strong directive implications: "Throw him out," or "Don't vote for him." In special contexts, where speaker and listener have agreed upon an *exact* and *verifiable* meaning of the word "un-American," the statement could be a report. Such contexts are rare.

2. "A policeman's lot is not a happy one."   —W. S. GILBERT

3. "Man is born free; and everywhere he is in chains."   —ROUSSEAU

4. Lightning strokes vary in length from 500 feet to two miles or more.

5. The performance will begin at 8:30 P.M. sharp.

6. "Books must be read as deliberately and reservedly as they were written." —H. D. THOREAU

7. "Activity is the only road to knowledge."   —G. B. SHAW

8. With smoker after smoker who has tried different cigarettes—and compared them for mildness, coolness and flavor—Mammals are the "choice of experience."

9. In man at rest, about sixteen breathing movements are made per minute.

10. "Some of the follies we commit because of false maps in our heads are so commonplace that we do not even think of them as remarkable. There are those who protect themselves from accidents by carrying a rabbit's foot in the pocket. Some refuse to sleep on the thirteenth floor of hotels."   —S. I. HAYAKAWA, *Language in Thought and Action*

III. Write the copy, draw (or describe) the illustrations you may need, and lay out a campaign (dinners, appointing of committees, personal solicitations, etc.) for a local fund-raising drive on behalf of the Red Cross, the Community Chest, or some such organization. Try sincerely to use appeals that will alter other people's behavior, in this case, cause them to contribute to the fund where they might otherwise not. Can one go too far in using affective appeals for even such worthy causes? If the answer is "Yes," what determines the limits within which one should stay?

IV. "Ownership" is defined in this chapter as a set of directive agreements recognized by society with respect to who may enjoy the use of what things. But the freedom to use and enjoy what is "mine" is limited according to the kind of property; e.g., I may drive "my" automobile only if it is duly registered with the state and if I have a driver's license. What are the differences in the extensional meanings of the word "my" in the following expressions:

my electric iron   *my* house
my real estate lot   *my* hotel room
my shares of General Motors stock   *my* original Rembrandt

8. The Language of Affective Communication

What I call the "auditory imagination" is the feeling for syllable and rhythm, penetrating far below the conscious levels of thought and feeling, invigorating every word; sinking to the most primitive and forgotten, returning to the origin and bringing something back, seeking the beginning and the end. It works through meanings, certainly, or not without meanings in the ordinary sense, and fuses the old and obliterated and the trite, the current, and the new and surprising, the most ancient and the most civilized mentality.   T. S. ELIOT

"What's all this about 'one man, one vote'?" asked the Nottingham miner.
"Why, one bloody man, one bloody vote," Bill replied.
"Well, why the 'ell can't they say so?"
                                                        HUGH R. WALPOLE

The language of science is instrumental in getting done the work necessary for life, but it does not tell us anything about what life feels like in the living. We can communicate scientific facts to each other without knowing or caring about each other's feelings; but before love, friendship, and community can be established among men so that we *want* to co-operate and become a society, there must be, as we have seen, a flow of sympathy between one man and another. This flow of sympathy is established, of course, by means of the affective uses of language. Most of the time, after all, we are not interested in keeping our feelings out of our discourse, but rather we are eager to express them as fully as we can. Let us examine, then, some more of the ways in which language can be made to work affectively.

Verbal Hypnotism

First, it should be pointed out again that fine-sounding speeches, long words, and the general *air* of saying something important are affective in result, regardless of what is being said. Often when we are hearing or reading impressively worded sermons, speeches, political addresses, essays, or "fine writing," we stop being critical altogether, and simply allow ourselves to feel as excited, sad, joyous, or angry as the author wishes us to feel. Like snakes under the influence of a snake charmer's flute, we are swayed by the musical phrases of the verbal hypnotist. If the author is a man to be trusted, there is no reason why we should not enjoy ourselves in this way now and then. But to listen or read in this way habitually is a debilitating habit.

There is a kind of churchgoer who habitually listens in this way, however. He enjoys any sermon, no matter what the moral principles recommended, no matter how poorly organized or developed, no matter how shabby its rhetoric, so long as it is delivered in an impressive tone of voice with proper musical and physical settings. Such listeners are by no means to be found only in churches. The writer has frequently been enraged when, after he has spoken before women's clubs on problems about which he wished to arouse thoughtful discussion, certain ladies have remarked, "That was such a lovely address, professor. You have such a nice voice."

Some people, that is, never listen to *what* is being said, since they are interested only in what might be called the gentle inward massage that the *sound* of words gives them. Just as cats and dogs like to be stroked, so do some human beings like to be verbally stroked at fairly regular intervals; it is a form of rudimentary sensual gratification. Because listeners of this kind are numerous, intellectual shortcomings are rarely a barrier to a successful career in public life, on the stage or radio, on the lecture platform, or in the ministry.

More Affective Elements

The affective power of repetition of similar sounds, as in "catchy" titles and slogans (*The Mind in the Making, Live Alone and Like It,* Roosevelt or Ruin) has already been mentioned. Somewhat higher on the scale are repetitions not only of sounds but of grammatical structures, as in:

First in war,
first in peace,
first in the hearts of his countrymen . . .

Government of the people,
by the people,
for the people . . .

Elements of discourse such as these are, from the point of view of scientific reporting, extraneous; but without them, these phrases would not have impressed people. Lincoln could have signified just as much for informative purposes had he said "government of, by and for the people," or even more simply, "a people's government." But he was not writing a scientific monograph. He hammers the word "people" at us three times, and with each apparently unnecessary repetition he arouses deeper and more affecting connotations of the word. While this is not the place to discuss in detail the complexities of the affective qualities of language that reside in sound alone, it is important to remember that many of the attractions of literature and oratory have a simple phonetic basis—rhyme, alliteration, assonance, crossed alliteration, and all the subtleties of rhythm. All these sound effects are used to reinforce wherever possible the other affective devices.

Another affective device is the *direct address* to the listener or reader, as: "Keep off the grass. This means you!" The most painful example of this is Jimmie Fidler's "And I *do* mean you." It seeks to engage the listener's attention and interest by making him feel that he personally is being addressed. But the use of this device is by no means limited to the advertising poster and radio announcer. It softens the impersonality of formal speeches and adds what is called the "personal touch." When a speaker or writer feels a special urgency about his message, he can hardly help using it. It occurs, therefore, in the finest rhetoric as well as in the simplest. Almost as common as the "you" device is the "we" device. The writer in this case allies the reader with himself, in order to carry the reader along with him in seeing things as he does: "*We* shall now consider next . . ." "Let *us* take, for example . . ." "*Our* duty is to go forward . . ." This device is particularly common in the politer forms of exhortation used by preachers and teachers and is found throughout this book.

In such rhetorical devices as the *periodic sentence* there is distortion of grammatical order for affective purposes. A periodic sentence is one in which the completion of the thought is, for the sake of the slight dramatic effect that can be produced by keeping the reader in suspense for a while, delayed. Then there are such devices as *antithesis,* in which strongly opposed notions are placed together or even laid side by side in parallel phonetic or grammatical constructions, so that the reader feels the contrast and is stirred by it: "Born a serf, he died a king." "The sweetest songs are those that tell of saddest thought." "The hungry judges soon the sentence sign, And wretches hang that jurymen may dine."

Metaphor and Simile

As we have seen, words have affective connotations in addition to their informative value, and this accounts for the fact that statements of the kind: "I've been waiting *ages* for you—you're an hour overdue!" "He's got *tons* of money!" "I'm so tired I'm simply *dead!*" —which are nonsensical if interpreted literally—nevertheless "make sense." The inaccuracy or inappropriateness of the informative connotations of our words are irrelevant from the point of view of affective communication. Therefore we may refer to the moon as "a piece of cheese," "a lady," "a silver ship," "a fragment of angry candy," or anything else, so long as the words arouse the desired feelings toward the moon or toward the whole situation in which the moon appears. This, incidentally, is the reason literature is so difficult to translate from one language to another—a translation that follows informative connotations will often falsify the affective connotations, and vice versa, so that readers who know both the language of the original and the language of the translation are almost sure to be dissatisfied, feeling either that the "spirit of the original has been sacrificed" or else that the translation is "full of inaccuracies."

During the long time in which *metaphor* and *simile* were regarded as "ornaments" of speech—that is, as if they were like embroidery, which improves the appearance of our linen but adds nothing to its utility—the psychology of such communicative devices was neglected. We tend to assume, in ways that will be discussed more fully in later chapters, that things that create in us the same responses are identical with each other. If, for example, we are revolted by the conduct of an acquaintance at dinner and we have had such a sense of revulsion before only when watching pigs at a trough, our first, unreflecting reaction is naturally to say, "He is a pig." So far as our feelings are concerned, the man and the pig are identical with each other. Again, the soft winds of spring may produce in us agreeable sensations; the soft hands of lovely young girls also produce agreeable sensations; therefore, "Spring has soft hands." This is the basic process by which we arrive at metaphor. Metaphors are not "ornaments of discourse"; they are direct expressions of evaluations and are bound to occur whenever we have strong feelings to express. They are to be found in special abundance, therefore, in all primitive speech, in folk speech, in the speech of the unlearned, in the speech of children, and in the professional argot of the theater, of gangsters, and other lively occupations.

So far as our feelings are concerned, there is no distinction between animate and inanimate objects. Our fright *feels* the same whether it is a creature or object that we fear. Therefore, in the expression of our feelings, a car may "lie down and die," the wind "kisses" our cheeks, the waves are "angry" and "roar" against the cliffs, the roads are icy and "treacherous," the mountains "look down" on the sea, machine guns "spit," revolvers "bark," volcanoes "vomit" fire, and the engine "gobbles" coal. This special kind of metaphor is called *personification* and is ordinarily described in textbooks of rhetoric as "making animate things out of inanimate." It is better understood, however, if we describe it as *not distinguishing between the animate and the inanimate*.

Simile

However, even at rudimentary stages of evaluation it becomes apparent that calling a person a pig does not take sufficiently into consideration the differences between the person and the pig. Further reflection compels one to say, in modification of the original statement, "He is *like* a pig." Such an expression is called a *simile* —the pointing out of the similarities in our feelings towards the person and the pig. The simile, then, is something of a compromise stage between the direct, unreflective expression of feeling and the report, but of course closer to the former than the latter.

Adequate recognition has never been given to the fact that what we call slang and vulgarism works on exactly the same principles as poetry does. Slang makes constant use of metaphor and simile: "sticking his neck out," "to rubberneck," "out like a light," "baloney," "shutterbug," "punch-drunk," "weasel puss," "keep your shirt on." The imaginative process by which phrases such as these are coined is the same as that by which poets arrive at poetry. In poetry, there is the same love of seeing things in scientifically outrageous but emotionally expressive language:

> The hunchèd camels of the night
> Trouble the bright
> And silver waters of the moon.
> —FRANCIS THOMPSON

> The snow doesn't give a soft white
> damn Whom it touches.
> —E. E. CUMMINGS

> . . . the leaves dead
> Are driven, like ghosts from an enchanter fleeing,
> Yellow, and black, and pale, and hectic red,
> Pestilence-stricken multitudes.
> —PERCY BYSSHE SHELLEY

Sweet are the uses of adversity,
Which like the toad, ugly and venomous,
Wears yet a precious jewel in his head;
And this our life exempt from public haunt,
Finds tongues in trees, books in the running brook,
Sermons in stones, and good in everything.
                              —WILLIAM SHAKESPEARE

    I saw Eternity the other night
    Like a great ring of pure and endless light.
                              —HENRY VAUGHAN

What is called slang, therefore, might well be regarded as the
poetry of everyday life, since it performs much the same function
as poetry; that is, it vividly expresses people's feelings about life
and about the things they encounter in life.

Dead Metaphor

Metaphor, simile, and personification are among the most useful
communicative devices we have, because by their quick affective
power they often make unnecessary the inventing of new words for
new things or new feelings. They are so commonly used for this
purpose, indeed, that we resort to them constantly without realizing that we are doing so. For example, when we talk about the
"head" of a cane, the "face" of a cliff, the "bowels" of a volcano,
the "arm" of the sea, the "hands" of a watch, the "branches" of a
river or an insurance company, we are using metaphor. A salesman
"covers" an area; an engine "knocks"; a theory is "built up" and
then "knocked down"; a government "drains" the taxpayers, and
corporations "milk" the consumers. Even in so unpoetical a source
as the financial page of a newspaper, metaphors are to be found:
stock is "watered," shares are "liquidated," prices are "slashed" or
"stepped up," markets are "flooded," the exchange is "bullish"; in
spite of government efforts to "hamstring" business and "strangle"
enterprise, there are sometimes "melons" to be "sliced"; although
this is—but here we leave the financial page—"pure gravy" for some,
others are left "holding the bag." The "rings" both of "political

rings" and "hydrocarbon rings" are metaphorical, as are the "chains" in "chain stores" and "chain reactions." Metaphors are so useful that they often pass into the language as part of its regular vocabulary. Metaphor is probably the most important of all the means by which language develops, changes, grows, and adapts itself to our changing needs. When metaphors are successful, they "die"—that is, they become so much a part of our regular language that we cease thinking of them as metaphors at all.

To object to arguments, as is often done, on the ground that they are based on metaphors or on "metaphorical thinking" is rarely just. The question is not whether metaphors are used, but whether the metaphors represent useful similarities.

Allusion

Still another affective device is *allusion*. If we say, for example, standing on a bridge in St. Paul, Minnesota, in the early morning:

> Earth has not anything to show more fair;
> Dull would he be of soul who could pass by
> A sight so touching in its majesty . . .

we are evoking, in the mind of anyone familiar with the poem such feelings as Wordsworth expressed at the sight of London in the early morning light in September 1802 and applying them to St. Paul. Thus, by a kind of implied simile, we can give expression to our feelings. Allusion, then, is an extremely quick way of expressing and also of creating in our hearers shades of feeling. With a Biblical allusion we can often arouse reverent or pious attitudes; with a historical allusion, such as saying that New York is "the modern Babylon," we can say quickly and effectively that we feel New York to be an extremely wicked and luxurious city, doomed to destruction because of its sinfulness; by a literary allusion, we can evoke the exact feelings found in a given story or poem as a way of feeling toward the event before us.

But allusions work as an affective device only when the hearer is familiar with the history, literature, people, or events alluded to.

Family jokes (which are almost always allusions to events or memories in the family's experience) have to be explained to outsiders; classical allusions in literature have to be explained to people not familiar with the classics. Nevertheless, whenever a group of people—the members of a single family or the members of a whole civilization—have memories and traditions in common, extremely subtle and efficient affective communications become possible through the use of allusion.

One of the reasons, therefore, that the young in every culture are made to study the literature and history of their own linguistic or national groups is that they may be able to understand and share in the communications of the group. Whoever, for example, fails to understand such statements as "He is a regular Benedict Arnold," or "The president of the corporation is only a Charlie McCarthy; the Bergen of the outfit is the general manager," is in a sense an outsider to the popular cultural traditions of contemporary America. Similarly, one who fails to understand passing allusions to well-known figures in European or American history, to well-known lines in Chaucer, Shakespeare, Milton, Wordsworth, or the King James version of the Bible, or to well-known characters in Dickens, Thackeray, or Mark Twain may be said in the same sense to be an outsider to an important part of the traditions of English-speaking people. The study of history and of literature, therefore, is not merely the idle acquisition of social polish, as practical men are fond of believing, but a necessary means both of increasing the efficiency of our communications and of increasing our understanding of what others are trying to communicate to us.

Irony, Pathos, and Humor

A somewhat more complex device, upon which much of humor, pathos, and irony depends, is the use of a metaphor, simile, or allusion that is so obviously inappropriate that a feeling of conflict is aroused: a conflict between our more obvious feelings towards that which we are talking about and the feelings aroused by the expression. In such a case, the conflicting feelings resolve themselves into a *third, new feeling.* Let us suppose, returning to our example above, that we are looking at an extremely ugly part of St. Paul, so that our obvious feelings are those of distaste. Then we arouse, with the Wordsworth quotation, the feeling of beauty and majesty. The result is a feeling suggested neither by the sight of the city alone nor by the allusion alone, but one that is a product of the *conflict* of the two—a sharp sense of incongruity that compels us either to laugh or to weep, depending on the rest of the context. There are many complex shades of feeling that can hardly be aroused in any other way. If a village poet is referred to as the "Mudville Milton," for example, the conflict between the inglorious connotations of "Mudville" and the glorious connotations of "Milton" produces an effect of the ludicrous, so that the poet is exposed to contempt, although, if Craigenputtock can produce a Carlyle, there is no reason that Mudville should not produce a Milton. This somewhat more complex device may be represented graphically by a diagram borrowed from mathematics:

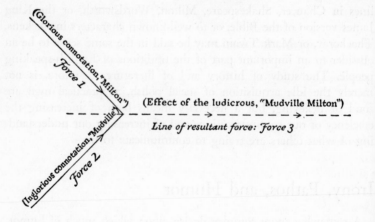

(Effect of the ludicrous, "Mudville Milton")

Line of resultant force: Force 3

The Affectiveness of Facts

The following account of an automobile accident is quoted from the Chicago *Sun-Times,* October 4, 1948:

One [victim], Alex Kuzma, 63, of 808 North Maplewood Avenue, was hit with such impact that his right forearm was carried off on the car of the hit-run motorist who struck him. Kuzma was struck Sunday as he crossed Chicago Avenue at Campbell Avenue. Witnesses saw the car slow down, douse its headlights and speed away. After searching futilely for the dead man's missing arm, police expressed belief it must have lodged in some section of the speeding auto.

There are few readers who will not have some kind of affective reaction to this story—at least a mild horror at the gruesomeness of the accident and some indignation at the driver who failed to stop after striking someone. Facts themselves, *especially at lower levels of abstraction,* can be affective without the use of special literary devices to make them more so.

There is, however, one important difference between the affectiveness of facts and the other affective elements in language. In the latter, the writer or speaker is expressing his own feelings; in the former, he is "suppressing his feelings"—that is to say, stating things in a way that would be verifiable by all observers, regardless of one's feelings.

Often, as in the example given, a report with accurately stated facts is more affective in result than outright and explicit judgments. By bringing the report down to even lower levels of abstraction— describing the blood on the victim's face and torn clothing, the torn ligaments hanging out of the remaining stump of his arm, and so on—one can make it even more affective. Instead of telling the reader, "It was a ghastly accident!" *we can make the reader say it for himself.* The reader is, so to speak, *made to participate in the communicative act by being left to draw his own conclusions.* A skillful writer is often, therefore, one who is especially expert at selecting the facts that are sure to move his readers in the desired ways. We are more likely to be convinced by such descriptive and factual writing than by a series of explicit judgments, because the writer does not ask us to take his word for it that the accident was "ghastly." Such a conclusion becomes, in a sense, our own discovery rather than his.

Levels of Writing

Reliance upon the affectiveness of facts—that is, reliance upon the reader's ability to arrive at the judgment we want him to arrive at—varies considerably, of course, according to the subject we are dealing with and the audience.

In this light, it is interesting to compare magazines and stories at different levels: the "pulp" and "confession" magazines, the "slicks" (*Good Housekeeping, McCall's, Esquire, Saturday Evening Post,* and so on), and the "quality" magazines (*Harper's, The New Yorker, The Nation,* for example). In the magazines of mass appeal, the writers rarely rely on the reader's ability to arrive at his own conclusions. In order to save any possible strain on the reader's intelligence, the writers *make the judgments for us.* The "slicks" do this less than the "pulps," while in the "quality" group, the tendency is to rely a great deal on the reader: to give no judgments at all when the facts "speak for themselves," or to give enough facts with every judgment so that the reader is free to make a different judgment if he so wishes.

The following passages from the August 1948 issue of *True Confessions* give an example of making the judgments for the reader so that he doesn't have to figure them out for himself:

Telling Mrs. Peters and Mrs. Jenks, watching grief engulf them, was nightmare enough, but telling Edie was worst of all. She just stood there in frozen silence, her eyes wide with horror and disbelief, her face getting whiter and whiter.

"I did everything possible to save them!" I cried. "It was an accident—an unpreventable accident!"

But Edie's eyes were bitterly accusing as she choked, *"Accident!* If you hadn't insisted on taking them, there would have been no accident!" Tears streamed down her ravaged face and her voice rose hysterically. "I never want to see you again as long as I live! You—*you murderer!*" she screamed.

I stared at her for what seemed a lifetime of horror before I turned and fled, a million shrieking demons screaming in my ear, *She's right! You're a murderer! Murderer!*

The coroner's verdict called the boat's overloading "a tragic error of judgment." . . . But nothing could lighten that feeling of guilt in my heart or remove the sound of Edie's voice screaming, "Murderer!" It rang in my ears day and night, making work impossible—sleep even more impossible. Until I sought forgetfulness in the only way I could find it—by getting blind drunk and staying that way.

I was lurching through the door of a cheap bar weeks later when . . .

✦ ✦ ✦

Jim was big and strong with huge shoulders and a great shock of yellow hair. Just looking at him made me excited and breathless. His great laugh could stir me to laughter. The touch of his hand filled me with a sweet, frightening delight. The day he invited me to the senior prom I thought I'd die of happiness.

Then I told Mother. I can still see her thin, fine-featured face pinched as if with frost. There was cold retreat in her eyes, and the wry smile on her lips made my heart turn over. . . .

The prose style of Ernest Hemingway is perhaps the classic example of the opposite technique—a highly sophisticated one, needless to say—of stating externally observable facts in the form of bare reports and of letting the reported facts have their impact on the reader. The following is the famous ending of *A Farewell to Arms:*

I went into the room and stayed with Catherine until she died. She was unconscious all the time, and it did not take her very long to die.

Outside the room, in the hall, I spoke to the doctor, "Is there anything I can do tonight?"

"No. There is nothing to do. Can I take you to your hotel?"

"No, thank you. I am going to stay here a while."

"I know there is nothing to say. I cannot tell you—"

"No," I said. "There's nothing to say."

"Good-night," he said. "I cannot take you to your hotel?"

"No, thank you."

"It was the only thing to do," he said. "The operation proved—"

"I do not want to talk about it," I said.

"I would like to take you to your hotel."

"No, thank you."

He went down the hall. I went to the door of the room.

"You can't come in now," one of the nurses said.

"Yes I can," I said.

"You can't come in yet."

"You get out," I said. "The other one too."

But after I had got them out and shut the door and turned off the light it wasn't any good. It was like saying good-by to a statue. After a while I went out and left the hospital and walked back to the hotel in the rain.

What Literature Is For

From what has been said, our first and most obvious conclusion is that since the expression of individual feelings is central to litera- ture, affective elements are of the utmost importance in all literary writing. In the evaluation of a novel, poem, play, or short story, as well as in the evaluation of sermons, moral exhortations, political speeches, and directive utterances generally, the usefulness of the given piece of writing as a "map" of actual "territories" is often secondary—sometimes quite irrelevant. If this were not the case, *Gulliver's Travels, Alice in Wonderland, The Scarlet Letter,* or Emerson's *Essays* would have no excuse for existence.

Secondly, when we say that a given piece of affective writing is true, we do not mean "scientifically true." It may mean merely that we agree with the sentiment; it may also mean that we believe that an attitude has been accurately expressed; again, it may mean that the attitudes it evokes are believed to be such as will lead us to better social or personal conduct. There is no end to the meanings "true" may have. People who feel that science and literature or science and religion are in necessary conflict do so because they habitually think in opposites of black and white, true and false, good and evil. To such people, if science is "true," then literature or religion is nonsense; if literature or religion is "true," science is merely "pretentious ignorance." What should be understood when people tell us that certain statements are "scientifically true" is that they are useful and verifiable formulations, suitable for the purposes of organized co-operative workmanship. What should be under- stood when people tell us that the plays of Shakespeare or the poems of Milton or Dante are "eternally true" is that they produce in us attitudes toward our fellow men, an understanding of ourselves, or feelings of deep moral obligation that are valuable to humanity under any conceivable circumstances.

Thirdly, let us consider an important shortcoming of the language of reports and of scientific writing. John Smith in love with Mary is not William Brown in love with Jane; William Brown in love with Jane is not Henry Jones in love with Anne; Henry Jones in love with Anne is not Robert Browning in love with Elizabeth Barrett. Each of these situations is unique; no two loves are exactly alike—in fact, no love even between the same people is *exactly* the same from day to day. Science, seeking as always laws of the widest possible applicability and the greatest possible generality, would abstract from these situations *only what they have in common*. But each of these lovers is conscious only of the *uniqueness* of his own feelings; each feels, as we all know, that he is the first one in the world ever to have so loved.

How is that sense of difference conveyed? It is here that affective uses of language play their most important part. The infinity of differences in our feelings towards all the many experiences that we undergo are too subtle to be reported; they must be expressed. And we express them by the complicated manipulation of tones of voice, of rhythms, of connotations, of affective facts, of metaphors, of allusions, of every affective device of language at our command.

Frequently the feelings to be expressed are so subtle or complex that a few lines of prose or verse are not enough to convey them. It is sometimes necessary, therefore, for authors to write entire books, carrying their readers through numbers of scenes, situations, and adventures, pushing their sympathies now this way and now that, arousing in turn their fighting spirit, their tenderness, their sense of tragedy, their laughter, their superstitiousness, their cupidity, their sensuousness, their piety. Only in such ways, sometimes, can the *exact* feelings an author wants to express be re-created in his readers. This, then, is the reason that novels, poems, dramas, stories, allegories, and parables exist: to convey such propositions as "Life is tragic" or "Susanna is beautiful," not by telling us so, but by putting us through a whole series of experiences that make us feel toward life or toward Susanna as the author did. *Literature is the most exact expression of feelings, while science is the most exact kind of reporting.* Poetry, which condenses all the affective resources of language into patterns of infinite rhythmical subtlety, may be said to be *the language of expression at its highest degree of efficiency.*

Symbolic Experience

In a very real sense, then, people who have read good literature have lived more than people who cannot or will not read. To have read *Gulliver's Travels* is to have had the experience, with Jonathan Swift, of turning sick at the stomach at the conduct of the human race; to read *Huckleberry Finn* is to feel what it is like to drift down the Mississippi River on a raft; to have read Byron is to have suffered with him his rebellions and neuroses and to have enjoyed with him his nose-thumbing at society; to have read *Native Son* is to know how it feels to be frustrated in the particular way in which Negroes in Chicago are frustrated. This is the great task that affective communication performs: it enables us to feel how others felt about life, even if they lived thousands of miles away and centuries ago. It is not true that we have only one life to live; if we can read, we can live as many more lives and as many kinds of lives as we wish.

Here, the reader may object by asking, are we not twisting language somewhat to talk about "living" other lives than one's own? In one sense, the objection is correct; two different meanings of the word "live" are involved in the expressions "living one's own life" and "living other people's lives in books." Human life, however, is "lived" at more than one level; we inhabit both the extensional world and the world of words (and other symbols). "Living other people's lives in books" means, as we shall use the expression here, *symbolic experience*—sometimes called "vicarious experience."

In the enjoyment and contemplation of a work of literary or dramatic art—a novel, a play, a moving picture—*we find our deepest enjoyment when the leading characters in the story to some degree symbolize ourselves.* Jessie Jenkins at the movie, watching Ann Sheridan being kissed by a handsome man, sighs as contentedly as if she herself were being kissed—and *symbolically,* she is. In other words, she identifies herself with Ann Sheridan and Ann Sheridan's role in the story. Humphrey Bogart fighting a crowd of villains is watched by thousands of men who clench their hands as if *they* were doing the fighting—which they are, *symbolically.* As we identify ourselves with the people in the story, the dramatist or the novelist puts us through *organized sequences of symbolic experiences.*

The differences between actual and symbolic experiences are great—one is not scarred by watching a moving-picture battle, nor is one nourished by watching people in a play having dinner. Furthermore, actual experiences come to us in highly disorganized fashion: meals, arguments with the landlady, visits to the doctor about one's fallen arches, and so on, interrupt the splendid course of romance. The novelist, however, *abstracts* only the events relevant to his story and then *organizes* them into a meaningful sequence. This business of abstracting (selecting) events and organizing them so that they bear some meaningful relationship to each other and to the central "theme" of a novel or play constitutes the "story-teller's art." Plot construction, development of character, narrative structure, climax, denouement, and all the other things one talks about in technical literary criticism have reference to this organizing of symbolic experiences so that the whole complex of symbolic experiences (i.e., the finished story or play) will have the desired impact on the reader.

All literary and dramatic enjoyment, whether of nursery tales in childhood or of moving pictures later on or of "great literature," appears to involve to some degree the reader's imaginative identification of himself with the roles portrayed and his projection of himself into the situations described in the story.[1] Whether a reader is able

[1] At what age does the capacity for imaginative identification of oneself with the roles portrayed in a story begin? The writer would suggest, on the basis of very limited observation, that it begins around the age of two or earlier. An interesting test case is to read the story of the Three Bears to a very small child to see when he begins to identify himself with Baby Bear.

to identify himself with the characters of a story depends both on the maturity of the story and the maturity of the reader. If a mature reader finds difficulty identifying himself with the hero of a cowboy story, it is because he finds the hero too simple-minded a character to serve as an acceptable symbol for himself, and the villains and the events too improbable to serve as symbols for his own enemies and his own problems. On the other hand, an immature reader, reading the same story, may have a deep need to imagine himself a courageous cowboy, and may also be too inexperienced or uneducated to know what kinds of people or events are probable or improbable—in which case he may enjoy the story enormously. Again, the immature reader, confronted with a story in which the central character is someone far removed from him in outlook and background (say, for example, an eighteenth-century French cardinal, involved in problems and events the reader has never heard of or thought about before) will find it impossible to find in the "hero" any kind of symbol for himself—and will therefore lay the book aside as "too dry."

One of the reasons for calling some people immature is that they are incapable of confronting defeat, tragedy, or unpleasantness of any kind. Such persons usually cannot endure an "unhappy ending" *even in a set of symbolic experiences*. Hence the widespread passion for happy endings in popular literature, so that even stories about unhappy events have to be made, in the end, to "come out all right." The immature constantly need to be reassured that everything will always come out all right.

Readers who mature as they grow older, however, steadily increase the depth and range and subtlety of their symbolic experiences. Under the guidance of skilled writers who have accurately observed the world and were able to organize their observations in significant ways, the mature reader may symbolically experience what it feels like to be a Chinese peasant woman, a Roman emperor, an early nineteenth-century poet, a Greek philosopher, an irresolute Prince of Denmark, or a dispossessed Mexican sharecropper. He may symbolically experience murder, guilt, religious exaltation, bankruptcy, the loss of friends, the discovery of gold mines or new philosophical principles, or the sense of desolation following a locust invasion in North Dakota. Each new symbolic experience means the enrichment of his insight into people and events.

The immature reader, satisfied with the narrow range of characters that popular literature offers for the reader to identify himself with (almost invariably handsome young men or beautiful young women of acceptable social status, income level, and skin color), and satisfied with the narrow range of symbolic experiences offered (love, love, and more love), may read abundantly the offerings of the drugstore newsstand and the gift-shop lending library all his life without appreciably increasing his knowledge or his sympathies.

If, on the other hand, we are mature readers, we progress in our reading, each new extension and exercise of our imaginations making possible still further extensions. Gradually, the "maps" which we have inside our heads become fuller, more accurate, pictures of the actual "territories" of human character and behavior under many different conditions and in many different times. Gradually, too, our increased insight gives us sympathy with our fellow human beings everywhere. The Kings of Egypt, the Tibetan priest behind his ceremonial mask, the Roman political exile, and the embittered Harlem youth are presented to us by the novelist, the poet, and the playwright, at levels of vivid and intimate description, so that we learn how they lived, what they worried about, and how they felt. When the lives of other people, of whatever time and place, are examined in this way, we discover to our amazement that they are all people. This discovery is the basis of all civilized human relationships. If we remain uncivilized—whether in community, industrial, national, or international relationships—it is largely because most of us have not yet made this discovery. Literature is one of the important instruments to that end.

Science and Literature

By means of scientific communication, then, with its international systems of weights and measures, international systems of botanical and zoological nomenclature, international mathematical symbols, we are enabled to exchange information with each other, pool our observations, and acquire collective control over our environment. By means of affective communication—by conversation and gesture when we can see each other, but by literature and other arts when we cannot—we come to understand each other, to cease being brutishly suspicious of each other, and gradually to realize the profound community that exists between us and our fellow men. Science, in short, makes us able to co-operate; the arts enlarge our sympathies so that we become willing to co-operate.

We are today equipped technologically to be able to get practically anything we want. But our wants are crude. There seems to be only one motivation strong enough to impel us to employ our technological capacities to the full, and that is the desire for "military security." The most expensive concerted national effort in every major nation goes into preparations for a war that nobody wants to start. The immediate task of the future, then, is not only to extend the use of scientific method into fields such as economics and politics where superstition now reigns and makes calamity inevitable. It is also to bring, through the affective power of the arts and of literature, civilizing influences to bear upon our savage wills. We must not only be *able* to work together; we must actively *want* to work together.

Applications

I. All literary criticism that tries to find out what exactly an author is saying presupposes, of course, knowledge of principles such as those discussed in this chapter. Their real application can only be in abundant and careful reading and in the development of taste through *consciousness of what is going on* in every piece of literature one reads, whether it be a magazine serial, a Katherine Mansfield short story, or an Elizabethan play.

A useful practice, even for an experienced reader, is to take short passages of prose and verse—especially passages he has long been familiar with—and to find out by careful analysis (a) what the author is trying to communicate; (b) what affective elements help him to convey his meaning; (c) what elements, if any, obscure his communication; and (d) how successful, on the whole, the author is in conveying his ideas and feelings to the reader. The following passages may serve as material for this kind of analysis:

1. "It was a crisp and spicy morning in early October. The lilacs and laburnums, lit with the glory fires of autumn, hung burning and flashing in the upper air, a fairy bridge provided by kind Nature for the wingless wild things that have their home in the tree tops and would visit together; the larch and the pomegranate flung their purple and yellow flames in brilliant broad splashes along the slanting sweep of the woodland; the sensuous fragrance of innumerable deciduous flowers rose upon the swooning atmosphere; far in the empty sky a solitary oesophagus slept upon motionless wing; everywhere brooded stillness, serenity, and the peace of God." —SAMUEL L. CLEMENS

2.
   Could man be drunk forever
    With liquor, love, and fights,
   Lief should I rouse at morning,
    And lief lie down of nights.

   But men at whiles are sober,
    And think by fits and starts,
   And if they think, they fasten
    Their hands upon their hearts.
      —A. E. HOUSMAN

3.
     Ars Poetica

A poem should be palpable and mute
As a globed fruit

Dumb
As old medallions to the thumb

Silent as the sleeve-worn stone
Of casement ledges where the moss has grown—

A poem should be wordless
As the flight of birds

   * * *

A poem should be motionless in time
As the moon climbs

Leaving, as the moon releases
Twig by twig the night-entangled trees,

Leaving, as the moon behind the winter leaves,
Memory by memory the mind—

A poem should be motionless in time
As the moon climbs

*   *   *

A poem should be equal to:
Not true

For all the history of grief
An empty doorway and a maple leaf

For love
The leaning grasses and two lights above the sea—

A poem should not mean
But be   —ARCHIBALD MACLEISH

4. "Already, in the architecture and layout of the new community, one sees the knowledge and discipline that the machine has provided turned to more vital conquests, more human consummations. Already, in imagination and plan, we have transcended the sinister limitations of the existing metropolitan environment. We have much to unbuild and much more to build; but the foundations are ready; the machines are set in place and the tools are bright and keen; the architects, the engineers, and the workmen are assembled. None of us may live to see the complete building, and perhaps in the nature of things the building can never be completed; but some of us will see the flag or the fir tree that the workers will plant aloft in ancient ritual when they cap the topmost story."   —LEWIS MUMFORD, *The Culture of Cities*

5.   Moving through the silent crowd
            Who stand behind dull cigarettes
            These men who idle in the road,
            I have a sense of falling light.

            They lounge at corners of the street
            And greet friends with a shrug of shoulder,
            And turn their empty pockets out,
            The cynical gestures of the poor.

            Now they've no work, like better men
            Who sit at desks and take much pay

They sleep long hours and rise at ten
To watch the hours that drain away.

I'm jealous of the weeping hours
They stare through with such hungry eyes.
I'm haunted by these images,
I'm haunted by their emptiness.

—STEPHEN SPENDER

6. "There is probably one purpose, and only one, for which the use
of force by a government is beneficent, and that is to diminish the total
amount of force in the world. It is clear, for example, that the legal
prohibition of murder diminishes the total amount of violence in the
world. And no one would maintain that parents should have unlimited
freedom to ill-treat their children. So long as some men wish to do
violence to others, there cannot be complete liberty, for either the wish
to do violence must be restrained, or the victims must be left to suffer.
For this reason, although individuals and societies should have the
utmost freedom as regards their own affairs, they ought not to have
complete freedom as regards their dealings with others. To give freedom
to the strong to oppress the weak is not the way to secure the greatest
possible amount of freedom in the world. This is the basis of the socialist revolt against the kind of freedom which used to be advocated by
laissez-faire economists."   —BERTRAND RUSSELL, *Political Ideals* *

II. The opening of a story or play or poem has special significance in
setting the point of view, establishing the mood, gaining the reader's
attention and interest. What can be inferred about the author's purpose
from these beginnings?

Haircut

I got another barber that comes over from Carterville and helps
me out Saturdays, but the rest of the time I can get along all right
alone. You can see for yourself that this ain't no New York City
and besides that, the most of the boys works all day and don't
have no leisure to drop in here and get themselves prettied up.

You're a newcomer, ain't you? I thought I hadn't seen you
round before. I hope you like it good enough to stay. As I say, we
ain't no New York City or Chicago, but we have pretty good times.
Not as good, though, since Jim Kendall got killed. When he was

alive, him and Hod Meyers used to keep this town in an uproar.
I bet they was more laughin' done here than any town its size in
America. . . ."

The rest of the story will be found in *The Love Nest and Other
Stories,* by Ring Lardner, Charles Scribner's Sons, New York.

Andrea del Sarto
called "The Faultless Painter"

But do not let us quarrel any more,
No, my Lucrezia; bear with me for once:
Sit down and all shall happen as you wish.
You turn your face, but does it bring your heart?
I'll work then for your friend's friend, never fear,
Treat his own subject after his own way,
Fix his own time, accept, too, his own price,
And shut the money into this small hand
When next it takes mine. . . .

The rest of this poem will be found in *The Poems of Robert Browning.*

Miss Brill

Although it was so brilliantly fine—the blue sky powdered with
gold and great spots of light like white wine splashed over the
Jardins Publiques—Miss Brill was glad she had decided on the fur.
The air was motionless, but when you opened your mouth there
was just a faint chill, like a chill from a glass of iced water before
you sip, and now and again a leaf came drifting—from nowhere,
from the sky. Miss Brill put up her hand and touched her fur.
Dear little thing! It was nice to feel it again. She had taken it out
of its box that afternoon, shaken out the moth-powder, given it a
good brush, and rubbed the life back into the dim little eyes.
"What has been happening to me?" said the sad little eyes. Oh,
how sweet it was to see them snap back at her again from the red
eiderdown! . . . But the nose, which was of some black composition, wasn't at all firm. It must have had a knock, somehow. Never
mind—a little dab of black sealing-wax when the time came—
when it was absolutely necessary . . . Little rogue! Yes, she really
felt like that about it. Little rogue biting its tail just by her left
ear. She could have taken it off and laid it on her lap and stroked
it. She felt a tingling in her hands and arms, but that came from
walking, she supposed. And when she breathed, something light

and sad—no, not sad, exactly—something gentle seemed to move in her bosom. . . .

The rest of this story will be found in *The Garden Party* by Katherine Mansfield, Alfred A. Knopf, Inc., New York.

Dr. Vinton

The sea pleased Dr. Vinton as no other single element ever had. He was up very early the first morning of the voyage, all shaved and dressed and ready before the room stewards had finished wiping down the corridors. It was a calm morning, a steady morning, and the alley-ways were humming with the faint note of progress that always fills a ship. Dr. Vinton was gratified to discover a calm sea through his porthole, and when he stepped forth from his state-room he was glad to find men already at work.

This feeling of satisfaction, of benignity, extended outward toward the world and toward his fellow men.

"Cleaning her up, eh?" he said, passing one of the stewards. Fraternization was good at any hour; it was particularly pleasing to Dr. Vinton before breakfast. He was glad, too, that he had remembered to refer to the ship as "her." . . .

The rest of this story will be found in *Quo Vadimus?* by E. B. White, Harper and Brothers, New York.

III. There are two kinds of identification which a reader may make with characters in a story. First, he may recognize in the story-character a more or less realistic representation of himself. (For example, the story-character is shown misunderstood by his parents, while the reader, because of the vividness of the narrative, recognizes his own experiences in those of the story-character.) Secondly, the reader may find, by identifying himself with the story-character, the fulfillment of his own desires. (For example, the reader may be poor, not very handsome, and not popular with girls, but he may find symbolic satisfaction in identifying himself with a story-character who is represented as rich, handsome, and madly sought after by hundreds of beautiful women.) It is not easy to draw hard-and-fast lines between these two kinds of identification, but basically the former kind (which we may call "identification by self-recognition") rests upon the *similarity* of the reader's experiences with those of the story-character, while the latter kind ("identification for wish-fulfillment") rests upon the *dissimilarity* between the reader's dull life and the story-character's interesting life. Many (perhaps most) stories engage (or seek to engage) the reader's identification by *both* means.

Study carefully a story in a love-story, confession, or a cowboy adventure magazine, analyzing plot and characterization to see in what ways and to what degree "identification by self-recognition" and "identification for wish-fulfillment" are produced in the reader by the author. Do *not* begin this analysis with literature of greater sophistication or higher literary quality, since the mechanisms are most clearly and simply revealed in the pulp magazines.

IV. The above exercise rests on the assumption that the reader, not being a pulp magazine fan, will have performed his analysis "from the outside," as one whose own emotions were not involved in the story analyzed. Next, the same task of analysis may be performed with a story, novel, or play which the reader has found interesting and absorbing. The reader might ask himself such questions as these: "What *in me* responded to what elements in the story? What does my enthusiasm for this story reveal about the story and about myself? Ten years from now, is it likely that I shall be nearly enough as I am now to continue to be moved and delighted by this story?"

V. Next, the reader might analyze a story or play which he likes *only moderately,* in the light of such questions as these: "Why do I respond only slightly to this story? Is there some gap in my own sympathies or experience? Is there some shortcoming in the story (style, improbability of plot, imperfection of plot construction, weakness of characterization, factual error, or whatever)?"

VI. If the reader *doesn't* identify himself with *any* of the characters or incidents in a story or play—and this is usually the case with satire, for instance—and yet he finds it an extremely interesting story, what are the means by which the reader's sympathies and interest are engaged?

9. Art and Tension

But my position is this: that if we try to discover what the poem is doing for the poet, we may discover a set of generalizations as to what poems do for everybody. KENNETH BURKE

A well-chosen anthology [of verse] is a complete dispensary of medicine for the more common mental disorders, and may be used as much for prevention as cure. ROBERT GRAVES

Bearing the Unbearable

Animals know their environment by direct experience only; man crystallizes his knowledge and his feelings in phonetic symbolic representations; by written symbols he accumulates knowledge and passes it on to further generations of men. Animals feed themselves where they find food, but man, co-ordinating his efforts with the efforts of others by linguistic means, feeds himself abundantly and with food prepared by a hundred hands and brought from great distances. Animals exercise but limited control over each other, but man, again by employing symbols, establishes laws and ethical systems, which are linguistic means of establishing order and predictability upon human conduct. Acquiring knowledge, securing food, establishing social order, these are activities which the biologist finds explainable as having a bearing upon survival. For human beings, each of these activities involves a symbolic dimension.

Let us attempt to state the functions of literature in scientifically verifiable terms—in other words, in terms of biological "survival value." Granted that this is a difficult task in the present state of psychological knowledge, it is necessary that we try to do so, since most explanations of the value or necessity of literature (or the other arts) take the form of purr-words—which are really no explanations at all. For example, Wordsworth speaks of poetry as "the breath and finer spirit of all knowledge"; Coleridge speaks of it as "the best words in the best order." The explanations of literature given by most teachers and critics follow a similar purr-word pattern, usually reducible to "You should read great literature because it is very, very great." If we are to give a scientific account of the functions of literature, we shall have to do better than that.

Having included under the term "literature" all the affective uses of language, we find not only as the result of the insights of students of literature and critics but also from recent psychological and psychiatric investigations that, from the point of view of the utterer, one of the most important functions of the utterance is the relieving of *tensions*. We have all known the relief that comes from uttering a long and resounding series of impolite vocables under the stress of great irritation. The same releasing of psychological tensions appears to be effected at all levels of affective utterance, if we are to believe what writers themselves have said about the creative process. The novel, the drama, the poem, like the oath or the expletive, arise, at least in part, out of internal necessity when the organism experiences a serious tension, whether resulting from joy, grief, disturbance, or frustration. And, as a result of the utterances made, the tension is, to a greater or less degree and perhaps only momentarily, mitigated.

A frustrated or unhappy animal can do relatively little about its tensions.[1] A human being, however, with an extra dimension (the world of symbols) to move around in, not only undergoes experience, but he also *symbolizes his experience to himself*. Our states of tension—especially the unhappy tensions—*become tolerable* as we manage to *state what is wrong—to get it said*—whether to a sympathetic friend, or on paper to a hypothetical sympathetic reader, or even to oneself. If our symbolizations are adequate and sufficiently skillful, our tensions are brought *symbolically under control*. To

[1] See the account of "substitutive, or symbolic" behavior among cats under conditions of experimentally induced neurosis in Jules Masserman's *Behavior and Neurosis* (1943). It can hardly be denied, in the face of Dr. Masserman's evidence, that an extremely rudimentary form of what might be called "pre-poetic" behavior, analogous to the treasuring of a lock of a loved one's hair, is to be found even among cats. The cats, when hungry, fondle the push-button that *used to* trip a mechanism that brought them food, although they appear to know (since they no longer move to the food box after touching the button) that it no longer works.

achieve this control, one may employ what Kenneth Burke has called "symbolic strategies"—that is, ways of reclassifying our experiences so that they are "encompassed" and easier to bear.[2] Whether by processes of "pouring out one's heart" or by "symbolic strategies" or by other means, we may employ symbolizations as mechanisms of relief when the pressures of a situation become intolerable.

As we all know, language is social, and for every speaker there may be hearers. The result is that an utterance that relieves a tension for the speaker can relieve a similar tension, should one happen to exist, in the hearer. There is enough similarity in human experience in different times and cultures, apparently, so that the symbolic manipulation by which John Donne, for example, "encompassed" his feelings of guilt in one of his Holy Sonnets enables us too, at another time and under another set of circumstances, to encompass our feelings of guilt about, in all probability, a different set of sins.

William Ernest Henley confronted the fact of his chronic invalidism—he had been ill since childhood and had spent long periods of his life in hospitals—by stating, in his well-known poem "Invictus," his refusal to be defeated:

> Out of the night that covers me,
>   Black as the pit from pole to pole,
> I thank whatever gods may be
>   For my unconquerable soul.
>
> In the fell clutch of circumstance
>   I have not winced nor cried aloud.
> Under the bludgeonings of chance
>   My head is bloody, but unbowed.
>
> Beyond this place of wrath and tears
>   Looms but the horror of the shade,
> And yet the menace of the years
>   Finds, and shall find me, unafraid.

[2] See Kenneth Burke, *Philosophy of Literary Form* (1941). An infielder for the Chicago White Sox some years ago made four errors in four consecutive chances. Naturally, he found his performance difficult to face. His "symbolic strategy" was reported by a Chicago *Times* writer who quoted the infielder as saying, "Anyway, I bet it's a *record!*"

It matters not how strait the gate,
  How charged with punishments the scroll,
I am the master of my fate:
I am the captain of my soul.

How, at a different time and under different circumstances, other people can use Henley's utterance to take arms against a different sea of troubles is shown by the fact that this poem is one of the favorite poems of American Negroes and is sometimes recited or sung chorally by Negro organizations. The extra meaning added to the word "black" in the second line when the poem is said by Negroes makes it perhaps an even more pointed utterance for the Negro reader than it was for the original author. Indeed, the entire poem takes on different meanings depending on what a reader, putting himself into the role of the speaker of the poem, projects into the words "the night that covers me."

Poetry has often been spoken of as an aid to sanity. Kenneth Burke calls it "equipment for living." It would appear that we can take these statements seriously and work out their implications in many directions. What are, for example, some of the kinds of symbolic manipulation by which we attempt to equip ourselves in the face of the constant succession of difficulties and tensions, great and small, that confront us day by day?

Some "Symbolic Strategies"

First of all, of course, there is what is called literary "escape"— a tremendous source of literature, poetry, drama, comic strips, and other forms of affective communication. Edgar Rice Burroughs, confined to a sickbed, symbolically traipsed through the jungle, in the person of Tarzan, in a series of breath-taking and triumphant adventures—and by means of this symbolic compensation made his sickbed endurable. At the same time he made life endurable for millions of undersized, frustrated, and feeble people. Whatever one may think of the author and the readers of the Tarzan stories, it is to be emphasized that in order to derive what shabby relief they offer from pain or boredom, it takes, both in the telling and in the reading of such stories, the symbolic process, and hence a *human* nervous system.

Let us take another example of symbolic strategy. When an angry or disgruntled employee calls his employer a "half-pint Hitler," is he not, in crude fashion, using a "strategy" which, by means of introducing his employer (a petty tyrant) into a perspective which includes Hitler (a great tyrant), symbolically reduces his employer to, as Kenneth Burke would say, manageable proportions? And did not Dante likewise, unable to punish his enemies as they deserved to be punished, symbolically put them in their places in the most uncomfortable quarters in Hell? There is a world of difference between the completeness and adequacy of such a simple epithet as "half-pint Hitler" and Dante's way of disposing of his enemies—and Dante accomplished many more things in his poem besides symbolically punishing his enemies—but are they not both symbolic manipulations by means of which the utterers derive a measure of relief, or relaxation of psychological tensions?

Let us take another example. Upton Sinclair was deeply disturbed by the stockyards as they were in 1906. One thing he could have done would have been to try to forget it; he could have buried himself in reading or writing about other things, such as idyllic lands long ago and far away or entirely nonexistent—as do the readers and writers of escape literature. Another thing he could have done would have been, by a different symbolic manipulation, to show that present evil was part of greater good "in God's omniscient plan." This has been the strategy of many religions as well as of many authors. Still another possibility would have been actually to reform conditions at the stockyards so that he could contemplate them with equanimity—but he would have had to be an important official in a packing company or in the government to initiate a change in conditions. What he did, therefore, was to *socialize his discontent*—pass it on to others—on the very good theory that if enough people felt angry or disgusted with the situation, they could collectively change the stockyards in such a way that one could adjust oneself to them. Sinclair's novel, *The Jungle,* upset so many people that it led to a federal investigation of the meat industry and to the enactment of legislation controlling some of its practices.

As is now well known, when anyone continues to experience many tensions, and these tensions are permitted to accumulate, they may lead to more or less serious psychological maladjustment. Adjustment, as modern psychology sees the process, is no static condition of unreflective bliss that comes from neither knowing nor caring what is wrong with the world. It is a dynamic, day-to-day, moment-to-moment process, and it involves changing the environment to suit one's personality as much as it involves adapting one's feelings to existing conditions. The greater resources one has for achieving and maintaining adjustment, the more successful will the process be. Literature appears to be one of the available resources.

Both the enjoyment and the production of poetry and literature, then, being human symbolic devices employed in the day-to-day process of maintaining adjustment and equipping ourselves for living, appear to be extensions of our adjustment mechanism beyond those provided for us by that part of our biological equipment which we have in common with lower animals. If a man were to spend years of his life trying to discover the chemical constituency of salt water *without* bothering to find out what has already been said on the subject in any elementary chemistry book, we should say that he was making very imperfect use of the resources which our symbolic systems have made available to us. Similarly, can it not be said that people, worrying themselves sick over their individual frustrations, constantly suffering from petty irritations and hypertensions, are making extremely imperfect use of the available human resources of adjustment when they fail to strengthen and quiet themselves through contact with literature and the other arts?

What all this boils down to, then, is that poetry (along with the other arts), whether it be good or bad and at whatever level or crudity or refinement, exists to fulfill a necessary biological function for a symbol-using class of life, that of *helping us to maintain psychological health and equilibrium.*

"Equipment for Living"

Psychiatrists recognize no distinct classes of the "sane" and the "unsane." Sanity is a matter of degree, and "sane" people are all capable of becoming more sane, or less, according to the experiences they encounter and the strength and flexibility of the internal equipment with which they meet them. Even as one's physical health has to be maintained by food and exercise, it would appear that one's psychological health too has to be maintained in the very course of living by "nourishment" at the level of affective symbols: literature that introduces us to new sources of delight; literature that makes us feel that we are not alone in our misery; literature that shows us our own problems in a new light; literature that suggests new possibilities for oneself and opens new areas of possible experience; literature that offers us a variety of "symbolic strategies" by means of which we can "encompass" our situations.

From such a point of view, certain kinds of literature, like certain kinds of processed and manufactured food, can be said to look very much like nourishment, but to contain none of the essential vitamin ingredients, so that great quantities can be consumed without affecting one's spiritual undernourishment. (One could mean by "essential vitamin ingredients" in this context, "maps" of actual "territories" of human experience, directives that are both realistic and helpful, and so on.) Certain kinds of popular fiction claim to throw light upon given problems in life—stories with such titles as "The Office Wife—Was She Playing Fair?"—but, like patent medicines, these offer apparent soothing to surface symptoms, and leave underlying causes undealt with. Other kinds of fiction, like drugs and liquor, offer escape from pain, and again leave causes untouched, so that the more of them you take the more you need. Fantasy-living—which is one of the important characteristics of schizophrenia—can be aggravated by the consumption of too much of this narcotic literature. Still other kinds of fiction, movies, radio stories, and the like, give a false, prettified picture of the world—a world that can be adjusted to *without effort*. But readers

who adjust themselves to this unreal world naturally become progressively less adjusted to the world as it is.

These are admittedly oversimplified examples, and it would be a
disaster to apply too crudely the principle of literature as an aid
to sanity. An immediate temptation that some might see in this
principle would be to say that, if literature is an instrument for
maintaining sanity, the writings of many not-too-sane geniuses will
have to be thrown out as unhealthy. It would seem, on the contrary, that the symbolic strategies devised by extremely tortured
people like Dostoevski or Donne or Shelley for the encompassing
of their situations are valuable in the extreme. They mixed themselves powerful medicines against their ills, and their medicines
not only help us to encompass whatever similar tortures we may
be suffering from, but may serve also as antitoxins lest we in future
have occasion so to suffer.

Furthermore, when a work of literature is said to be "permanent,"
"lasting," or "great," does it not mean that the symbolic strategy
by which the author encompassed his disturbance (achieved his
equilibrium) works for other people troubled by other disturbances
at other times and places? Is it possible, for example, to read Sinclair's strategic handling of the Chicago stockyards without awareness that it applies more or less adequately to other people's disturbances about factory workers in Turin, or Manchester, or Kobe,
or Montreal? And if it applies especially well to, say, Detroit, does
not the Detroiter regard Sinclair's book as having lasting value?
And if, under changing conditions, there are no longer social situations which arouse similar tensions, or if the strategies seem no
longer adequate, do we not consider the author to be "dated," if
not "dead"? [3] But if an author has adequately dealt with tensions

---

[3] *The Jungle* is, in the writer's opinion, very much "dated" in some respects and
in other respects still powerful. Translated into many languages, it was been widely
read by working classes all over the world. The symbolic strategies of works of
great literary art are usually, unlike those of *The Jungle,* too complex and subtle
for such a rough analysis as has been attempted here. *The Jungle* has been chosen
for discussion because books like this, which are far from being great masterpieces
and yet give a great deal of profoundly felt insight into segments of human experience, are especially helpful in the understanding of the theories of literature
proposed in this chapter. The strategies, being not too subtle, can be clearly seen
and described.

that people under all times and conditions appear to experience, do we not call his writings "universal" and "undying"?

The relationship between literature and life is a subject about which little is known scientifically at the present time. Nevertheless, in an unorganized way, we all feel that we know something about that relationship, since we have all felt the effects of some kind of literature at some time in our lives. Most of us have felt, even if we have not been able to prove, that harmful consequences can arise from the consumption of such literary fare as is offered in the movies, in soap operas, in popular magazines, and in the so-called comic books. But the imperfection of our scientific knowledge is revealed by the fact that, when there is widespread argument as to whether or not comic books should be banned, equally imposing authorities on both sides are able to "prove" their cases; some say that comic books stimulate the child's imagination in unhealthy ways and lead them into crime, while others say that the crimes are committed by psychopathic children who would have committed them anyway, and that comic books, by offering to normal children a symbolic release of their aggressive tendencies, actually help to calm them down. It appears to be anybody's guess.

Nevertheless, is it not possible that if students of literature and psychology approach the problem of the relationship between imaginative representations and human behavior from a mental hygiene point of view, they will some day be able to state, in the interests of everyday sanity, what kinds of literature contribute to maturity and what kinds help to keep us permanently infantile and immature in our evaluations?

Art as Order

At least one other important element enters into our pleasure both in the writing and reading of literature—but about this there is still less available scientific knowledge. It pertains to what are called the artistic or esthetic values of a work of the imagination.

In Chapter 8, we spoke of the relationships, for example in a novel, of the incidents and characters to each other—that is, the meaningful arrangement of experiences that make a novel different from a jumbled narrative. Before we speak of a narrative as a "novel" and therefore as a "work of art," we must be satisfied that, regardless of whether or not we could "live the story" through imaginative identification with the characters, the incidents are arranged in some kind of *order*. Even if we don't happen to like the story, if we find a complex, but discernible and interesting, order to the incidents in a novel, we are able to say, "It certainly is beautifully put together." Indeed, sometimes the internal order and neat relationships of the parts to each other in a novel may be so impressive that we enjoy it in spite of a lack of sympathy with the kinds of incidents or people portrayed. Why is order interesting almost of itself?

The writer would suggest that if an answer is found to this question, it will have to be found in terms of human symbolic processes and the fact that symbols of symbols, symbols of symbols of symbols, and so on, can be manufactured indefinitely by the human nervous system. This fact, already explained in Chapter 2 (and to be explained further in Chapter 10), can be given a special application that may enable us to understand the functions of literature.

Animals, as we have remarked, live in the extensional world— they have no symbolic world to speak of. There would seem to be no more "order" in an animal's existence than the order of physical events as they impinge on its life. Man, however, both *lives* (at the extensional level) and *talks about his life to himself* (at the symbolic level, either with words, or in the case of painters and musicians and dancers, with nonverbal symbols). A human being is not satisfied simply to know his way around extensionally; he can hardly help talking to himself about what he has seen and felt and done.

The data of experience, when talked about, are full of contradictions. Mrs. Robinson loves her children, but ruins them through misdirected love; the illiterate peasants of a Chinese village show greater social and personal wisdom than the educated people of great cities; people say crime doesn't pay, but in some cases it pays extremely well; a young man by temperament a scholar and a poet feels compelled to commit a political murder; a faithful wife of twenty years deserts her husband for no apparent reason; a ne'er-do-well acts courageously in a dangerous situation—these and a thousand other contradictions confront us in the course of our lives. Unordered, and bearing no relationship to each other, our statements about experience are not only disconnected, but they are difficult to use.

Insofar as we are aware of these contradictions, this disorder among our statements is itself a source of tension. Such contradictions provide us with no guide to action; hence they leave us with the tensions of indecision and bewilderment. These tensions are not resolved until we have, *by talking to ourselves about our talking* (symbolizing our symbols), "fitted things together," so that, as we say, things don't seem to be "meaningless" any more. Religions, philosophies, science, and art are equally, and through different methods, ways of resolving the tensions produced by the contradictory data of experience by talking about our talking, then talking about our talking about our talking, and so on, until some kind of *order* has been established among the data.

Talking about things, talking about talking, talking about talking about talking, etc., represent what we shall call talking at different *levels of abstraction*. The imposition of order upon our pictures of the world is, it appears, what we mean by "understanding." When we say that a scientist "understands" something, does it not mean that he has ordered his observations at the objective, descriptive, and higher inferential levels of abstraction into a workable system in which all levels are related to other levels in terms of a few powerful generalizations? When a great religious leader or philosopher is said to "understand" life, does it not mean that he has also ordered his observations into a set of attitudes, often crystallized into exceedingly general and powerful directives? And when a novelist is said to "understand" the life of any segment of humanity (or humanity as a whole), has he not also ordered his observations at many different levels of abstraction—the particular and concrete, the general, and the more general? (Fuller explanation of "levels of abstraction" will be found in Chapter 10, to follow.) But the novelist presents that order not in a scientific, ethical, or philosophical system of highly abstract generalizations, but in a set of symbolic experiences at the descriptive level of affective reports, involving the reader's feelings through the mechanism of identification. And these symbolic experiences, in the work of any competent novelist, are woven together to frame a consistent set of attitudes, whether of scorn, or compassion, or admiration of courage, or sympathy with the downtrodden, or a sense of futility, depending on his outlook.

Some of the ways of organizing a set of experiences for literary purposes are purely mechanical and external: these are the "rules" governing the proper construction of the novel, the play, the short story, the sonnet, and so on. But more important are the ways of organization suggested by the materials of the literary work—the experiences which the writer wishes to organize. When the materials of a story do not fit into the conventional pattern of a novel, the novelist may create a new organization altogether, more suited to the presentation of his experiences than the conventional patterns. In such a case, critics speak of the materials as "creating their own form." The reason a poem, novel, or play assumes the shape it ultimately does is the concern of the technical literary critic. He studies the interplay of external and internal demands which finally shape the materials into a "work of art."

To symbolize adequately and then to order into a coherent whole one's experiences constitute an integrative act. The great novelist or dramatist or poet is one who has successfully integrated and made coherent vast areas of human experience. Literary greatness requires, therefore, great extensional awareness of the range of human experience as well as great powers of ordering that experience meaningfully. This is why the discipline of the creative artist is endless: there is always more to learn, both about human experience (which is the material to be ordered) and about the techniques of his craft (which are the means of ordering).

From the point of view of the reader, the fact that language is social is again of central importance. The ordering of experiences and attitudes accomplished linguistically by the writer produces, in the reader, some ordering of his own experiences and attitudes. The reader becomes, as a result of this ordering, somewhat better organized himself. That's what art is for.

Applications

I. Compare the following excerpts with the point of view expressed in this chapter:

1. "The end of writing is to instruct; the end of poetry is to instruct by pleasing."   —SAMUEL JOHNSON, *Preface to Shakespeare*

2. "A classic is a work which gives pleasure to the minority which is intensely and permanently interested in literature. It lives on because the minority, eager to renew the sensation of pleasure, is eternally curious and is therefore engaged in an eternal process of rediscovery. A classic does not survive for any ethical reason. It does not survive because it conforms to certain canons, or because neglect would kill it. It survives because it is a source of pleasure and because the passionate few can no more neglect it than a bee can neglect a flower. The passionate few do not read 'the right things' because they are right. That is to put the cart before the horse. 'The right things' are the right things solely because the passionate few *like* reading them. . . ."

"Nobody at all is quite in a position to choose with certainty among modern works. To sift the wheat from the chaff is a process that takes an exceedingly long time. Modern works have to pass before the bar of the taste of successive generations; whereas, with classics, which have been through the ordeal, almost the reverse is the case. *Your taste has to pass before the bar of the classics.* That is the point. If you differ with a classic, it is you who are wrong, and not the book. If you differ with a modern work, you may be wrong or you may be right, but no judge is authoritative to decide. Your taste is unformed. It needs guidance and it needs authoritative guidance."

          —ARNOLD BENNETT, *Literary Taste: How to Form It*

3. "The view that the mental experience of the reader is the poem itself leads to the absurd conclusion that a poem is non-existent unless experienced and that it is re-created in every experience. There thus would not be one *Divine Comedy* but as many Divine Comedies as there are and were and will be readers. We end in complete skepticism and anarchy and arrive at the vicious maxim of *De gustibus non est disputandum.* If we should take this view seriously, it would be impossible to explain why one experience of a poem by one reader should be better than the experience of any other reader and why it is possible

to correct the interpretation of another reader. It would mean the definite end of all teaching of literature which aims at enhancing the understanding and appreciation of a text. . . .

"The psychology of the reader, however interesting in itself or useful for pedagogical purposes, will always remain outside the object of literary study—the concrete work of art—and is unable to deal with the question of the structure and value of the work of art."

—RENE WELLEK and AUSTIN WARREN, *Theory of Literature*

4. "The business of art is to reveal the relation between man and his circumambient universe, at the living moment. As mankind is always struggling in the toils of old relationships, art is always ahead of the 'times,' which themselves are always far in the rear of the living moment.

"When van Gogh paints sunflowers, he reveals, or achieves, the vivid relation between himself, as man, and the sunflower, as sunflower, at that quick moment of time. His painting does not represent the sunflower itself. We shall never know what the sunflower is. And the camera will *visualize* the sunflower far more perfectly than van Gogh can.

"The vision on the canvas is a third thing, utterly intangible and inexplicable, the offspring of the sunflower itself and van Gogh himself. The vision on the canvas is for ever incommensurable with the canvas, or the paint, or van Gogh as a human organism, or the sunflower as a botanical organism. You cannot weigh nor measure nor even describe the vision on the canvas. . . .

"It is a revelation of the perfected relation, at a certain moment, between a man and a sunflower. . . . And this perfected relation between man and his circumambient universe is life itself, for mankind. . . . Man and the sunflower both pass away from the moment, in the process of forming a new relationship. The relation between all things changes from day to day, in a subtle stealth of change. Hence art, which reveals or attains to another perfect relationship, will be for ever new.

"If we think about it, we find that our life *consists in* this achieving of a pure relationship between ourselves and the living universe about us. This is how I 'save my soul' by accomplishing a pure relationship between me and another person, me and other people, me and a nation, me and a race of men, me and animals, me and the trees or flowers, me and the earth, me and the skies and sun and stars, me and the moon: an infinity of pure relations, big and little. . . . This, if we knew it, is our life and our eternity: the subtle, perfected relation between me and my whole circumambient universe. . . .

"Now here we see the beauty and the great value of the novel. Philosophy, religion, science, they are all of them busy nailing things down, to get a stable equilibrium. Religion, with its nailed down One God . . . ; philosophy, with its fixed ideas; science with its 'laws': they, all of them, all the time, want to nail us on some tree or other.

"But the novel, no. The novel is the highest example of subtle interrelatedness that man has discovered. . . ."

—D. H. LAWRENCE, "Morality and the Novel," in *Phoenix*

II. In the light of what has been said in this chapter, study the following poems to see:

a. What tensions of his own the author seems to be trying to resolve.

b. What symbolic strategies he employs.

c. Whether these strategies might be applicable to other people and other situations.

d. To what extent the author has succeeded in ordering his experiences into a coherent, meaningful whole.

In what particular ways, if any, is each of these poems likely to serve as "equipment for living"?

Ozymandias

I met a traveler from an antique land
Who said: Two vast and trunkless legs of stone
Stand in the desert. Near them, on the sand,
Half sunk, a shattered visage lies, whose frown,
And wrinkled lip, and sneer of cold command,
Tell that its sculptor well those passions read
Which yet survive, (stamped on these lifeless things),
The hand that mocked them and the heart that fed;
And on the pedestal these words appear:
'My name is Ozymandias, king of kings;
Look on my works, ye Mighty, and despair!'
Nothing beside remains. Round the decay
Of that colossal wreck, boundless and bare,
The lone and level sands stretch far away.

—PERCY BYSSHE SHELLEY

Salutation

O generation of the thoroughly smug
  and thoroughly uncomfortable,
I have seen fishermen picnicking in the sun,

I have seen them with untidy families,
I have seen their smiles full of teeth
    and heard ungainly laughter.
And I am happier than you are,
And they were happier than I am;
And the fish swim in the lake
    and do not even own clothing.

—EZRA POUND

Lessons of the War

NAMING OF PARTS

Today we have naming of parts. Yesterday,
We had daily cleaning. And tomorrow morning
We shall have what to do after firing. But today,
Today we have naming of parts. Japonica
Glistens like coral in all of the neighboring gardens,
    And today we have naming of parts.

This is the lower sling swivel. And this
Is the upper sling swivel, whose use you will see
When you are given your slings. And this is the piling swivel,
Which in your case you have not got. The branches
Hold in the gardens their silent, eloquent gestures,
    Which in our case we have not got.

This is the safety-catch, which is always released
With an easy flick of the thumb. And please do not let me
See anyone using his finger. You can do it quite easy
If you have any strength in your thumb. The blossoms
Are fragile and motionless, never letting anyone see
    Any of them using their finger.

And this you can see is the bolt. The purpose of this
Is to open the breech, as you see. We can slide it
Rapidly backwards and forwards; we call this
Easing the spring. And rapidly backwards and forwards
The early bees are assaulting and fumbling the flowers:
    They call it easing the Spring.

They call it easing the Spring: it is perfectly easy
If you have any strength in your thumb: like the bolt,
And the breech, and the cocking-piece, and the point of balance,

Which in our case we have not got; and the almond-blossom
Silent in all of the gardens and the bees going backwards and forwards,
  For today we have naming of parts.

                       —HENRY REED

III. Read, ponder, and digest:

'Terence, this is stupid stuff:
You eat your victuals fast enough;
There can't be much amiss, 'tis clear,
To see the rate you drink your beer.
But oh, good Lord, the verse you make,
It gives a chap the belly-ache.
The cow, the old cow, she is dead;
It sleeps well, the horned head:
We poor lads, 'tis our turn now
To hear such tunes as killed the cow.
Pretty friendship 'tis to rhyme
Your friends to death before their time
Moping melancholy mad:
Come, pipe a tune to dance to, lad.'

  Why, if 'tis dancing you would be,
There's brisker pipes than poetry.
Say, for what were hop-yards meant,
Or why was Burton built on Trent?
Oh many a peer of England brews
Livelier liquor than the Muse,
And malt does more than Milton can
To justify God's ways to man.
Ale, man, ale's the stuff to drink
For fellows whom it hurts to think:
Look into the pewter pot
To see the world as the world's not.
And faith, 'tis pleasant till 'tis past:
The mischief is that 'twill not last.
Oh I have been to Ludlow fair
And left my necktie God knows where,
And carried half way home, or near,
Pints and quarts of Ludlow beer:
Then the world seemed none so bad,

And I myself a sterling lad;
And down in lovely muck I've lain,
Happy till I woke again.
Then I saw the morning sky:
Heigho, the tale was all a lie;
The world, it was the old world yet,
I was I, my things were wet,
And nothing now remained to do
But begin the game anew.

Therefore, since the world has still
Much good, but much less good than ill,
And while the sun and moon endure
Luck's a chance, but trouble's sure,
I'd face it as a wise man would,
And train for ill and not for good.
'Tis true, the stuff I bring for sale
Is not so brisk a brew as ale:
Out of a stem that scored the hand
I wrung it in a weary land.
But take it: if the smack is sour,
The better for the embittered hour;
It should do good to heart and head
When your soul is in my soul's stead;
And I will friend you, if I may
In the dark and cloudy day.

There was a king reigned in the East:
There, when kings will sit to feast,
They get their fill before they think
With poisoned meat and poisoned drink.
He gathered all that springs to birth
From the many-venomed earth;
First a little, thence to more,
He sampled all her killing store;
And easy, smiling, seasoned sound,
Sate the king when healths went round.
They put arsenic in his meat
And stared aghast to watch him eat;
They poured strychnine in his cup
And shook to see him drink it up:

They shook, they stared as white's their shirt:
Them it was their poison hurt.
—I tell the tale that I heard told.
Mithridates, he died old.

—A. E. HOUSMAN

BOOK TWO

Language and Thought

A great deal of attention has been paid . . . to the technical languages in which men of science do their specialized thinking . . . But the colloquial usages of everyday speech, the literary and philosophical dialects in which men do their thinking about the problems of morals, politics, religion and psychology—these have been strangely neglected. We talk about "mere matters of words" in a tone which implies that we regard words as things beneath the notice of a serious-minded person.

This is a most unfortunate attitude. For the fact is that words play an enormous part in our lives and are therefore deserving of the closest study. The old idea that words possess magical powers is false; but its falsity is the distortion of a very important truth. Words do have a magical effect—but not in the way that the magicians supposed, and not on the objects they were trying to influence. Words are magical in the way they affect the minds of those who use them. "A mere matter of words," we say contemptuously, forgetting that words have power to mould men's thinking, to canalize their feeling, to direct their willing and acting. Conduct and character are largely determined by the nature of the words we currently use to discuss ourselves and the world around us.

ALDOUS HUXLEY, *Words and Their Meanings*

10. How We Know What We Know

The crucial point to be considered in a study of language behavior is the relationship between language and reality, between words and not-words. Except as we understand this relationship, we run the grave risk of straining the delicate connection between words and facts, of permitting our words to go wild, and so of creating for ourselves fabrications of fantasy and delusion.
WENDELL JOHNSON

Bessie, The Cow

The universe is in a perpetual state of flux. The stars are in constant motion, growing, cooling, exploding. The earth itself is not unchanging; mountains are being worn away, rivers are altering their channels, valleys are deepening. All life is also a process of change, through birth, growth, decay, and death. Even what we used to call "inert matter"—chairs and tables and stones—is not inert, as we now know, for, at the submicroscopic level, it is a whirl of electrons. If a table looks today very much as it did yesterday or as it did a hundred years ago, it is not because it has not changed, but because the changes have been too minute for our coarse perceptions. To modern science there is no "solid matter." If matter looks "solid" to us, it does so only because its motion is too rapid or too minute to be felt. It is "solid" only in the sense that a rapidly rotating color chart is "white" or a rapidly spinning top is "standing still." Our senses are extremely limited, so that we constantly have to use instruments such as microscopes, telescopes, speedometers, stethoscopes, and seismographs to detect and record occurrences which our senses are not able to record directly. The way in which we happen to see and feel things is the result of the peculiarities of our nervous systems. There are "sights" we cannot see, and, as even children know today with their high-frequency dog whistles, "sounds" that we cannot hear. It is absurd, therefore, to imagine that we ever perceive anything "as it really is."

Inadequate as our senses are, with the help of instruments they tell us a great deal. The discovery of microörganisms with the use of the microscope has given us a measure of control over bacteria; we cannot see, hear, or feel radio waves, but we can create and transform them to useful purpose. Most of our conquest of the external world, in engineering, in chemistry, and in medicine, is due to our use of mechanical contrivances of one kind or another to increase the capacity of our nervous systems. In modern life, our unaided senses are not half enough to get us about in the world. We cannot even obey speed laws or compute our gas and electric bills without mechanical aids to perception.

To return, then, to the relations between words and what they stand for, let us say that there is before us "Bessie," a cow. Bessie is a living organism, constantly changing, constantly ingesting food and air, transforming it, getting rid of it again. Her blood is circulating, her nerves are sending messages. Viewed microscopically, she is a mass of variegated corpuscles, cells, and bacterial organisms; viewed from the point of view of modern physics, she is a perpetual dance of electrons. What she is in her entirety, we can never know; even if we could at any precise moment say what she was, at the next moment she would have changed enough so that our description would no longer be accurate. It is impossible to say completely what Bessie or anything else really *is*. Bessie is no static "object," but a dynamic process.

The Bessie that we experience, however, is something else again. We experience only a small fraction of the total Bessie: the lights and shadows of her exterior, her motions, her general configuration, the noises she makes, and the sensations she presents to our sense of touch. *And because of our previous experience, we observe resemblances in her to certain other animals to which. in the past, we have applied the word "cow."*

The Process of Abstracting

The "object" of our experience, then, is not the "thing in itself," but *an interaction between our nervous systems (with all their imperfections) and something outside them.* Bessie is unique—there is nothing else in the universe exactly like her in all respects. But our nervous systems, automatically *abstracting* or selecting from the process-Bessie those features of hers in which she resembles other animals of like size, functions, and habits, *classify* her as "cow."

When we say, then, that "Bessie is a cow," we are only noting the process-Bessie's resemblances to other "cows" and *ignoring differences.* What is more, we are leaping a huge chasm: from the dynamic process-Bessie, a whirl of electro-chemico-neural eventfulness, to a relatively static "idea," "concept," or *word,* "cow." The reader is referred to the diagram entitled "The Abstraction Ladder," which he will find on page 169.[1]

As the diagram illustrates, the "object" we see is an abstraction of the lowest level, but it is still an abstraction, since it leaves out characteristics of the process that is the real Bessie. The *word* "Bessie" (cow_1) is the lowest *verbal* level of abstraction, leaving out further characteristics—the differences between Bessie yesterday and Bessie today, between Bessie today and Bessie tomorrow—and selecting only the similarities. The word "cow" selects only the similarities between Bessie (cow_1), Daisy (cow_2), Rosie (cow_3), and so on, and therefore leaves out still more about Bessie. The word "livestock" selects or abstracts only the features that Bessie has in common with pigs, chickens, goats, and sheep. The term "farm asset" abstracts only the features Bessie has in common with barns, fences, livestock, furniture, generating plants, and tractors, and is therefore on a very high level of abstraction.

The reason we must concern ourselves with the process of abstracting is that the study of language is all too often regarded as

[1] The "abstraction ladder" is based on "The Structural Differential," a diagram originated by A. Korzybski to explain the process of abstracting. For a fuller explanation both of the diagram and the process it illustrates, see his *Science and Sanity: An Introduction to Non-Aristotelian Systems and General Semantics* (1933), especially Chapter XXV.

being a matter of examining such things as pronunciation, spelling, vocabulary, grammar, and sentence structure. The methods by which composition and oratory are taught in old-fashioned school systems seems to be largely responsible for this widespread notion that the way to study words is to concentrate one's attention exclusively on words.

But as we know from everyday experience, learning language is not simply a matter of learning words; it is a matter of correctly relating our words to the things and happenings for which they stand. We learn the language of baseball by playing or watching the game *and studying what goes on*. It is not enough for a child to learn to *say* "cookie" or "dog"; he must be able to use these words in their proper relationship to nonverbal cookies and nonverbal dogs before we can grant that he is learning the language. As Wendell Johnson has said, "The study of language begins properly with a study of what language is about."

Once we begin to concern ourselves with what language is about, we are at once thrown into a consideration of how the human nervous system works. When we call Beau (the Boston terrier), Pedro (the Chihuahua), Snuffles (the English bulldog), and Shane (the Irish wolfhound)—creatures that differ greatly in size, shape, appearance, and behavior—by the same name, "dog," our nervous system has obviously gone to work *abstracting* what is common to them all, ignoring for the time being the differences among them.

Why We Must Abstract

This process of abstracting, of leaving characteristics out, is an indispensable convenience. To illustrate by still another example, suppose that we live in an isolated village of four families, each owning a house. A's house is referred to as *maga;* B's house is *biyo;* C's is *kata,* and D's is *pelel*. This is quite satisfactory for ordinary purposes of communication in the village, unless a discussion arises about building a new house—a spare one, let us say. We cannot refer to the projected house by any one of the four words we have for the existing houses, since each of these has too specific a meaning. We must find a *general* term, at a higher level of abstraction,

ABSTRACTION LADDER

Start reading from the bottom *UP*

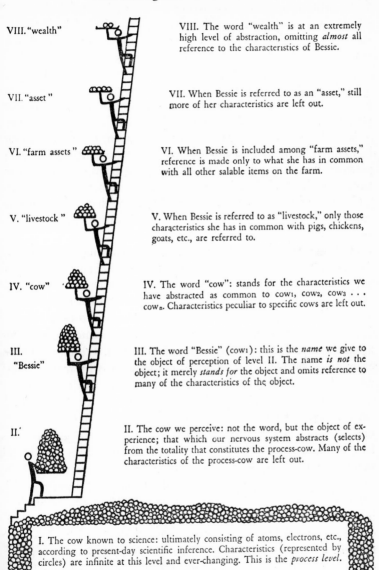

VIII. "wealth"

VII. "asset"

VI. "farm assets"

V. "livestock"

IV. "cow"

III. "Bessie"

II.

VIII. The word "wealth" is at an extremely high level of abstraction, omitting *almost* all reference to the characteristics of Bessie.

VII. When Bessie is referred to as an "asset," still more of her characteristics are left out.

VI. When Bessie is included among "farm assets," reference is made only to what she has in common with all other salable items on the farm.

V. When Bessie is referred to as "livestock," only those characteristics she has in common with pigs, chickens, goats, etc., are referred to.

IV. The word "cow": stands for the characteristics we have abstracted as common to cow_1, cow_2, cow_3 ... cow_n. Characteristics peculiar to specific cows are left out.

III. The word "Bessie" (cow_1): this is the *name* we give to the object of perception of level II. The name *is not* the object; it merely *stands for* the object and omits reference to many of the characteristics of the object.

II. The cow we perceive: not the word, but the object of experience; that which our nervous system abstracts (selects) from the totality that constitutes the process-cow. Many of the characteristics of the process-cow are left out.

I. The cow known to science: ultimately consisting of atoms, electrons, etc., according to present-day scientific inference. Characteristics (represented by circles) are infinite at this level and ever-changing. This is the *process level*.

that means "something that has certain characteristics in common with *maga, biyo, kata,* and *pelel,* and yet is not A's, B's, C's, or D's." Since this is much too complicated to say each time, an *abbreviation* must be invented. Let us say we choose the noise, *house.* Out of such needs do our words come—they are a form of shorthand. The invention of a new abstraction is a great step forward, since it *makes discussion possible*—as, in this case, not only the discussion of a fifth house, but of all future houses we may build or see in our travels or dream about.

A producer of educational films once remarked to the writer that it is impossible to make a shot of "work." You can shoot Joe hoeing potatoes, Frank greasing a car, Bill spraying paint on a barn, but never just "work." "Work," too, is a shorthand term, standing, at a higher level of abstraction, for a characteristic that a multitude of activities, from dishwashing to navigation to running an advertising agency to governing a nation, have in common.

The indispensability of this process of abstracting can again be illustrated by what we do when we "calculate." The word "calculate" originates from the Latin word *calculus,* meaning "pebble," and comes to have its present meaning from such ancient practices as that of putting a pebble into a box for each sheep as it left the fold, so that one could tell, by checking the sheep returning at night against the pebbles, whether any had been lost. Primitive as this example of calculation is, it will serve to show why mathematics works. Each pebble is, in this example, an abstraction representing the "oneness" of each sheep—its numerical value. And because we are abstracting from extensional events on clearly understood and uniform principles, the numerical facts about the pebbles are also, barring unforeseen circumstances, numerical facts about the sheep. Our x's and y's and other mathematical symbols are abstractions made from numerical abstractions, and are therefore abstractions of still higher level. And they are useful in predicting occurrences and in getting work done because, since they are abstractions properly and uniformly made from starting points in the extensional world, the relations revealed by the symbols will be, again barring unforeseen circumstances, relations existing in the extensional world.

On Definitions

Definitions, contrary to popular opinion, tell us nothing about things. They only describe people's linguistic habits; that is, they tell us what noises people make under what conditions. Definitions should be understood as *statements about language.*

House. This is a word, at the next higher level of abstraction, that can be substituted for the more cumbersome expression, "Something that has characteristics in common with Bill's bungalow, Jordan's cottage, Mrs. Smith's tourist home, Dr. Jones's mansion . . ."
Red. A feature that rubies, roses, ripe tomatoes, robins' breasts, uncooked beef, and lipsticks have in common is abstracted, and this word expresses that abstraction.
Kangaroo. Where the biologist would say "herbivorous mammal, a marsupial of the family Macropodidae," ordinary people say "kangaroo."

Now it will be observed that while the definitions of "house" and "red" given here point *down* the abstraction ladder (see the charts) to *lower* levels of abstraction, the definition of "kangaroo" remains at the same level. That is to say, in the case of "house," we could if necessary go and *look* at Bill's bungalow, Jordan's cottage, Mrs. Smith's tourist home, and Dr. Jones's mansion, and figure out for ourselves what features they seem to have in common; in this way, we might begin to understand under what conditions to use the word "house." But all we know about "kangaroo" from the above is that where some people say one thing, other people say another. That is, when we stay at the *same* level of abstraction in giving a definition, we do not give any information, unless, of course, the listener or reader is already sufficiently familiar with the defining words so that he can work himself down the abstraction ladder. Dictionaries, in order to save space, have to assume in many cases such familiarity with the language on the part of the reader. But where the assumption is unwarranted, definitions at the same level of abstraction are worse than useless. Looking up "indifference" in some cheap pocket dictionaries, we find it defined as "apathy"; we look up "apathy" and find it defined as "indifference."

Even more useless, however, are the definitions that go *up* the abstraction ladder to higher levels of abstraction—the kind most of us tend to make automatically. Try the following experiment on an unsuspecting friend:

> "What is meant by the word *red?*"
> "It's a color."
> "What's a *color?*"
> "Why, it's a quality things have."
> "What's a *quality?*"
> "Say, what are you trying to do, anyway?"

You have pushed him into the clouds. He is lost.

If, on the other hand, we habitually go *down* the abstraction ladder to *lower* levels of abstraction when we are asked the meaning of a words, we are less likely to get lost in verbal mazes; we will tend to "have our feet on the ground" and know what we are talking about. This habit displays itself in an answer such as this:

> "What is meant by the word *red?*"
> "Well, the next time you see a bunch of cars stopped at an intersection, look at the traffic light facing them. Also, you might go to the fire department and see how their trucks are painted."

"Let's Define Our Terms"

An extremely widespread instance of an unrealistic (and ultimately superstitious) attitude toward definitions is found in the common academic prescription, "Let's define our terms so that we shall all know what we are talking about." As we have already seen in Chapter 4, the fact that a golfer, for example, cannot define golfing terms is no indication that he cannot understand and use them. *Conversely, the fact that a man can define a large number of words is no guarantee that he knows what objects or operations they stand for in concrete situations.* People often believe, having defined a word, that some kind of understanding has been established, ignoring the fact that *the words in the definition often conceal even more serious confusions and ambiguities than the word defined*. If we happen to discover this fact and try to remedy matters by defining the defining words, and then, finding ourselves still confused, go on to define the words in the definitions of the defining words, and so on, we quickly find ourselves in a hopeless snarl. The only way to avoid this snarl is *to keep definitions to a minimum and to point to extensional levels wherever necessary—and in writing and speaking, this means giving specific examples of what we are talking about.*

Ultimately, no adequate definition of "apple pie" can be given in words—one has to examine and taste an actual apple pie. The same goes for more abstract words. If we have never felt love, if we have never felt strongly about a moral principle nor felt the satisfactions of seeing a moral principle observed, we may verbally define "love" or "justice" until doomsday, but we shall still not know what they mean.

Chasing Oneself in Verbal Circles

In other words, the kind of "thinking" we must be extremely wary of is that which *never* leaves the higher verbal levels of abstraction, the kind that never points *down* the abstraction ladder to lower levels of abstraction and from there to the extensional world:

"What do you mean by *democracy?*"
"Democracy means the preservation of human rights."
"What do you mean by *rights?*"
"By rights I mean those privileges God grants to all of us—I mean man's inherent privileges."
"Such as?"
"Liberty, for example."
"What do you mean by *liberty?*"
"Religious and political freedom."
"And what does that mean?"
"Religious and political freedom is what we have when we do things the *democratic* way."

Of course it is possible to talk meaningfully about democracy, as Jefferson and Lincoln have done, as Charles and Mary Beard do in *The Rise of American Civilization,* as Frederick Jackson Turner does in *The Frontier in American History,* as Lincoln Steffens does in his *Autobiography,* as David Lilienthal does in *TVA: Democracy on the March*—to name only the first examples that come to mind— but such a sample as the above is not the way to do it. The trouble with speakers who never leave the higher levels of abstraction is not only that they fail to notice when they are saying something and when they are not; they also produce a similar lack of discrimination in their audiences. Never coming down to earth, they frequently chase themselves around in verbal circles, unaware that they are making meaningless noises.

This is by no means to say, however, that we must never make extensionally meaningless noises. When we use directive language, when we talk about the future, when we utter ritual language or engage in social conversation, we often make utterances that have no extensional verifiability. It must not be overlooked that our highest ratiocinative and imaginative powers are derived from the fact that symbols *are* independent of things symbolized, so that we are free not only to go quickly from low to extremely high levels of abstraction (from "canned peas" to "groceries" to "commodities" to "national wealth") and to manipulate symbols even when the things they stand for cannot be so manipulated ("If all the freight cars in the country were hooked up to each other in one long line . . ."), but we are also free to manufacture symbols at will even if they stand only for abstractions made from other abstractions and not for anything in the extensional world. Mathematicians, for example, often play with symbols that have no extensional content, just to find out what can be done with them; this is called "pure mathematics." And pure mathematics is far from being a useless pastime, because mathematical systems that are elaborated with no extensional applications in mind often prove later to be applicable in useful and unforeseen ways. Mathematicians, however, when they are dealing with extensionally meaningless symbols, usually know what they are doing. We likewise *must* know what we are doing.

Nevertheless, all of us (including mathematicians), when we speak the language of everyday life, often make meaningless noises without knowing that we are doing so. We have already seen what confusions this can lead to. The fundamental purpose of the abstraction ladder, as shown both in this chapter and the next, is to make us aware of the process of abstracting.

The Distrust of Abstractions

We may, using our abstraction ladder, allocate statements as well as words to differing levels of abstraction. "Mrs. Plotz makes good potato pancakes" may be regarded as a statement at a fairly low level of abstraction, although, to be sure, it leaves out many characteristics, such as (1) what one means by "goodness" in potato pancakes, and (2) the infrequent occasions when her pancakes fail to turn out well. "Mrs. Plotz is a good cook," is a statement at a higher level of abstraction, covering Mrs. Plotz's skill not only with potato pancakes, but also with roasts, pickles, noodles, strudels, and so on, nevertheless omitting *specific* mention of what she can accomplish. "Chicago women are good cooks," is a statement at a still higher level of abstraction; it is one that can be made (if at all) on the basis of the observation of the cooking of a statistically significant number of Chicago women. "The culinary art has reached a high state in America," would be a still more highly abstract statement, and if made at all, would have to be based not only on the observation of the Mrs. Plotzes of Chicago, New York, San Francisco, Denver, Albuquerque, and Chattanooga, but also on the observation of the quality of meals served in hotels and restaurants, the quality of training given in departments of home economics in high schools and colleges, the excellence of the writings on culinary art in American books and magazines, and many other relevant facts.

It is to be regretted, although it is understandable, that there exists a tendency in our times to speak contemptuously of "mere abstractions." The ability to climb to higher and higher levels of abstraction is a distinctively human trait, without which none of our philosophical or scientific insights would be possible. In order to have a science of chemistry, one *has* to be able to think of "H_2O," leaving out of consideration for the time being the wetness of water, the hardness of ice, the pearliness of dew, and the other extensional characteristics of H_2O at the objective level. In order to have a study called "ethics," one has to be able to think of what ethical behavior has in common under different conditions and in different civilizations; one has to abstract that which is common to the behavior of the ethical carpenter, the ethical politician, the ethical businessman, the ethical soldier, and that which is common to the laws of conduct of the Buddhist, the Judaist, the Confucian, and the Christian. Thinking that is most abstract can also be that which is most generally useful. The famous injunction of Jesus, "And as ye would that men should do to you, do ye also to them likewise," is, from this point of view, a brilliant generalization of more particular directives—a generalization at so high a level of abstraction that it appears to be applicable to all men in all cultures.

But high level abstractions acquire a bad reputation because they are so often used, consciously or unconsciously, to confuse and befuddle people. A grab among competing powers for oil resources may be spoken of as "protecting the integrity of small nations." (Remember the "Greater East Asia Co-prosperity Sphere"?) An unwillingness to pay social security taxes may be spoken of as "maintaining the system of free enterprise." Depriving the Negro of his vote in violation of the Constitution of the United States may be spoken of as "preserving states' rights." The consequence of this free, and often irresponsible, use of high level abstractions in public controversy and special pleading is that a significant portion of the population has grown cynical about *all* abstractions.

But, as the abstraction ladder has shown, *all we know is abstractions*. What you know about the chair you are sitting in is an abstraction from the totality of that chair. When you eat white bread, you cannot tell by the taste whether or not is has been "enriched by vitamin B" as it says on the wrapper; you simply have to trust that the process (from which the words "vitamin B" are abstracted) is actually there. What you know about your wife—even if she has been your wife for thirty years—is again an abstraction. Distrusting all abstractions simply does not make sense.

The test of abstractions then is not whether they are "high" or "low level" abstractions, but *whether they are referrable to lower levels.* If one makes a statement about "culinary arts in America," one should be able to refer the statement down the abstraction ladder to particulars of American restaurants, American domestic science, American techniques of food preservation, and so on down to Mrs. Plotz in her kitchen. If one makes a statement about "civil rights in Wisconsin," one should know something about national, state, and local statutes, about the behavior of policemen, magistrates, judges, academic authorities, hotel managers, and the general public in Wisconsin, whose acts and whose decisions affect that minimum of decent treatment in the courts, in politics, and in society that we call "civil rights." *A preacher, a professor, a journalist, or politician whose high level abstractions can systematically and surely be referred to lower level abstractions is not only talking, he is saying something.* As *Time* would say, no windbag, he.

"Dead-Level Abstracting"

Professor Wendell Johnson of the State University of Iowa, in his *People in Quandaries,* discusses a linguistic phenomenon which he calls "dead-level abstracting." Some people, it appears, remain more or less permanently stuck at certain levels of the abstraction ladder, some on the lower levels, some on the very high levels. There are those, for example, who go in for "persistent low-level abstracting":

Probably all of us know certain people who seem able to talk on and on without ever drawing any very general conclusions. For example, there is the back-fence chatter that is made up of he said and then I said and then she said and I said and then he said, far into the afternoon, ending with, "Well, that's *just* what I told him!" Letters describing vacation trips frequently illustrate this sort of language, detailing places seen, times of arrival and departure, the foods eaten and the prices paid, whether the beds were hard or soft, etc.

A similar inability to get to higher levels of abstraction character-
izes certain types of mental patients who suffer, as Johnson says
"a general blocking of the abstracting process." They go on indefinitely, reciting insignificant facts, never able to pull them together to frame a generalization to give a meaning to the facts.

Other speakers remain stuck at higher levels of abstraction, with
little or no contact with lower levels. Such language remains permanently in the clouds. As Johnson says:

It is characterized especially by vagueness, ambiguity, even utter
meaninglessness. Simply by saving various circulars, brochures, free
copies of "new thought" magazines, etc. . . . it is possible to accumulate in a short time quite a sizable file of illustrative material. Much
more, of course, is to be found on library shelves, on newsstands, and
in radio programs. Everyday conversation, classroom lectures, political
speeches, commencement addresses, and various kinds of group forums
and round-table discussions provide a further abundant source of *words
cut loose from their moorings.* [Italics supplied.]

(The writer heard recently of a course in esthetics given at a
large middlewestern university in which an entire semester was
devoted to Art and Beauty and the principles underlying them, and
during which the professor, even when asked by students, persistently declined to name specific paintings, symphonies, sculptures
or objects of beauty to which his principles might apply. "We are
interested," he would say, "in principles, not in particulars.")

There are psychiatric implications to dead-level abstracting on
higher levels, too, since it is inevitable that, when maps proliferate
wildly without any reference to a territory, the result can only be
delusion. But whether at higher or lower levels, dead-level abstracting is, as Johnson says, always dull:

The low-level speaker frustrates you because he leaves you with no
directions as to what to do with the basketful of information he has
given you. The high-level speaker frustrates you because he simply
doesn't tell you what he is talking about. . . . Being thus frustrated,
and being further blocked because the rules of courtesy (or of at-
tendance at class lectures) require that one remain quietly seated until
the speaker has finished, there is little for one to do but daydream,
doodle, or simply fall asleep.

It is obvious, then, that interesting speech and interesting writing, as well as clear thinking and consequent psychological adjustment, require the constant interplay of higher and lower level abstractions, and the constant interplay of the verbal levels with the nonverbal ("object") levels. In science, this interplay goes on constantly, hypotheses being checked against observations, predictions against extensional results. (Scientific *writing,* however, as exemplified in technical journals, offers some appalling examples of *almost* dead-level abstracting—which is the reason so much of it is hard to read. Nevertheless, the interplay between verbal and nonverbal, experimental levels does continue, or else it would not be science.) The work of good novelists and poets also represents this constant interplay between higher and lower levels of abstraction. A "significant" novelist or poet is one whose message has a high level of *general* usefulness in providing insight into life; but he gives his generalizations an impact and a power to convince through his ability to observe and describe actual social situations and states of mind. A memorable literary character, such as Sinclair Lewis's George F. Babbitt, has *descriptive* validity (at a low level of abstraction) as the picture of an individual, as well as a *general* validity as a picture of a "typical" American businessman. The great political leader is also one in whom there is interplay between higher and lower levels of abstraction. The ward heeler knows politics only at lower levels of abstraction: what promises or what acts will cause what people to vote as desired; his loyalties are not to principles (high-level abstractions) but to persons (e.g., political bosses) and immediate advantages (low-level abstractions). The so-called impractical political theorist knows the high-level abstractions ("democracy," "civil rights," "social justice") but is not well enough acquainted with facts at lower levels of abstraction to get himself elected county register of deeds. But the political leaders to whom states and nations remain permanently grateful are those who were able, somehow or other, to achieve simultaneously higher-level aims ("freedom," "national unity," "justice") *and* lower-level aims ("better prices for potato farmers," "higher wages for textile workers," "judicial reform," "soil conservation").

The interesting writer, the informative speaker, the accurate thinker, and the well-adjusted individual, operate on all levels of the abstraction ladder, moving quickly and gracefully and in orderly fashion from higher to lower, from lower to higher—with minds as lithe and deft and beautiful as monkeys in a tree.

Applications

I. Starting with the one at the lowest level of abstraction, arrange the following statements in order of increasing abstraction.

1. I like motoring better than flying.
2. I like Studebaker cars.
3. I like American motor cars better than English cars.
4. I like my 1949 Studebaker Commander four-door sedan.
5. I like travel.

1. Joe keeps all our household appliances in working condition.
2. Joe is a mechanical genius.
3. Joe is very handy with tools.
4. Joe is a 100 per cent real American boy.
5. Yesterday Joe replaced a burned-out condenser in the radio.
6. Joe is an awfully useful person to have around.
7. Joe keeps that radio in working condition.

II. Apply the following terms to events in the extensional world; i.e., go down the abstraction ladder to the things and happenings these words may point to.

| National honor | The Battle of Gettysburg | Art |
| Sportsmanship | Jurisdictional dispute | Philosophy |

III. Analyze, in terms of levels of abstraction, the following passages:

1. "A *phobia* is a recurrent and persistent fear of a particular object or situation which in 'objective' reality presents no actual danger to the subject—although (cf. Case 1) in his unconsciously equated experience the patient may conceive the symbolized danger to be overwhelming. Phobias, indeed, are originally derived from situation-related fears, and differ from the latter only in their 'rationality,' symbolic spread, and generalization to remote aspects of the situation. For instance, fear of a rampant tiger is directly understandable, but it is justifiable to con-

sider abnormal the reactions of a severely aleurophobic patient who exhibits fear within a mile of a well-protected zoo, cannot bear the approach of a kitten, and experiences anxiety when any animal of the genus *Felis* is shown on a motion picture screen. In neither the 'normal' or 'abnormal' instance, be it noted, need the fear be based on a direct experience with the 'object' feared, although in both the tiger is, of course, symbolically equated with physical danger. The difference lies in this: that the phobia, unlike the fear, is based on no rational conscious reasons whatever, but springs from experiences deeply repressed and not necessarily related to a direct attack by a big or little cat at any time in the patient's life. To illustrate:

"Case 7: Anne A———, an eighteen-year-old girl was brought to the psychiatric out-patient clinic by her . . ."

—JULES MASSERMAN, *Principles of Dynamic Psychiatry*

SAMPLE ANALYSIS: The author starts with a definition of phobia that names the general conditions under which a fear may be called a phobia. The second sentence is also general and adds information about the origin of a phobia and shows how it differs from "situation-related fears." So far the author seems to be writing at a high level of abstraction without much progress up or down the abstraction ladder. The third sentence goes, however, down the abstraction ladder to a specific example, capable of being visualized by the reader ("rampant tiger") and also gives examples of specific situations (zoo, kitten, moving pictures) where fear may be termed a phobia. After more general explanations, there is a case history of a specific patient, Anne A———, reporting facts at still lower (descriptive) levels of abstraction. Whether or not other scientists agree with Dr. Masserman in calling this case a phobia, we at least know that, when *he* uses the word, this is the kind of case *he* is talking about. So far as relationships between higher and lower levels of abstraction are concerned, this passage is a good extensionally-directed definition of phobia.

2. "A function . . . is a table giving the relation between two variable quantities, where a change in one implies some change in the other. The cost of a quantity of meat is a function of its weight; the speed of a train, a function of the quantity of coal consumed; the amount of perspiration given off, a function of the temperature. In each of these illustrations, a change in the second variable: weight, quantity of coal

consumed, and temperature, is correlated with a change in the first variable: cost, speed, and volume of perspiration. The symbolism of mathematics permits functional relationships to be simply and concisely expressed. Thus $y = x$, $y = x^2$, $y = \sin x$, $y = \operatorname{csch} x$, $y = e^x$ are examples of functions."

—KASNER and NEWMAN, *Mathematics and the Imagination*

3.   CONTRACTORS—GENERAL (cont'd)
        Amer Home Builders Inc 6236 S Cot Grv MI dwy 3-4212
        American Processors 1623 W Lake.......MO nro 6-1829
        Amer Roof Truss Co 6850 S Stony Isl.....PL aza 2-1772
        Ames Arthur E 7416 S Inglsid..........TR iangl 4-6796
        Amoroso Banny & Sons 933 S Hoyne......SE ely 3-7258
        Andersen Agnar 2301 N Keating........BE lmnt 5-0900
                —Chicago *Classified Telephone Directory*

4. *"Causes of Calamities.* By causes of a calamity are meant two kinds of conditions. First there is *the necessary condition* or cause, without which the calamity cannot occur. Second, there are *supplementary conditions,* that do not hinder or neutralize but rather facilitate the realization of the consequences of the necessary condition, thus making *the necessary cause a sufficient cause.* The necessary cause of an infectious disease, say diphtheria, is infection. But if a person is inoculated against it, he may be in closest contact with the germs and yet remain uninfected. Inoculation is an *adverse* supplementary condition neutralizing the results of the necessary cause of diphtheria. This is the reason why, besides the necessary cause, an absence of adverse, and the presence of favoring supplementary conditions also are elements of the causation of such a calamity.

"From this standpoint, the following factors are the necessary causes and supplementary conditions of each type of calamity studied. . . .

"Causes of Famine. Necessary cause: inability of a given society to procure the food required by all its members. Supplementary conditions: *A.* The unfavorable play of natural forces such as drought, flood, fire, earthquakes, invasions of locusts or similar pests, epidemics, and other cosmic and biological processes. *B.* A disastrous constellation of sociocultural forces, e.g., invasion, war, revolution, dislocation of trade and commerce, breakdown of transportation and distribution of food, lack of organization for a possible food emergency; carelessness, laziness, ignorance, etc.

"As soon as enough of these supplementary conditions make real the potential inability of the society to procure food for its members, famine emerges. Its necessary cause remains this inability, but it is actualized by different combinations of supplementary conditions."

—PITIRIM A. SOROKIN, *Man and Society in Calamity* *

5. "And Shem lived after he begat Arphaxad five hundred years, and begat sons and daughters.

"And Arphaxad lived five and thirty years, and begat Salah;

"And Arphaxad lived after he begat Salah four hundred and three years, and begat sons and daughters.

"And Salah lived thirty years, and begat Eber.

"And Salah lived after he begat Eber four hundred and three years, and begat sons and daughters.

"And Eber lived four and thirty years, and begat Peleg. . . ."

—Genesis, 11:11-18

6. "There is nevertheless a sense in which the modes of signifying are interdependent. When the situation does not itself supply the clues needed for the direction of behavior, the organism or other organisms may supplement the situation by signs. And if signs in a number of modes of signifying are produced, these do depend on each other in certain ways. The prescription of an action is not of much help under these circumstances unless the object to which the action is to be directed is appraised, designated, and identified. There is a sense then in which in a highly problematic situation where behavior needs full direction, prescriptions require appraisals and appraisals require statements to a degree to which statements do not require appraisals or appraisals require prescriptions. To put the same point in another way, an organism which requires direction by signs must as a minimum have such signs as direct its behavior to the kind of objects it needs and their location; it can then try out their relevance and how to act on them in case these objects are not further signified appraisively and prescriptively. But the organism would often be quite helpless in its behavior if it merely had a sign that something was good or must be treated in a certain way without this something being designated, for behavior would then be without orientation. For this reason prescriptions rest on appraisals and appraisals on statements in a way in which statements do not need to be followed by appraisals and appraisals by

prescriptions. These interrelations will become more evident when we consider the relations of such types of discourse as are found in science, art, religion; in that context we will also consider the dependence of formators upon signs in the other modes of signifying."

—CHARLES W. MORRIS, *Signs, Language and Behavior* *

7. "Behold, a sower went forth to sow;

"And when he sowed, some seeds fell by the wayside, and the fowls came and devoured them up:

"Some fell upon stony places, where they had not much earth: and forthwith they sprung up, because they had no deepness of earth:

"And when the sun was up, they were scorched; and because they had no root, they withered away.

"And some fell among thorns; and the thorns sprung up, and choked them:

"But other fell into good ground, and brought forth fruit, some an hundredfold, some sixtyfold, some thirtyfold.

"Who hath ears to hear, let him hear."   —Matthew, 13:3-9

8.   Let Observation, with extensive view,
      Survey mankind, from China to Peru;
      Remark each anxious toil, each eager strife,
      And watch the busy scenes of crowded life;
      Then say how hope and fear, desire and hate
      O'erspread with snares the clouded maze of fate,
      Where wavering man, betray'd by vent'rous pride
      To tread the dreary paths without a guide,
      As treach'rous phantoms in the mist delude,
      Shuns fancied ills, or chases airy good;
      How rarely Reason guides the stubborn choice,
      Rules the bold hand or prompts the suppliant voice;
      How nations sink, by darling schemes oppress'd,
      When Vengeance listens to the fool's request.

                                        —SAMUEL JOHNSON

9.   *From "Rain after a Vaudeville Show"*

      The last pose flickered, failed. The screen's dead white
      Glared in a sudden flooding of harsh light

---

* Reprinted from *Signs, Language and Behavior* by Charles Morris by permission of the publisher, Prentice-Hall, Inc., 70 Fifth Avenue, New York 11, N. Y. Copyright 1946 by Prentice-Hall, Inc.

Stabbing the eyes; and as I stumbled out
The curtain rose. A fat girl with a pout
And legs like hams, began to sing "His Mother."
Gusts of bad air rose in a choking smother;
Smoke, the wet steam of clothes, the stench of plush,
Powder, cheap perfume, mingled in a rush.
I stepped into the lobby—and stood still
Struck dumb by sudden beauty, body and will.
Cleanness and rapture—excellence made plain—
The storming, thrashing arrows of the rain!

—STEPHEN VINCENT BENÉT *

IV. Alfred Korzybski in *Science and Sanity* points out that consciousness of abstracting enables us, among other things, to become aware of
what happens when we go from low to higher levels of abstraction with
a single term. For example, to worry about worry or to fear fear may
lead to morbid responses but, with another group of words, the higher
level of abstraction reverses or annuls the lower level effects as in "hatred
of hatred." Consider the responses that are likely to be the outcome
when you

1. are curious about curiosity.
2. doubt your doubts.
3. are nervous about your nervousness.
4. reason about reasoning.
5. try to know about knowing.
6. are impatient with your impatience.

* From *Rain after a Vaudeville Show*. Copyright, 1918, 1920, 1923, 1925, 1929,
1930, 1931, by Stephen Vincent Benét.

11. The Little Man Who Wasn't There

As I was going up the stair
I met a man who wasn't there.
He wasn't there again to-day.
I wish, I wish he'd stay away.

HUGHES MEARNS

Everybody is familiar with the fact that the ordinary man does
not see things as they are, but only sees certain fixed types. . . .
Mr. Walter Sickert is in the habit of telling his pupils that they
are unable to draw any individual arm because they think of it
as an arm; and because they think of it as an arm they think
they know what it ought to be. T. E. HULME

How Not To Start a Car

The following story appeared in the Chicago *Daily News* of September 8, 1948:

TORONTO (AP)—Angered when his automobile broke down, Gordon Metcalf, 29, smashed his fist through his rear window and died of wounds. The coroner said several arteries were severed in the forearm of the 200-pound man, and he had suffered serious loss of blood when he reached the hospital in a taxicab. The 1927 model car had given Metcalf considerable expense and trouble since he bought it a few weeks ago, police said.

Let us examine the mechanism of this man's reaction. He got angry at the car just as he might have got angry at a person, horse, or mule that was stubborn and unco-operative. He thereupon proceeded to "teach" that car a "lesson." Although the reaction is unreflecting and automatic, it is nevertheless a rather complicated one, since it involves (1) his making up an abstraction about his car ("that mean old car"), and then (2) his reacting to his own abstraction rather than to the actualities of the car itself.

People in primitive societies often act in similar ways. When crops fail or rocks fall upon them, they "make a deal with"—offer sacrifices to—the "spirits" of vegetation or of the rocks, in order to obtain better treatment from them in the future. All of us, however, have certain reactions of similar kinds: sometimes, tripping over a chair, we kick it and call it names; some people, indeed, when they fail to get letters, get angry at the postman. In all such behavior, we *confuse* the abstraction which is *inside* our heads with that which is *outside* and act as if the abstraction *were* the event in the outside world. We create in our heads an imaginary chair that maliciously trips us and then "punish" the extensional chair that bears ill will to nobody; we create an imaginary, inferential postman who is "holding back our mail" and bawl out the extensional postman who would gladly bring us letters if he had any to bring.

Confusion of Levels of Abstraction

In a wider sense, however, we are confusing levels of abstraction —confusing that which is inside our heads with that which is outside—all the time. For example, we talk about the yellowness of a pencil as if the yellowness were a "property" of the pencil and not a product, as we have seen, of the *interaction* of something outside our skins with our nervous systems. We confuse, that is to say, the two lowest levels of the abstraction ladder (see p. 169) and treat them as one. Properly speaking, we should not say, "The pencil is yellow," which is a statement that places the yellowness in the pencil; we should say instead, "That which has an effect on me which leads me to say 'pencil' also has an effect on me which leads me to say 'yellow.'" We don't have to be that precise, of course, in the language of everyday life, but it should be observed that the latter statement takes into consideration the part our nervous systems play in creating whatever pictures of reality we may have in our heads, while the former statement does not.

Now this habit of confusing that which is inside our skins and that which is outside is essentially a relic of prescientific patterns of thinking. The more advanced civilization becomes, the more conscious we must be that our nervous systems *automatically leave out characteristics* of the events before us. If we are not aware of characteristics left out, if we are not conscious of the process of abstracting, we make *seeing and believing a single process*. If, for example, you react to the twenty-second rattlesnake you have seen in your life as if it were identical with the abstraction you have in your head as the result of the last twenty-one rattlesnakes you have seen, you may not be far out in your reactions. But civilized life provides our nervous systems with more complicated problems than rattlesnakes to deal with. There is a case cited by Korzybski in *Science and Sanity* of a man who suffered from hay fever whenever there were roses in the room. In an experiment, a bunch of roses was produced unexpectedly in front of him, and he immediately had a violent attack of hay fever, despite the fact that the "roses" in this case were *made of paper*. That is, his nervous system saw-and-believed in one operation.

But words, as we have seen by means of the abstraction ladder, are still higher levels of abstraction than the "objects" of experience. The more words at extremely high levels of abstraction we have, then, the more conscious we must be of this process of abstracting. For example, the word "rattlesnake" leaves out every important feature of the actual rattlesnake. But if the word is vividly remembered as part of a whole complex of terrifying experiences with an actual rattlesnake, the word itself is capable of arousing the same feelings as an actual rattlesnake. There are people, therefore, who turn pale at the *word*.[1]

---

[1] A recent musical comedy ("High Button Shoes") contains a routine in which a comedian gets an attack of sneezing at the mention of the words "fresh country air" and "ragweed." The fact that this theme of reacting to words as things is extremely common in the humor of comic strips, movies, and radio shows demonstrates, I believe, not only that such reactions are widespread, but also that most people in the audience have enough of a tendency in this direction to recognize in the comedy characterizations *an exaggeration of their own reactions*.

This, then, is the origin of word-magic. The word "rattlesnake" and the actual creature are felt to be *one and the same thing,* because they arouse the same reactions. This sounds like nonsense, of course, and it is nonsense. But from the point of view of a pre-scientific logic, it has its justification. As Lévy-Bruhl explains in his *How Natives Think,* primitive "logic" works on such a principle. The creature frightens us; the word frightens us; therefore the creature and the word are "the same"—not actually the same, per-haps, but there is a "mystic connection" between the two. This sense of "mystic connection" is Lévy-Bruhl's term for what we have called "necessary connection" in our discussion in Chapter 2 of naïve attitudes towards symbols. As a consequence of this naïveté, "mystical power" is attributed to words. There come to be "fearful words," "forbidden words," "unspeakable words"—words taking on the characteristics of the things they stand for. Such feelings as these about the power of words are, as we have already seen, probably in part responsible for such social phenomena as the strenuous campaign in the early 1930's to bring back prosperity through fre-quent reiteration of the *words,* "Prosperity is around the corner!"

The commonest form of this confusion of levels of abstraction, however, is illustrated by our reacting to the twenty-second Repub-lican we encounter in our lives as if he were identical with the ab-straction "Republican" inside our heads. "If he's Republican, he must be O.K."—or "an old fogey," we are likely to say, confusing the extensional Republican with our abstraction "Republican," which is the product not only of the last twenty-one "Republicans" we have met, but also of all that we have been *told* about "Republicans."

"Jews"

To make the principles clearer, we shall use an example that is loaded with prejudices for many people: "Mr. Miller is a *Jew.*" On hearing this, some "Christians" have marked hostile reactions, instantaneously, for example, putting themselves on guard against Mr. Miller's expected sharp financial practices. That is to say, a "Christian" of this kind confuses his high-level abstraction, "Jew," with the extensional Mr. Miller and behaves towards Mr. Miller as if he were identical with that abstraction. (See the abstraction ladder, p. 169.) "Jew" is only *one* of thousands upon thousands of abstractions which may be applied to Mr. Miller, to whom such terms as "left-hander," "parent," "amateur golfer," "teetotaler," "Bostonian," and so on may possibly be equally applied. But the prejudiced person is unaware of all but the one abstraction—perhaps in most contexts the least important one—"Jew." Certainly he is unaware that "Jew" is one of the most sloppily constructed abstractions in the language, i.e., one of the most difficult to refer systematically down the abstraction ladder to lower levels of abstraction. (Try it some time. Does "Jew" refer to a "race," a religion, a nationality, a physical type, a state of mind, a caste? If not these, what?)

Now it happens that the word "Jew" has powerful affective connotations in Christian culture as the result of a number of historical accidents associating "Jews" with money. The kinds of historical accident that resulted in this association will be discussed in a subsequent chapter; for the moment it will suffice to observe the way in which the affective connotations of the word are employed in such expressions as, "He *jewed* me out of ten dollars," "Don't be such a *jew*," "I *jewed* down the price." In some circles, it is not uncommon for mothers to discipline disobedient children by saying to them, "If you don't behave, I'll sell you to the old Jew man."

Let us return to our hypothetical Mr. Miller, who has been introduced as a "Jew." To a person for whom these affective connotations are very much alive—and there are many such—and who habitually confuses that which is inside his nervous system with that which is outside, Mr. Miller is a man "not to be trusted." If Mr. Miller succeeds in business, that "proves" that "Jews are smart"; if Mr. Johansen succeeds in business, it only proves that Mr. Johansen is smart. If Mr. Miller fails in business, it is alleged that he nevertheless has "money salted away somewhere." If Mr. Miller is strange or foreign in his habits, that "proves" that "Jews don't assimilate." If he is thoroughly American—i.e., indistinguishable from other natives —he is "trying to pass himself off as one of us." If Mr. Miller fails

to give to charity, that is because "Jews are tight"; if he gives gen-
erously, he is "trying to buy his way into society." If Mr. Miller lives
in the Jewish section of town, that is because "Jews are so clannish";
if he moves to a locality where there are no other Jews, that is because "they try to horn in everywhere." In short, Mr. Miller is
automatically condemned, no matter who he is or what he does.

But Mr. Miller may be, for all we know, rich or poor, a wife
beater or a saint, a stamp collector or a violinist, a farmer or a
physicist, a lens grinder or an orchestra leader. If, as the result of
our automatic reactions, we put ourselves on guard about our *money*
immediately upon meeting Mr. Miller, we may offend a man
from whom we might have profited financially, morally, or spiritually, or we may fail to notice his attempts to run off with our wife
—that is, we shall act with complete inappropriateness to the *actual*
situation at hand. Mr. Miller is not identical with our notion of
"Jew," *whatever our notion of "Jew" may be.* The "Jew," created
by intensional definition of the *word, simply is not there.*

John Doe, the "Criminal"

Another instance of the confusion of levels of abstraction is to be
found in cases like this: Let us say that here is a man, John Doe,
who is introduced as one "who has just been released after three
years in the penitentiary." This is already on a fairly high level of
abstraction, but it is nevertheless a *report.* From this point, however,
many people *immediately and unconsciously* climb to still higher
levels of abstraction: "John Doe is an *ex-convict* . . . he's a criminal!" But the word "criminal" is not only on a much higher level
of abstraction than "the man who spent three years in the penitentiary," but it is also, as we have seen before in Chapter 3, a
judgment, with the implied prediction, "He has committed a crime
in the past and will probably commit more crimes in future." The
result is that when John Doe applies for a job and is forced to
state that he has spent three years in the penitentiary, prospective
employers, automatically confusing levels of abstraction, may say to
him, "You can't expect me to give jobs to criminals!"

John Doe, for all we know from the report, may have undergone a complete reformation or, for that matter, may have been unjustly imprisoned in the first place; nevertheless, he may wander in vain, looking for a job. If, in desperation, he finally says to himself, "If everybody is going to treat me like a criminal, I might as well become one," and goes out and commits a robbery, the blame can hardly be said to be entirely his.

The reader is familiar with the way in which rumor grows as it spreads. Many of the exaggerations of rumor are again due to this inability on the part of some people to refrain from climbing to higher levels of abstraction—from reports to inferences to judgments—and then confusing the levels. According to this kind of "reasoning":

Report. "Mary Smith didn't get in until two last Saturday night."
Inference. "I bet she was out tearing around!"
Judgment. "She's a worthless hussy. I never did like her looks. I knew it the moment I first laid eyes on her."

Basing our actions towards our fellow human beings on such hastily abstracted judgments, it is no wonder that we frequently make life miserable not only for others, but for ourselves.

As a final example of this type of confusion, *notice the difference between what happens when a man says to himself, "I have failed three times," and what happens when he says, "I am a failure!"*

Delusional Worlds

Consciousness of abstracting prepares us in advance for the fact that things that look alike are *not* alike, for the fact that things that have the same name are *not* the same, for the fact that judgments are *not* reports. In short, it prevents us from acting like fools. Without consciousness of abstracting—or rather, without the habit of *delaying reactions,* which is the product of a deep awareness that seeing is not believing—we are completely unprepared for the differences between roses and paper roses, between the intensional

"Jew" and the extensional Mr. Miller, between the intensional "criminal" and the extensional John Doe.

Such delayed reactions are a sign of adulthood. It happens, however, that as the result of miseducation, bad training, frightening experiences in childhood, obsolete traditional beliefs, propaganda, and other influences in our lives, all of us have what might be termed "areas of insanity" or, perhaps better, "areas of infantilism." There are certain subjects about which we can never, as we say, "think straight," because we are "blinded by prejudice." Some people, for example, as the result of a childhood experience, cannot help being frightened by the mere sight of a policeman—any policeman; the terrifying "policeman" inside their heads "is" the extensional policeman outside, who probably has no designs that anyone could regard as terrifying. Some people turn pale at the sight of a spider—any spider—even a nice, harmless one safely enclosed in a bottle. Some people automatically become hostile at the *words* "un-American," "fascist," or "communist."

The picture of reality created inside our heads by such unconsciousness of abstracting is not at all a "map" of any existing "territory." It is a delusional world. In this never-never land, all "Jews" are out to cheat you; all "capitalists" are overfed tyrants, smoking expensive cigars and gnashing their teeth at labor unions. In this world, too, all snakes are poisonous, automobiles can be disciplined by a well-directed sock in the eye, and every stranger with a foreign accent is a spy. Some of these people who spend too much of their time in such delusional worlds eventually get locked up, but, needless to say, there are many of us still at large.

How do we reduce such areas of infantilism in our thought? One way is to know deeply that there is no "necessary connection" between words and what they stand for. For this reason, the study of a foreign language is always good for us, even if it has no other uses. Other ways have already been suggested: to be aware of the process of abstracting and *to realize fully that words never "say all" about anything*. The abstraction ladder—an adaptation of a diagram originated by Alfred Korzybski to illustrate visually the relationship between words, "objects," and events—is designed to help us understand and remain conscious of the process of abstracting.

Applications

It was suggested at the end of Chapter 2 that examples of language in action be collected in a scrapbook or on filing cards. Enough general principles of the relationship between language and behavior have now been presented to expand the collection to include illustrations of many different linguistic principles. The following sample headings will suggest some of the clippings and quotations one might look for:

Straight reports.

Stories featuring inferences, with full awareness that they are inferences.

Stories featuring inferences in such a way that they may be mistaken for reports.

Reacting to judgments as if they were reports.

Shifts of meaning resulting from changes in context.

Snarl-words and purr-words mistaken for reports.

Slanting.

Quarrels over nonsense questions.

Social conversation.

Over-reacting to affective connotations of words.

Directives mistaken for reports.

Disillusionment caused by directives imperfectly understood.

Dead-level abstracting.

Meaningless use of high-level abstractions.

Higher- and lower-level abstractions properly related.

Seeing-and-believing.

The little man who wasn't there.

Other headings will occur to the reader as he reviews the chapters to follow. The study of the relationships between language and behavior is one that can be pursued at any time anywhere—in an office, at school, at church, behind (or in front of) a hosiery counter, at parties, at meetings, in all one's reading, and in the course of intimate family or personal relationships. Even a desultory collection of examples of language-in-action, if carefully noted and pasted down and pondered over, will help in enabling the reader to understand what the writer of this book is saying *and why he wants to say it*. Collectors of such examples will no doubt find reasons for wishing to refine, expand, or correct some of the statements made in this book. Further progress in the scientific study of the relationships between language and behavior depends upon such corrections and improvements of the present generalizations. The reader's co-operation is earnestly invited.

12. The Society
Behind Our Symbols

*That we should practise what we preach is generally admitted;
but anyone who preaches what he and his hearers practise must
incur the gravest moral disapprobation.*

LOGAN PEARSALL SMITH

"One Born Every Minute"

Most words in everyday discussion and controversy that are laden
with affective connotations are incredibly complex both in the feelings they express and the reactions they arouse. In order to understand, even partially, some of the complexities involved, let us continue with our discussion of the word "Jew," exploring some of the
socioeconomic bypaths into which it will lead us. Such an exploration will serve to illustrate how much more we need to know than
dictionaries can tell us before we begin to know what is behind
some of the words we use.

Whenever people of a pre-monetary culture (farmers, fishermen,
and other rural folk who live on what they produce, swap the sur-
plus, and rarely handle money) come into contact with people
skilled in money and credit transactions (those who understand
bookkeeping, interest, mortgages, notes, banking, and such matters),
the latter are likely to take advantage of the former. The former are
handlers of economic things (potatoes, fish, coconuts), and the
latter are *handlers of economic symbols* (notes, bills, futures, covering the exchange of potatoes, fish, coconuts). The thing-handlers,
even if they have not been taken advantage of, are likely to feel
suspicious and uneasy in dealings with the symbol-handlers. The
former are not skilled in computing interest; many have difficulty

with simple addition and subtraction; the words in the fine print of
sales agreements and contracts are over their heads. Hence, the
thing-handlers usually attribute their financial disappointments to
the "unscrupulousness" and "cunning" of the shopkeepers, moneylenders, and traders.

The experiences of many Polynesian and Asiatic people with
skilled Chinese merchants, of rural Japanese with city slickers from
Tokyo and Osaka, of rural Mediterranean folk with Syrian traders,
of rural Americans with the "Connecticut Yankee" (who sold, it
will be remembered, "wooden nutmegs" to unsuspecting yokels),
of farmers everywhere with bankers, and of rural Americans and
Europeans with Jewish tradesmen and moneylenders, have been
very much alike. Those who couldn't understand figures have resented (often with good reason) the clever city people who could.
The words "Chinese merchant," "Osaka merchant," "Syrian," "Connecticut Yankee," "moneylender," "banker," and "Jew," have therefore had almost identical connotations at various times and in
various parts of the world. All these words (and there are many
more like them depending on what part of the world you are in)
represent, for back-country people, the semiliterate man's resentment of the verbally facile urban trader, his baffling percentages
and papers, and his whole mysterious system of economic symbols.
The farmer who can never figure out the whys and wherefores
of all the deductions that make his milk-checks smaller from month
to month, the miner who is mystified by the fact that the longer
he works the more money he seems to owe to the company store,
the Polynesian native who put a cross on a piece of paper only to
find that he has virtually sold himself into slavery on a plantation—
all such victims of ignorance have reason to hate the symbol-handler.

To many illiterate Christian folk, the "Jew" is the classic symbol
of the hated economic symbol-handler, and they use the word to
express their resentment of symbol-handlers *whether the particular
symbol-handlers they resent happen to be Jews or not.* Jews, a small
minority in medieval Christendom, were often in symbol-handling
occupations. There is no mystery why this should have been so.
Christian prohibitions against Jewish land-ownership prevented
them from becoming farmers. The exclusion of Jews from craft-

guilds prevented many of them from going into the organized skilled trades. Moreover, a Jew never knew when a pogrom might start, which meant that he would have to fly for his life, leaving everything behind except his shirt and starting over again in a strange town. Skill in trading—that is, the ability to handle economic symbols—like the equipment necessary for tailoring or watch-making (also traditional Jewish occupations)—is something you can take with you when you have to flee. The development of symbol-handling ("middleman") skills was one of the very few economic courses open to Jews.

Furthermore, the medieval Christian world did not tolerate, except to non-Christians, the occupation of banking (moneylending). Nevertheless, moneylenders were necessary to the development of business. Hence, it became the standard practice of Christians to borrow money from Jews to satisfy their business requirements, meanwhile calling them names to satisfy their consciences—just as, during Prohibition in the United States, it was fairly common practice to patronize bootleggers to satisfy one's thirst, meanwhile denouncing them for "lawlessness" on all public occasions to satisfy one's conscience.

In addition, many princes and noblemen who owed large sums of money to Jewish moneylenders made the happy discovery that it was easy to avoid the payment of their debts by arousing the superstitious populace to torturing and massacring the Jews on the pretext of "crusades against the infidel." After such incidents, the Jews would be either dead or willing to cancel the debts owed them in order to save their lives. Such business risks would further increase the interest rates, even as the risk of police raids increased the price of bootleg liquor. The increased interest rates would further infuriate the Christians. The word "Jew," therefore, came to have increasingly powerful affective connotations, expressing at once the terror felt by Christians toward non-Christians and the resentment felt by people everywhere toward moneylenders, who are almost always felt to be "grasping," "unscrupulous," and "cunning." The moral objections to moneylending disappeared, of course, especially after people began to found new forms of Christianity, partly in order that they might freely engage in that profession. Nevertheless, the affective connotations of the word "Jew" survived and have remained, even to this day, to connect Jews, in the minds of illiterate and semiliterate Christians, with the evils of the economic symbol-handling occupations.[1]

There has been, then, some reason in history for using the figure of the "Jew" as a symbol of the economic symbol-handler. Today, however, in a society such as ours almost completely dominated by economic symbol-handlers and their subordinates (that is, the entire white-collar class, from corporation presidents down, whose days are devoted almost entirely to paper-work), it is ridiculous to select Jews as being peculiarly representative of the symbol-handling occupations.

Marginal Businessmen

But well-educated urban people who are symbol-handlers themselves also have prejudices against Jews. They often contend, and demonstrate with some evidence, that not all, but a significant number, of Jews in business have characteristic ways of behaving that they find disagreeable. They feel justified, therefore, in approaching Jews with at least a minimum of cautious reservation.

But the "Jewish" characteristics they describe are not Jewish. What they usually describe are the characteristics of *marginal businessmen*. The marginal businessman is one who does not belong in the *established* profitable business of a community. In the United States, he is often a fairly recent immigrant or a member of a minority group. (Members of the majority don't have to go

---

[1] Even among literate Christians who regard themselves as too intelligent to share vulgar prejudices, an attenuated form of this identification of Jews as symbol-handlers persists to a remarkable degree. Jews, the writer was told by a faculty-wife at a tea in a university community recently, are extraordinarily adept at handling words and figures and ideas, but they are not skillful in any work requiring manual dexterity. On another occasion the writer learned from a department manager in a large Jewish-owned department store, first, that his employers were very kind and good to him, and secondly, that they, like all Jews, having great brains for figures, were much too smart to do any manual work themselves. Just as he was saying this, a Jewish stock-clerk staggered by under a huge load of shoe boxes.

into marginal businesses; they can usually find employment in established enterprises.) Starting as a rule with little capital or none, marginal businessmen go into neighborhoods that are too unpromising or into enterprises that have too uncertain a future for larger, established companies to be bothered with. Chili parlors, small restaurants (Italian, Greek, Chinese), Jewish dry-goods stores and delicatessens, shoe-repairing shops, second-hand and junk businesses of all kinds, and almost all services for the Negro trade are the commonest examples of marginal business at the present time. Many unscheduled airlines are also marginal businesses in the same sense.

Jewish businessmen in the United States (and in many other nations, for discrimination against and persecution of the Jew is common throughout Christendom) are largely either in marginal enterprises or in enterprises that were marginal until relatively recently. The predominance of Jews in the ready-to-wear garment industry is due to the fact that they got into it at a time when most people made their own clothes. They also got started in the moving picture business at a time when it was so marginal that few people ever imagined that it would ever emerge from the penny arcade. Success in marginal business requires one or more of the following: (1) finding an undeveloped market that established businesses have ignored or overlooked; (2) having the foresight (or luck) to get into a type of business that is not profitable now, but eventually will be; (3) being sufficiently aggressive, skillful, and shrewd in business to survive even under the most unfavorable conditions; (4) being willing to work twice as hard as the next man.

Trying to achieve success in marginal business, then, imposes similar disciplines on all people who go into it, regardless of color or creed. And similar disciplines produce similar character traits. At the present time, many Negroes in Chicago have become, and many more are becoming, successful businessmen, starting in marginal enterprises. Among the more recent successful Negro enterprises are insurance (white firms have for a long time turned down Negro customers) and publishing (white magazines have rarely taken into consideration the interests and wants of the Negro reader). Many more successful Negro businesses will no doubt follow. What is interesting is that many Negro businessmen who have submitted to the disciplines of marginal business show most of the characteristics popularly attributed to Jews: for example, (1) a single-minded absorption with making money, preferably the quickest way; (2) extreme aggressiveness and shrewdness, and an unwillingness to pay high wages; (3) a tendency to be somewhat overproud of the money they have made; (4) a tendency to adhere firmly to the principle that "business is business"—in other words, a willingness to sacrifice considerations of sentiment or humanitarianism or even ethics if necessary in the interests of profit. (The owner of a marginal, non-network radio station—he was neither a Jew nor a Negro—once said to the writer in justifying his broadcasting of some questionable advertising, "When we are big and rich, we'll be able to afford to be ethical.")

Indeed, America's reputation throughout the nineteenth century as a "money-mad," "uncultivated," and "materialistic" society rests largely on the fact that America was very much a "land of opportunity." In other words, it was a place where the marginal businessman had before him many chances of success, with newly found natural resources, new inventions, and large, promising marginal areas (such as the frontier) to exploit, offering everyone a constant hope of quick riches. The discipline of the marginal businessman (rather than that, say, of the corporation official) was the standard training of the nineteenth-century American businessman, who believed emphatically in the "business is business" principle, who believed in being "wide awake," and who believed in going into business for himself and "wearing no man's collar." *Most of the traits that contemporary upper-class Americans find objectionable in Jews are traits that were held up for admiration and emulation throughout the nineteenth century by the entire American business community.*

Climbing the Social Ladder

The success of a marginal businessman is almost always greeted with mixed feelings. He may have become rich, but he has usually had to work too hard to have had time to acquire the polish and the social mannerisms of those who have had their money longer. If he was an immigrant, he may still speak with a foreign accent; if he rose from the lower class, he may still retain lower class manners or tastes; if he started as a lower class immigrant (as many successful American marginal businessmen have), he enters the society of the wealthy and cultured with two strikes against him. As he climbs the socioeconomic ladder, he is subject to the contempt of the aristocrat for the *parvenu*—even if the aristocrat (as is usually the case in Chicago) is himself only one generation removed from marginal business, his grandpappy being a Swede who ran up a small carpentry shop into a big furniture factory.

The attitudes of the upper class are reflected and often intensified in the lower and middle classes of the majority group. The latter especially tend to feel that the marginal businessman, by working so very hard, uses unfair tactics. The impressive industriousness of Japanese market-gardeners in California and of Jewish shopkeepers has always aroused resentment on the part of those who prefer to stop working after an eight-hour day. The marginal businessman is also resented for being "clever." What is not sufficiently appreciated is that he has to use his head in order to be able to survive at all.

Today, many Negro children are being told, as Jewish children have been told for generations, "You have to be twice as smart and work twice as hard as the next man in order to get half as far." Consequently, many more Negro businessmen in the next few decades are going to prove (as some have already) to be both extremely resourceful and extremely hard-working. But both their resourcefulness and their hard work will largely be unnoticed by white people, since so many of them "know" that Negroes are stupid and lazy.

The disadvantage of calling the characteristics of marginal businessmen "Jewish characteristics" lies not only in the errors we may make in evaluating individual Jews. An even graver disadvantage is the resulting *misdirection of attention*. The word "Jewish" draws attention away from the observation of the effects of economic and social pressures as they affect *all* people. The belief in special "Jewish" characteristics is an enormous obstacle to the understanding of human nature and society.

Negro Anti-Semitism

The prejudices on the part of Negroes against Jews represents the ultimate confusion resulting from such socioeconomic facts as have been mentioned. In New York, Detroit, and Chicago, many shops in Negro neighborhoods are owned by Jews, Negro neighborhoods being marginal business areas and Jews being often in marginal business. A considerable proportion of Negroes in large Northern cities are back-country folk, recently arrived from the rural regions of the South. Like rural immigrants from Lithuania, Poland, Germany, or Mexico, Negro country folk are capable of being victimized by small-loan sharks, sellers of gaudy and short-lived "de luxe living and dining room suites," and merchants who offer you a $39.95 watch for one dollar down and a dollar a week for the next fifteen years. Hence the resentment of the helpless "thing-handler" for the shrewd "symbol-handler" is combined with the resentment that any customer must feel for the practices of some marginal businessmen. This combined resentment is channeled, as the result of the Christian traditions mentioned earlier, against "the Jews."

(A Chicago Negro who came from the South during World War II was complaining of the prices charged by an Italian marginal grocer. "The damn Jew," he said. "But," his friends said to him, "Serrano isn't a Jew; he's Italian." "I don't care what he is," he answered. "He's still a Jew to me.")

Fortunately, many Jewish businessmen in the Negro communities understand the situation. Many have established cordial relationships and a reputation for fair dealing with customers. They have often united to bring pressure to bear on unethical businessmen in order to change their practices. Many Jewish businessmen are in the forefront of the demand for improved economic opportunities for Negroes and have set the example themselves not only by hiring Negro help, but also by training Negroes and placing them in positions of high executive responsibility. However, prejudice being as irrational as it is, and marginal business being as exacting as it is, the habit of "blaming the Jews" will not quickly die out of the Negro community. As Negro businessmen gradually take over the business in the Negro community, however, the consumer will discover (as some of them are already discovering) that some Negro marginal businessmen will display the same extremes of aggressive and unscrupulous business conduct that some marginal Jews have displayed. In such a case, exploited Negroes will probably develop a prejudice against all Negro businessmen—which will not be a very much more intelligent reaction, but it will at least take some of the heat off the Jews.[2]

Maps Versus Territories

From the point of view of the ideology of the business community, the fact that marginal businessmen need not remain marginal forever is *the* great fact about America. According to the most conservative spokesman of American business, America is a great country *because* a newsboy may some day become the president of a large corporation, *because* a man may start with a peddler's cart and wind up with a big chain of department stores. Such successes are a large part of what most of us mean when we say "equality of opportunity" and the "free enterprise system." Moreover, the fact that liberals and conservatives alike—and even many socialists—promise vehemently to help the "small businessman" attests to the universality in America of the belief that the door must never be closed to marginal business. Meanwhile, however, the leaders of some labor unions—especially some craft unions—under cover of pious talk about helping "the working man and the small businessman," make it impossible for many a marginal enterprise to operate;

[2] In South Africa, Indians occupy many marginal business positions. When, in January 1949, Negro resentment against oppression burst into violence at Durban and Johannesburg, the rioting was directed not against the whites, whose oppression of Negroes is far worse than is practiced anywhere in the United States, but against the Indians.

and associations of powerful (nonmarginal) business interests, also under cover of stirring verbalizations about the "little businessman," often send lobbyists to Washington and to state capitals to help big businesses get even bigger.

These mixed attitudes towards the marginal businessman which show themselves both in our social life and in business appear to rest ultimately on a mixed attitude towards free enterprise itself. How free should free enterprise be? Some businessmen mean by "free enterprise," "free and open competition, and let the best man win." Others mean "free to enter into agreements *not to compete*." Still others use either meaning of the word "free" (and several other meanings besides) without ever noticing the extent to which it covers, in their thinking, entirely contradictory notions. The same man who talks with pride of the achievements of the "competitive system" often supports "fair trade" agreements (which are agreements not to compete) and grow furious about the "chiselers" who actually compete by the handiest and most obvious device that business offers, namely, price-cutting.

But the businessman is by no means alone in his inconsistency. In the conflict of motives and interests in which we are all involved in our economic and social life in a highly restless society, maintaining orderly relationships between verbal "maps" and nonverbal "territories" is an extremely difficult—perhaps for many people a hopeless—task. Of course we want everyone to have a chance to be rich—but the colored Mr. Jones is getting rich and I am not, so damn Jones for not knowing his place! Of course we want the little businessman to have the chance to become a big businessman —but we hate "Big Business"! Of course, we want a free competitive system—but we don't like the way some people compete (i.e., successfully)! Of course, we believe in the dignity of labor— but what *could* that woman have been thinking of, inviting that truckdriver's wife to our A.A.U.W. meeting? Of course, we believe in equality and I am certainly as good as anybody else—but the *nerve* of those shanty Irish thinking they're as good as me! Of course, we must show the rest of the world that we are a peace-loving nation—but we must have the greatest air force in the world in addition to the atomic bomb! Of course we believe in the brotherhood of man—who the hell says we don't?

Inconsistencies of thought and feeling are, perhaps, inevitable in human affairs. Our higher-level abstractions are, even in the best of us, slightly out of kilter with our lower-level abstractions. But both meaningful utterance *and personal and social integration* depend upon the existence, as stated in Chapter 8, of *orderly* relationships between our higher- and lower-level abstractions. This is a thought that should, if properly absorbed, keep the reader quiet for at least a week. It has kept the writer quiet, on a number of topics, for even longer periods.

Applications

Because this chapter has touched on matters about which many people have strong feelings, perhaps it will be useful to the reader to go over the following statements and indicate which assertions the writer did NOT make in the chapter.

1. It is better to be an illiterate but honest "thing-handler" than a slick and dishonest "symbol-handler."
2. City people always try to make suckers of country people.
3. Jews are smarter than Gentiles and Japanese are smarter than either.
4. You have to be a crook to succeed in marginal business.
5. Negroes are intelligent and industrious.
6. There are times when the marginal businessman feels he cannot afford to be ethically meticulous.
7. Some Jewish merchants in the Negro community unfairly exploit their Negro customers.
8. Negro customers will be better treated when businesses in the Negro community are owned entirely by Negroes.
9. American business was founded largely by marginal businessmen.
10. Big businessmen who talk about "free enterprise" are hypocrites
11. "Free enterprise" is a meaningless abstraction.
12. Our socioeconomic problems will be solved if we agree on the correct definition of such words as "free enterprise" and "fair business practices."

13. Most people in America feel that the marginal businessman is essential to the free enterprise system.

14. The free enterprise system contains so many inherent contradictions that it should be abandoned.

15. Swedes are social climbers.

16. The way to abolish race prejudice is to abolish marginal business.

17. Marginal businessmen, regardless of their racial origin, confront similar problems.

18. Negroes are rarely very intelligent.

19. A conscientious study of the dictionary definitions of a term gives us insight into social processes.

20. We should all love our fellow men.

13. Classification

When a legal distinction is determined ... between night and day, childhood and maturity, or any other extremes, a point has to be fixed or a line has to be drawn, or gradually picked out by successive decisions, to mark where the change takes place. Looked at by itself without regard to the necessity behind it, the line or point seems arbitrary. It might as well be a little more to the one side or the other. But when it is seen that a line or point there must be, and that there is no mathematical or logical way of fixing it precisely, the decision of the legislature must be accepted unless we can say that it is very wide of any reasonable mark. OLIVER WENDELL HOLMES

For of course the true meaning of a term is to be found by observing what a man does with it, not by what he says about it.
P. W. BRIDGMAN

Giving Things Names

The figure below shows eight objects, let us say animals, four large and four small, a different four with round heads and another four with square heads, and still another four with curly tails and another four with straight tails. These animals, let us say, are scampering about your village, but since at first they are of no importance to you, you ignore them. You do not even give them a name.

One day, however, you discover that the little ones eat up your grain, while the big ones do not. A differentiation sets itself up, and abstracting the common characteristics of A, B, C, and D, you decide to call these *gogo;* E, F, G, and H you decide to call *gigi.* You chase away the *gogo,* but leave the *gigi* alone. Your neighbor, however, has had a different experience; he finds that those with square heads bite, while those with round heads do not. Abstracting the common characteristics of B, D, F, and H, he calls them *daba,* and A, C, E, and G he calls *dobo.* Still another neighbor discovers, on the other hand, that those with curly tails kill snakes, while those with straight tails do not. He differentiates them, abstracting still another set of common characteristics: A, B, E, and F are *busa,* while C, D, G, and H are *busana.*

Now imagine that the three of you are together when E runs by. You say, "There goes the *gigi*"; your first neighbor says, "There goes the *dobo*"; your other neighbor says, "There goes the *busa.*" Here immediately a great controversy arises. What is it really, a *gigi,* a *dobo,* or a *busa?* What is its *right name?* You are quarreling violently when along comes a fourth person from another village who calls it a *muglock,* an edible animal, as opposed to *uglock,* an inedible animal—which doesn't help matters a bit.

Of course, the question, "What is it *really? What is its right name?"* is a nonsense question. By a nonsense question is meant one that is not capable of being answered. Things can have "right names" only if there is a necessary connection between symbols and things symbolized, and we have seen that there is not. That is to say, in the light of your interest in protecting your grain, it may be necessary for you to distinguish the animal E as a *gigi;* your neighbor, who doesn't like to be bitten, finds it practical to distinguish it as a *dobo;* your other neighbor, who likes to see snakes killed, distinguishes it as a *busa.* What we call things and where we draw the line between one class of things and another depend upon the interests we have and the purposes of the classification. For example, animals are classified in one way by the meat industry, in a different way by the leather industry, in another different way by the fur industry, and in a still different way by the biologist.

None of these classifications is any more final than any of the others; each of them is useful for its purpose.

This holds, of course, regarding everything we perceive. A table "is" a table to us, because we can understand its relationship to our conduct and interests; we eat at it, work on it, lay things on it. But to a person living in a culture where no tables are used, it may be a very big stool, a small platform, or a meaningless structure. If our culture and upbringing were different, that is to say, our world would not even look the same to us.

Many of us, for example, cannot distinguish between pickerel, pike, salmon, smelts, perch, crappies, halibut, and mackerel; we say that they are "just fish, and I don't like fish." To a seafood connoisseur, however, these distinctions are real, since they mean the difference to him between one kind of good meal, a very different kind of good meal, or a poor meal. To a zoologist, even finer distinctions become of great importance, since he has other and more general ends in view. When we hear the statement, then, "This fish is a specimen of the pompano, *Trachinotus carolinus,*" we accept this as being "true," even if we don't care, not because that is its "right name," but because that is how it is *classified* in the most complete and most general system of classification which people most deeply interested in fish have evolved.

When we name something, then, we are classifying. *The individual object or event we are naming, of course, has no name and belongs to no class until we put it in one.* To illustrate again, suppose that we were to give the *extensional* meaning of the word "Korean." We would have to point to all "Koreans" living at a particular moment and say, "The word 'Korean' denotes at the present moment these persons: A_1, A_2, A_3 . . . A_n." Now, let us say, a child, whom we shall designate as Z, is born among these "Koreans." *The extensional meaning of the word "Korean," determined prior to the existence of Z, does not include Z.* Z is a new individual belonging to no classification, since all classifications were made without taking Z into account. Why, then, is Z also a "Korean"? *Because we say so.* And, saying so—fixing the classification—we have determined to a considerable extent future attitudes toward Z. For example, Z will always have certain rights in Korea;

he will always be regarded in other nations as an "alien" and will be subject to laws applicable to "aliens."

In matters of "race" and "nationality," the way in which classifications work is especially apparent. For example, the present writer is by "race" a "Japanese," by "nationality" a "Canadian," but, his friends say, "essentially" an "American," since he thinks, talks, behaves, and dresses much like other Americans. Because he is "Japanese," he is excluded by law from becoming a citizen of the United States; because he is "Canadian," he has certain rights in all parts of the British Commonwealth; because he is "American," he gets along with his friends and teaches in an American institution of higher learning without any noticeable special difficulties. Are these classifications "real"? Of course they are, and *the effect that each of them has upon what he may and may not do constitutes their "reality."*

There was, again, the story some years ago of the immigrant baby whose parents were "Czechs" and eligible to enter the United States by quota. The child, however, because it was born on what happened to be a "British" ship, was a "British subject." The quota for Britishers was full for that year, with the result that the new-born infant was regarded by immigration authorities as "not admissible to the United States." How they straightened out this matter, the writer does not know. The reader can multiply instances of this kind at will. When, to take another example, is a person a "Negro"? By the definition accepted in the United States, any person with even a small amount of "Negro blood"—that is, whose parents or ancestors were classified as "Negroes"—is a "Negro." *It would be exactly as justifiable to say that any person with even a small amount of "white blood" is "white."* Why do they say one rather than the other? Because the former system of classification *suits the convenience of those making the classification.*

There are few complexities about classifications at the level of dogs and cats, knives and forks, cigarettes and candy, but when it comes to classifications at high levels of abstraction, for example, those describing conduct, social institutions, philosophical and moral problems, serious difficulties occur. When one person kills another, is it an act of murder, an act of temporary insanity, an act of homicide, an accident, or an act of heroism? As soon as the process of classification is completed, our attitudes and our conduct are to a considerable degree determined. We hang the murderer, we lock up the insane man, we free the victim of circumstances, we pin a medal on the hero.

The Blocked Mind

Unfortunately, people are not always aware of the way in which they arrive at their classifications. Unaware of the characteristics of the extensional Mr. Miller not covered by classifying him as "a Jew" and attributing to Mr. Miller all the characteristics *suggested* by the affective connotations of the term with which he has been classified, they pass final judgment on Mr. Miller by saying, "Well, a Jew's a Jew. There's no getting around that!"

We need not concern ourselves here with the injustices done to "Jews," "Roman Catholics," "Republicans," "red-heads," "chorus girls," "sailors," "brass-hats," "Southerners," "Yankees," "school-teachers," "government regulations," "socialistic proposals," and so on, by such hasty judgments or, as it is better to call them, fixed reactions. "Hasty judgments" suggests that such errors can be avoided by thinking more slowly; this, of course, is not the case, for some people think very slowly with no better results. What we are concerned with is the way in which we block the development of our own minds by such automatic reactions.

To continue with our example of the people who say, "A Jew's a Jew. There's no getting around that!"—they are, as we have seen, confusing the denoted, extensional Jew with the fictitious "Jew" inside their heads. Such persons, the reader will have observed, can usually be made to admit, on being reminded of certain "Jews" whom they admire—perhaps Albert Einstein, perhaps Hank Green-berg, perhaps Jascha Heifetz, perhaps Benny Goodman—that "there are exceptions, of course." They have been compelled by experience, that is to say, to take cognizance of at least a few of the multitude of "Jews" who do not fit their preconceptions. At this point, how-ever, they continue triumphantly, "But exceptions only prove the rule!" [1]—which is another way of saying, "Facts don't count." In extremely serious cases of people who "think" in this way, it can sometimes be observed that the best friends they have may be Isaac Cohens, Isidor Ginsbergs, and Abe Sinaikos; nevertheless, in explaining this, they will say, "I don't think of them as Jews at all. They're just friends." In other words, the fictitious "Jew" inside their heads remains unchanged *in spite of their experience*.

People like this *cannot learn from experience*. They continue to vote "Republican" or "Democratic," no matter what the Republicans or Democrats do. They continue to object to "socialists," no matter what the socialists propose. They continue to regard "mothers" as sacred, no matter which mother. A woman who had been given up both by physicians and psychiatrists as hopelessly insane was being considered by a committee whose task it was to decide whether or not she should be committed to an asylum. One member of the committee doggedly refused to vote for commitment. "Gentlemen," he said in tones of deepest reverence, "you must remember that this woman is, after all, a mother." Similarly such people continue to hate "Protestants," no matter which Protestant. Unaware of characteristics left out in the process of classification, they overlook, when the term "Republican" is applied to both the party of Abraham Lincoln and the party of Warren Harding, the rather important differences between them: "If the Republican party was good enough for Abe Lincoln, it's good enough for me!"

Cow₁ Is Not Cow₂

How do we prevent ourselves from getting into such intellectual blind alleys, or, finding we are in one, how do we get out again? One way is to remember that practically all statements in ordinary conversation, debate, and public controversy taking the form, "Republicans are Republicans," "Business is business," "Boys will be

---

[1] This extraordinarily fatuous saying originally meant, "The exception *tests* the rule"—*Exceptio probat regulam*. This older meaning of the word "prove" survives in such an expression as "automobile proving ground."

boys," "Women drivers are women drivers," and so on, are *not true*. Let us put one of these back into a context in life.

"I don't think we should go through with this deal, Bill. Is it altogether fair to the railroad company?"

"Aw, forget it! *Business is business,* after all."

Such an assertion, although it looks like a "simple statement of fact," is not simple and is not a statement of fact. The first "business" *denotes* transaction under discussion; the second "business" invokes the *connotations* of the word. The sentence is a *directive,* saying, "Let us treat this transaction with complete disregard for considerations other than profit, as the word 'business' suggests." Similarly, when a father tries to excuse the mischief done by his sons, he says, "Boys will be boys"; in other words, "Let us regard the actions of my sons with that indulgent amusement customarily extended toward those whom we call 'boys,'" though the angry neighbor will say, of course, "Boys, my eye! They're little hoodlums; that's what they are!" These too are not informative statements but *directives, directing us to classify the object or event under discussion in given ways, in order that we may feel or act in the ways suggested by the terms of the classification.*

There is a simple technique for preventing such directives from having their harmful effect on our thinking. It is the suggestion made by Korzybski that we add "index numbers" to our terms, thus: Englishman$_1$, Englishman$_2$, . . . ; cow$_1$, cow$_2$, cow$_3$, . . . ; Frenchman$_1$, Frenchman$_2$, Frenchman$_3$, . . . ; communist$_1$, communist$_2$, communist$_3$, . . . The terms of the classification tell us what the individuals in that class have in common; THE INDEX NUMBERS REMIND US OF THE CHARACTERISTICS LEFT OUT. *A rule can then be formulated as a general guide in all our thinking and reading: Cow$_1$* IS NOT *cow$_2$; Jew$_1$* IS NOT *Jew$_2$; politician$_1$* IS NOT *politician$_2$, and so on. This rule, if remembered, prevents us from confusing levels of abstraction and forces us to consider the facts on those occasions when we might otherwise find ourselves leaping to conclusions which we may later have cause to regret.*

"Truth"

Most intellectual problems are, ultimately, problems of classification and nomenclature. Some years ago there was a dispute between the American Medical Association and the Antitrust Division of the Department of Justice as to whether the practice of medicine was a "profession" or "trade." The American Medical Association *wanted* immunity from laws prohibiting "restraint of trade"; therefore, it insisted that medicine *is* a "profession." The Antitrust Division *wanted* to stop certain economic practices connected with medicine, and therefore it insisted that medicine *is* a "trade." Partisans of either side accused the other of perverting the meanings of words and of not being able to understand plain English.

Can farmers operate oil wells and still be "farmers"? In 1947 the attorney general of the state of Kansas sued to dissolve a large agricultural co-operative, Consumers Co-operative Association, charging that the corporation, in owning oil wells, refineries, and pipe-lines, was exceeding the statutory privileges of purchasing co-operatives under the Co-operative Marketing Act, which permits such organizations to "engage in any activity in connection with manufacturing, selling, or supplying to its members machinery, equipment or supplies." The attorney general held that the co-operative, under the Act, could not handle, let alone process and manufacture, general farm supplies, but only those supplies used in the marketing operation. The Kansas Supreme Court decided unanimously in favor of the defendant (CCA). In so deciding, the court held that gasoline and oil *are* "farm supplies," and producing crude oil *is* "part of the business of farming."

"This court," said the decision, "will take judicial notice of the fact that in the present state of the art of farming, gasoline . . . is one of the costliest items in the production of agricultural commodities. . . . Anyway, gasoline and tractors are here, and this court is not going to say that motor fuel is not a supply necessary to carrying on of farm operations. . . . Indeed it is about as well put as can be on Page 18 of the state's Exhibit C where the defendant (CCA) says: 'Producing crude oil, operating pipe-lines and refineries, are also part of the business of farming. It is merely producing synthetic hay for iron horses. It is "off-the-farm farming" which the farmer, in concert with his neighbors, is carrying on. . . . Production of power farming equipment, then, is logically an extension of the farmers' own farming operations.'" (Italics supplied.)

Is a harmonica player a "musician"? Until 1948, the American Federation of Musicians had ruled that the harmonica was a "toy." Professional harmonica players usually belonged, therefore, to the American Guild of Variety Artists. Even as distinguished a musician as Larry Adler, who has often played the harmonica as a solo instrument with symphony orchestras, was by the union's definition "not a musician." In 1948, however, the AFM, finding that harmonica players were getting popular and competing with members of the union, decided that they were "musicians" after all—a decision that did not sit well with the president of AGVA, who promptly declared jurisdictional war on the AFM.

Is aspirin a "drug" or not? In some states, it is legally classified as a "drug," and therefore can be sold only by licensed pharmacists. If people want to be able to buy aspirin in groceries, lunchrooms, and pool halls (as they can in other states), they must have it reclassified as "not a drug."

Is medicine a "profession" or a "trade"? Is the production of crude oil "a part of farming"? Is a harmonica player a "musician"? Is aspirin a "drug"? The way in which such questions are commonly settled is by appeals to dictionaries to discover the "real meanings" of the words involved. It is also common practice to consult past legal decisions and all kinds of learned treatises bearing on the subject. The decision finally rests, however, not upon appeals to past authority, but upon *what people want*. If they want the AMA to be immune from antitrust action, they will go to the Supreme Court if necessary to get medicine "defined" as a "profession." If they want the AMA prosecuted, they will get a decision that it is a "trade." (They got, in this case, a decision from the Court that it did not matter whether the practice of medicine was a "trade" or not; what mattered was that the AMA had, as charged, *restrained the trade* of Group Health Association, Inc., a co-operative to *procure* medical services for its members. The antitrust action was upheld.)

If people want agricultural co-operatives to operate oil wells, they will get the courts to define the activity in such a way as to make it possible. If the public at large doesn't care, the decision whether a harmonica player is or is not a "musician" will be made by the stronger trade union. The question whether aspirin is or is not a "drug" will be decided neither by finding the dictionary definition of "drug" nor by staring long and hard at an aspirin tablet. It will be decided on the basis of where and under what conditions people want to buy their aspirin.

In any case, society as a whole ultimately gets, on all issues of wide public importance, the classifications it wants, even if it has to wait until all the members of the Supreme Court are dead and an entirely new court is appointed. When the desired decision is handed down, people say, "Truth has triumphed." *In short, society regards as "true" those systems of classification that produce the desired results.*

The scientific test of "truth," like the social test, is strictly practical, except for the fact that the "desired results" are more severely limited. The results desired by society may be irrational, superstitious, selfish, or humane, but the results desired by scientists are only that our systems of classification produce predictable results. Classifications, as amply indicated already, determine our attitudes and behavior toward the object or event classified. When lightning was classified as "evidence of divine wrath," no courses of action other than prayer were suggested to prevent one's being struck by lightning. As soon, however, as it was classified as "electricity," Benjamin Franklin achieved a measure of control over it by his invention of the lightning rod. Certain physical disorders were formerly classified as "demonic possession," and this suggested that we "drive the demons out" by whatever spells or incantations we could think of. The results were uncertain. But when those disorders were classified as "bacillus infections," courses of action were suggested that led to more predictable results. Science seeks only the *most generally useful* systems of classification; these it regards for the time being, until more useful classifications are invented, as "true."

Applications

I. There is a psychological test which can be made the basis for an interesting exercise in one's own home—especially in a home with children. Lay on a table an assortment of objects from all over the house: hammer, screw driver, toy hammer, toy screw driver, pipe, bubble pipe, kitchen equipment, metal spoon, plastic spoon, electrical equipment parts, scissors, fishing or sports equipment, and so forth, until you have twenty-five or more objects. Ask your friends to divide the objects into two piles, and to do this at least five times, using different systems of classification each time—but don't suggest the systems. Make a note of the systems of classification used and the order in which they come (e.g., painted and unpainted; metal and non-metal; toys and non-toys). Make notes, too, on the points at which people show marked indecision (e.g., do toy hammers belong with tools or non-tools? is an object made of hard molded rubber a plastic or a non-plastic?) and note also what objects seem to remain unclassifiable. When classifications are made that you don't understand, ask about them.

Write up the results, drawing any conclusions you can.

II. 1. What is meant when someone says, "What people ordinarily call rabbits are really hares, and what they call hares are really rabbits"?

2. When a corporation is classified as a "person" what are the characteristics of "persons" (as the word is understood in everyday, non-legal speech) attributed to corporations? What are the characteristics of "persons" left out of consideration in this classification?

3. Under what circumstances are tomatoes classified as "fruit" and under what circumstances as a "vegetable"? How else can they be classified?

4. When is an athlete an "amateur"? Investigate the rules for determining "amateur standing" in three or four different areas of sport (football, boxing, tennis, polo, and so forth) and the various methods used to give substantial compensation to "amateurs" in such ways as not to jeopardize their "amateur standing." Why, in college football, do we not put athletes on a straight, professional, salary basis, or, on the other hand, make the sport "completely amateur," i.e., without material compensation of any kind?

5. "Is motherhood an act of God? This question, involving all the profundities of metaphysics, faith, and physiology, might well give pause

to anyone, however learned. The answer YES would surely affront count-less atheists, agnostics. The answer NO would just as surely anger multitudes of the pious. Yet several men were actually confronted with this question last week and expected to make a public reply.

"Actress Helen Hayes, wife of Playwright Charles MacArthur, lately withdrew from the play *Coquette,* then on the road, saying: 'I am going to have a baby.' Producer Jed Harris ordered the play closed without notice. Five members of the cast at once demanded extra salary, said that Mr. Harris had violated the rules of Actors' Equity Association.

"The question depended on the Equity contract clause stating: 'The management is not responsible for fire, strikes, or an act of God.' Mr. Harris declared the expected MacArthur baby was certainly 'an act of God.' The protesting actors said it was no such thing.

"Equity arbitrators then met, discussed God and his acts. Appalled by the cosmic dimensions of their dilemma, they adjourned, wordless."

—*Time,* October 7, 1929

Advise the Equity arbitrators on the course of action most likely to secure general approval.

6. Comment on the following story from the Chicago *Sun-Times,* May 17, 1949:

"Washington (UP)—The House voted Monday to make the word 'wife' mean 'husband' too—sometimes. It passed and sent to the Senate a bill extending to dependent husbands of woman veterans the same pay and privileges given to dependent wives of men veterans. It was done by defining the word wife to mean husband, too, when that's necessary."

III. Study carefully a page of jokes in a popular magazine, the script of a radio variety show, or the text of a musical comedy, and note the extent to which humor is dependent upon sudden and unexpected *shifts of classification.* (For example, a comedy drummer may suddenly start beating time on someone's head, thus *reclassifying* a head as a "musical instrument.") Here are a few examples to start with:

1. JIM: Who was that lady I seen you with last night?
   SLIM: That wasn't no lady. That was my wife.

2. "Let us not be too particular. It is better to have old second-hand diamonds than none at all."   —SAMUEL L. CLEMENS

3. A lady from the West was the dinner guest of an old Boston family.

"Where is it you come from?" asked the hostess.

"Idaho," answered the guest.

"I hope you don't mind my saying this," said the hostess, "but in Boston we pronounce it 'Ohio.'"

4. "William Faulkner recalls a ball game once played in Mississippi. It was played in a cow pasture and ended abruptly when a runner slid into what he thought was third base."

—BENNETT CERF, *Try and Stop Me*

5. "A pigeon came home very late for dinner one evening, with his feathers bedraggled, and his eyes bloodshot. 'I was out minding my own business,' he explained, 'when bingo! I get caught in a badminton game!'"

—BENNETT CERF, *Try and Stop Me*

14. The Two-Valued Orientation

People with college educations, the student said, know more, and hence are better judges of people. But aren't you assuming, I asked, that a college education gives not only what we usually call "knowledge" but also what we usually call "shrewdness" or "wisdom"? Oh, he said, you mean that there isn't any use in going to college! FRANCIS P. CHISHOLM

Let him [the student] be made to understand that to confess the flaw he discovers in his own argument, though it is still unnoticed except by himself, is an act of judgment and sincerity, which are the principal qualities he seeks; that obstinacy and contention are vulgar qualities, most often seen in meanest souls; that to change his mind and correct himself, to give up the bad side at the height of his ardor, are rare, strong, and philosophical qualities. MONTAIGNE

In such an expression as "We must listen to *both* sides of every question," there is an assumption, frequently unexamined, that every question has, fundamentally, only two sides. We tend to think in opposites, to feel that what is not "good" must be "bad" and that what is not "bad" must be "good." This feeling is heightened when we are excited or angry. During war times, for example, it is often felt that whoever is not a "100 per cent patriot" *must* be a "foreign agent." Children manifest this same tendency. When they are taught English history, for example, the first thing they want to know about every ruler is whether he was a "good king" or a "bad king." In popular literature and movie scenarios written for childish mentalities, there are always "heroes" on the one hand, to be cheered, and "villains" on the other, to be hissed. Much popular political thought is based upon the opposition of "Americanism" (whatever that may mean) against "foreign -isms" (whatever that may mean). This tendency to see things in terms of two values only, affirmative and negative, good and bad, hot and cold, love and hate, may be termed the *two-valued orientation*.

The Two-Valued Orientation and Combat

Now, in terms of a single desire, there are only two values, roughly speaking: things that gratify or things that frustrate that desire. If we are starving, there are only two kinds of things in the world so far as we are concerned at the moment: edible things and inedible things. If we are in danger, there are the things that we fear and the things that may help and protect us. At primitive levels of existence, in our absorption in self-defense or food-seeking, there are, in terms of those limited desires, only two categories possible: things that give us pain and things that give us pleasure. Life at such levels can be folded neatly down the middle, with all good on one side, all bad on the other, and *everything is accounted for*, because things that are irrelevant to our interests escape our notice altogether.

When we are fighting, moreover, we are reduced at once to such a two-valued orientation. For the time being, nothing in the world exists except ourselves and our opponent. Dinner tomorrow, the beauties of the landscape, the interested bystanders—all are forgotten. We fight, therefore, with all the intensity we are capable of; our muscles are tense, our hearts beat much faster than usual, our veins swell, changes occur in the chemical composition of our blood in anticipation of possible damage. Indeed, the two-valued orientation, which under conditions of great excitement shows as many "physical" manifestations as "mental," may be regarded as an inevitable accompaniment to combat.

In the life of many primitive and warlike peoples, whose existence is a perpetual fight with the elements, with enemies, with wild animals, or with hostile spirits supposed to reside in natural objects, the two-valued orientation appears to be the normal orientation. Every act of a man's life in such a society is strictly governed by ritual necessity or taboo. There is, as cultural anthropologists have shown, little freedom in some types of primitive existence, since strict compulsions about "good" and "bad" govern every detail of life. One must, for example, hunt and fish in specified ways with specified ceremonials in order to achieve success; one must avoid walking on people's shadows; one must avoid stirring the pot from right to left instead of left to right; one must avoid calling people by their given names lest the name be overheard by evil spirits. A bird flying over the village is either "good luck" or "bad luck." Nothing is meaningless or accidental under such evaluative systems, because everything one sees, if it comes to notice at all, *must* be accounted for under one of the two values.

The trouble with such thought, of course, is that there is never any way of evaluating any new experience, process, or object other than by such terms as "good magic" or "bad magic." Any departure from custom is discouraged on the ground that it is "unprecedented" and therefore "bad magic." For this reason, many primitive peoples have apparently static civilizations in which each generation duplicates almost exactly the ways of life of previous generations—hence they become what is known as "backward" peoples. They have in their language no means of progressing towards new evaluations, since all things are viewed only in terms of two sets of values.[1]

The Two-Valued Orientation in Politics

Under a two-party political system such as we have in the United States, there is abundant occasion for uttering two-valued pronouncements. The writer has often listened to political speeches as given over sound-trucks in crowded Chicago streets and been impressed with the thoroughness with which Republicans (or Democrats) have been castigated and the Democrats (or Republicans) praised. Not a shadow of faint praise or even of extenuation is offered

---

[1] This is not to say that primitive peoples are "not intelligent." It simply means that lack of cultural intercommunication has deprived them of the opportunity to pool their knowledge with other peoples, so that they have had little occasion to develop the linguistic machinery which would offer finer evaluations needed for the accurate pooling of knowledge. Civilized people, insofar as they are civilized, have advanced not because of superior native intelligence, but because they have inherited the products of centuries of widest cultural intercommunication.

to the opposing party. When the writer asked a candidate for state representative why this was so, he was told, "Among our folks, it don't pay to be subtle." Fortunately, most voters regard this two-valuedness of political debate as "part of the game," especially around election time, so that it does not appear to have uniformly harmful consequences; overstatements on either side are at least partially canceled out by overstatements on the other. Nevertheless, there remains a portion of the electorate—*and this portion is by no means confined to the uneducated*—who take the two-valued orientation seriously. These are the people (and the newspapers) who speak of their opponents as if they were enemies of the nation rather than fellow-Americans with differing views as to what is good for the nation.

On the whole, however, a two-valued *orientation* in politics is difficult to maintain in a two-party system of government. The parties have to co-operate with each other between elections and therefore have to assume that members of the opposition are something short of fiends in human form. The public, too, in a two-party system, sees demonstrated the fact that the dire predictions of Republicans regarding the probable results of Democratic rule, and the equally dire predictions of the Democrats regarding Republican rule, are never more than partially fulfilled. Furthermore, criticism of the administration is not only possible, it is energetically encouraged by the opposition. Hence the majority of people can never quite be convinced that one party is "wholly good" and the other "wholly bad."

But whenever a political party feels that it is *so entirely right that no other party has any business existing*—and such a party gets control—there is immediate silencing of opposition. In such a case the party declares its philosophy to be the official philosophy of the nation and its interest to be the interests of the people as a whole. "Whoever is an enemy of the National Socialist party," as the Nazis said, "is an enemy of Germany." Even if you loved Germany greatly, but still didn't agree with the National Socialists as to what was good for Germany, you were liquidated. *Under the one-party system, the two-valued orientation, in its most primitive form, becomes the official national outlook*.

Hitler chose as the key terms of his system "Aryan," as representing all that was good, and "non-Aryan" (or "Jewish") as representing all that was evil. He and his propaganda ministry went systematically to work applying these terms to almost everything they could think of. The two-valued assumption is explicitly stated over and over again:

Discussion of matters affecting our existence and that of the nation must cease altogether. Anyone who dares to question the rightness of the National Socialist outlook will be branded as a traitor. (Herr Sauckel, Nazi Governor of Thuringia, June 20, 1933.)

Everyone in Germany is a National Socialist—the few outside the party are either lunatics or idiots. (Adolf Hitler, at Klagenfurt, Austria, on April 4, 1938. Quoted by New York *Times,* April 5, 1938.)

Everyone not using the greeting "Heil Hitler" or using it only occasionally and unwillingly, shows he is an opponent of the Fuehrer or a pathetic turn-coat . . . The German people's only greeting is "Heil Hitler." Whoever does not use it must recognize that he will be regarded as outside the community of the German nation. (Labor Front chiefs in Saxony, December 5, 1937.)

National Socialists say: Legality is that which does the German people good; illegality is that which harms the German people. (Dr. Frick, Minister of the Interior.)

Anyone or anything that stood in the way of Hitler's wishes was "Jewish," "degenerate," "corrupt," "democratic," "internationalist," and, as a crowning insult, "non-Aryan." On the other hand, everything that Hitler chose to call "Aryan" was by definition noble, virtuous, heroic, and altogether glorious. Courage, self-discipline, honor, beauty, health, and joy were "Aryan." Whatever he called upon people to do, he told them to do "to fulfill their Aryan heritage."

An incredible number of things were examined in terms of this two-valued orientation: art, books, people, calisthenics, mathematics, physics, dogs, cats, architecture, morals, cookery, religion. If Hitler approved, it was "Aryan"; if he disapproved, it was "non-Aryan" or "Jewish-dominated."

We request that every hen lay 130 to 140 eggs a year. The increase can not be achieved by the bastard hens (non-Aryan) which now populate German farm yards. Slaughter these undesirables and replace them. . . . (Nazi Party News Agency, April 3, 1937.)

The rabbit, it is certain, is no German animal, if only for its painful timidity. It is an immigrant who enjoys a guest's privilege. As for the lion, one sees in him indisputably German fundamental characteristics. Thus one could call him a German abroad. (General Ludendorff, in *Am Quell Deutscher Kraft.*)

Proper breathing is a means of acquiring heroic national mentality. The art of breathing was formerly characteristic of true Aryanism and known to all Aryan leaders . . . Let the people again practice the old Aryan wisdom. (Berlin *Weltpolitische Rundschau,* quoted in *The Nation.*)

Cows or cattle which were bought from Jews directly or indirectly may not be bred with the community bull. (Mayor of the Community of Koenigsdorf, Bavaria. *Tegernseerzeitung,* Nazi Party organ, October 1, 1935.)

There is no place for Heinrich Heine in any collection of works of German poets. . . . When we reject Heine, it is not because we consider every line he wrote bad. The decisive factor is that this man was a Jew. Therefore, there is no place for him in German literature. (*Schwarze Korps.*)

Because the Japanese were, before and during World War II, on friendly terms with Hitler's Germany, they were classified as "Aryans." This was an absurd enough classification, but of itself it probably did little harm to Hitler's cause. He made the additional error, however, of classifying some branches of physics as "Aryan" and other branches as "non-Aryan." It was the "non-Aryan" physics, unfortunately for him, that produced the theories that eventually produced the atomic bomb.

The connection between the two-valued orientation and combat is also apparent in the history of Nazism. From the moment Hitler achieved power, he told the German people that they were "surrounded by enemies." Long before World War II started, the German people were called upon to act as if a war were already in progress. Everyone, including women and children, was pressed into "war" service of one kind or another. In order to keep the combative sense from fizzling out for want of tangible enemies before the start of actual warfare, the people were kept fighting at home against alleged "enemies within the gates": principally the Jews, but also anyone else whom the Nazi happened to dislike. Education, too, was made explicitly warlike in intent:

There is no such thing as knowledge for its own sake. Science can only be the soldierly training of our minds for service to the nation. The university must be a battleground for the organization of the intellect. Heil Adolf Hitler and his eternal Reich! (Rector of Jena University.)

The task of universities is not to teach objective science, but the militant, the warlike, the heroic. (Dr. Drieck, headmaster of the Mannheim public schools.) [2]

The official National Socialist orientation never permitted a relaxation of the two-valued conviction that nothing is too good for the "good," and nothing is too bad for the "bad," and *that there is no middle ground.* "Whoever is not for us is against us!"

Man's Inhumanity to Man

The cruelties of the Nazi treatment of Jews and other "enemies" —the wholesale executions, the gas chambers, the "scientific" experiments in torture, starvation, and vivisection performed on political prisoners—have often taxed the credulity of the outside world. Stories of Nazi prison camps and death chambers are still regarded in some quarters as wartime anti-Nazi fabrications.

To the student of two-valued orientations, however, these stories are credible. If good is "absolutely good" and evil is "absolutely evil," the logic of a primitive, two-valued orientation demands that "evil" be exterminated by every means available. Murdering Jews

[2] The National Socialist pronouncements quoted in this chapter are from a collection of such utterances compiled by Clara Leiser and published under the title *Lunacy Becomes Us,* by Adolf Hitler and his Associates (Liveright Publishing Corporation, 1939).

becomes, under this orientation, a moral duty—to be carried out systematically and conscientiously. This appears to be, from the evidence produced at the Allied trials of war criminals, how the task was regarded. Many Nazi prison guards and executioners carried out their ghastly tasks, not in rage or in fiendish glee, but simply as matters of duty. So completely had the abstraction "Jew" blotted out all other perceptions, killing Jews became pretty much a matter of course. Aldous Huxley has said that it is the function of propaganda to enable people to do in cold blood things that they could otherwise do only in the heat of passion. Two-valued propaganda, seriously believed, has precisely this effect. One becomes completely convinced that "the dirty rats have it coming" and that "there is only one thing to do with them."

The Soviet One-Party System

There can be no doubt that communism started out in Russia with ideals far different from those of such avowed believers in force, fraud, and oppression as the German National Socialists. However much one may disagree with their views, it is apparent that Karl Marx, the ideological father of communism, and Lenin, his most influential disciple, were seriously and earnestly devoted to the cause of the underdog and looked forward to the day when there would be no underdogs (the "classless society"). Nevertheless, the Russian communists were so convinced of the rightness of their views that they set up a one-party state, defining their own abstractions as "Truth" and all dissenting, or partially dissenting, sets of abstractions as "wrong," "evil," "bourgeois," and "reactionary." The consequences are well known. The suppression of dissent, the "liquidation" of dissenters, the absence of freedom of thought and speech, the laying down of official pronouncements as to what is permissible not only in political thought but also in artistic, literary, philosophical, and scientific thought, have been almost as thorough and humorless in Russia as they were in Hitler's Germany.

The mechanism of the two-valued orientation requires a one-party system (why waste one's time listening to error when one knows the "Truth"?). The one-party system, in order to maintain itself, has to crack down on dissent and to pretend that it never makes a mistake. It appears, therefore, that it doesn't matter much whether one starts with noble or ignoble ideals if one is gravely two-valued in his approach: the end results are startlingly alike.

From the official Soviet point of view (as from the Nazi point of view just quoted), there is no such thing as knowledge for its own sake. Scientific theories, story themes in literature or the movies, trends in music or painting, like political opinions, are either praised as being "progressive," "democratic," "scientific," "materialist," "heroic," "socialist," and "pro-Soviet," or blamed for being "bourgeois," "decadent," "idealist" ("antiscientific"), "imperialist," "reactionary," "capitalist," and "fascist." There is a growing insistence on the existence of a "Soviet" science as opposed to "bourgeois" science, just as there was for the Nazis an "Aryan" as opposed to "non-Aryan" science. For example, Professor A. Zhebrak, the geneticist who incurred the displeasure of *Pravda* for his scientific views, is denounced in the following terms:

Zhebrak, as a Soviet scientist, ought to have unmasked the class meaning of the struggle taking place in connection with the problem of genetics. But, blinded by bourgeois prejudice, by a contemptible subservience to bourgeois science, he adopted the views of the enemy camp. . . . For A. Zhebrak there exists such a thing as "pure science." (Quoted by Joseph P. Lash in *New Republic,* January 3, 1949.)

In an address in September 1946 on "The Responsibility of the Soviet Writer," A. Zhdanov said that art can have no aims of its own apart from the glorification of the Soviet way of life and the merciless and unrelenting exposure of the evils of bourgeois culture. Writers, painters, and musicians whose works were not immediately comprehensible to the masses were denounced for "formalism." A "formalist" artist is one who is more concerned with achieving artistic excellence than with putting across a social message. "Formalism," then, is a bourgeois error, and, by the whoever-is-not-for-us-is-against-us principle, the formalist artist was declared to be "against us"—a "traitor" to the "true spirit" of Soviet art. Quite a shake-up in the arts followed Zhdanov's pronouncement:

Painters were warned against following such "formalists" as Picasso, Matisse and the Cubists, and the excellent collection of French Impressionists in Moscow was closed to the public and stored away in the cellar.

A decree of the Central Committee denounced formalism in music and ordered the reconstruction of all work in music to make it comprehensible to the Soviet people. . . . Such world-famous composers as Shostakovich, Prokofiev and Khatchaturian were condemned for music which was "antidemocratic," "alien to the Soviet people and its artistic taste" and reeking "strongly of the spirit of the contemporary modernist bourgeois music of Europe and America which reflects the marasmus of bourgeois culture." The director of the Moscow Conservatory of Music was ousted and Khatchaturian was replaced as chairman of the Union of Soviet Composers. . . .

The Soviet literary critic, M. Egolin, explaining to Moscow writers the significance of Zhdanov's address, made patriotism the keynote. . . . It is their [the Soviet writers'] duty to show "the way in which will power and strength of character are developed, in which average people, overcoming the hardships and burdens of war, perform great deeds, become heroes." . . . Poetry, it is decreed, must be permeated with Soviet optimism and noble striving. Moods of sorrow and discouragement, an individualistic preoccupation with love and personal destiny are considered alien to the Soviet outlook. (Joseph P. Lash, in *New Republic,* January 10, 1949.)

Because of the artificially imposed barriers to communication between the Soviet Union and the outside world, it is difficult to know how far this two-valuedness is being carried into Russian life. Perhaps clues are offered by such stories as the following:

moscow (AP)—The time has come, Soviet stylists were told today, to create clothing fashions "not reckoned on the corrupted boulevard tastes of the capitalist West." Society writer A. Donskikh, in "The Moscow Bolshevik," called on stylists to "begin working creatively on styles of clothing, simple and at the same time pretty, and corresponding to the increased cultural needs of the Soviet people." (New York *Herald Tribune,* December 29, 1948.)

Soviet Art, official organ of the Soviet Arts Committee, last week published an exposé of conditions under the big top. "Only by fully unmasking . . . in the arenas of Soviet circuses alien bourgeois tendencies can Soviet circus art achieve a new renaissance and become a genuine expression of the strength of our great fatherland," the article said. Circus managers were attacked for "trying to replace the healthy Soviet circus, with its ideology, optimism and purposefulness, with empty, formalistic imitations."

The worst offenders were the Western clowns. The article specifically attacked the famed Fratellinis, "reactionary and bourgeois (clowns) and classical exponents of buffoon games." A Russian critic who recently praised them was severely taken to task for "not revealing the ideological character of Western clownism." (*Time*, March 14, 1949.)

Defeating One's Own Ends

Convictions of a two-valued kind are far from being unknown in our own country. The resulting behavior, when carried out to its logical conclusion, is certainly horrible from any humanitarian point of view. But there is an even graver objection from what might be called a technological point of view, namely, that action resulting from two-valued orientations notoriously fails to achieve its objectives. The mobs, during World War I, that descended upon dissenting pacifist or religious groups in order to compel by force to kiss the flag did not advance the cause of national defense, but weakened it by creating burning resentments among those minorities. Southern lynch mobs do not solve the Negro problem; they simply make matters worse. What hardens "hardened criminals" is usually the way they are treated by a two-valued society and two-valued policemen. In short, the two-valued orientation produces the combative spirit, *and nothing else*. When guided by it for any purpose other than fighting, we practically always achieve results *opposite* from those intended.

Nevertheless, some orators and editorial writers employ the crude, unqualified two-valued orientation with extraordinary frequency, although in the alleged interests of peace, prosperity, good government, and other laudable aims. Do such writers and speakers do this because they know no better? Or are they so contemptuous of their audiences that they feel that "it don't pay to be subtle"? Another possibility is that they are sincere; like some physicians at the mention of "socialized medicine," they cannot help having two-valued reactions when certain hated subjects come into their minds. Another explanation, less pleasant to think about but in many instances highly probable, is that all the two-valued furore and spread-eagle oratory are a means of diverting public attention from more immediate issues. One can, by making an uproar about "atheism in the state university," "communists on the government pay roll," "theft of atomic information," or "who was to blame for Pearl Harbor," keep people from noticing what is going on with respect to such immediate problems as housing legislation, misuse of highway funds, forest and soil conservation, and the appointment of stooges for public utility companies to public utility regulating commissions.

The Multi-Valued Orientation

Except in quarrels and violent controversies, the language of everyday life shows what may be termed a multi-valued orientation. We have *scales* of judgment. Instead of "good" and "bad," we have "very bad," "bad," "not bad," "fair," "good," "very good"; instead of "sane" and "insane," we have "quite sane," "sane enough," "mildly neurotic," "neurotic," "almost psychotic," "psychotic." If we have only two values, for example, "law-abiding" and "law-breaking," we have only two ways of acting toward a given legal situation; the former are freed, and the latter are, let us say, executed. The man who rushes a traffic light is, of course, under such a dispensation, "just as much a law-breaker as a murderer" and will therefore have to get the same punishment. If this seems absurd, one has only to recall the medieval heresy trials in which the "orthodox" were freed and the "heretics" put to death—with the result that pious men who made slight theological errors through excess of Christian zeal were burned to as black a crisp as infidels or desecrators of the church. As soon as additional distinctions between *degrees* of offense are established, additional possibilities are thrown open, so that a minor traffic offense may mean a one-dollar fine; vagrancy, ten days; smuggling, two to five years in prison; grand larceny, five to fifteen years—that is, as many *degrees* of punishment as there are *degrees* of guilt recognized.

The greater the number of distinctions, the greater becomes the number of courses of action suggested to us. This means that we become increasingly capable of reacting *appropriately* to the many complex situations life presents. The physician does not lump all people together into the two classes of the "healthy" and the "ill." He distinguishes an indefinite number of conditions that may be described as "illness" and has an indefinite number of treatments or combinations of treatments. But the witch-doctor did one song and dance for all illnesses.

The two-valued orientation is an orientation based ultimately, as we have seen, on a single interest. But human beings have many interests: they want to eat, to sleep, to have friends, to publish books, to sell real estate, to build bridges, to listen to music, to maintain peace, to conquer disease. Some of these desires are stronger than others, and life presents a perpetual problem of weighing one set of desires against others and making choices: "I like having the money, but I think I would like having that car even better." "I'd like to fire the strikers, but I think it's more important to obey the labor board." "I'd like to obey the labor board, but I think it's more important that those strikers be taught a lesson." "I don't like standing in line for tickets, but I do want to see that show." For weighing the various and complicated desires that civilization gives rise to, an increasingly finely graduated scale of values is necessary, as well as foresight, lest in satisfying one desire we frustrate even more important ones. The ability to see things in terms of more than two values may be referred to as a *multi-valued orientation*.

The Multi-Valued Orientation and Democracy

The multi-valued orientation shows itself, of course, in almost all intelligent or even moderately intelligent public discussion. The editors of responsible papers, such as the New York *Times,* New York *Herald-Tribune,* Chicago *Sun-Times,* Milwaukee *Journal,* St. Louis *Post-Dispatch,* San Francisco *Chronicle,* Louisville *Courier-*

Journal—to name only a few—and the writers for reputable magazines, such as *Fortune, New Republic, Harper's, Atlantic Monthly, Commonweal,* or *The Nation,* almost invariably avoid the unqualified two-valued orientation. They may condemn communism, but they try to see what makes communists act as they do. They may denounce the actions of a foreign power, but they do not forget the extent to which American actions may have provoked the foreign power into behaving as it did. They may attack a political administration, but they do not forget its positive achievements. It does not matter whether it is from fair-mindedness or timidity that some writers avoid speaking in terms of angels and devils, pure "good" and pure "evil." The important thing is that they do, and by so doing they keep open the possibility of adjusting differences, reconciling conflicting interests, and arriving at just estimates. There are people who object to this "shilly-shallying" and insist upon an "outright yes or no." They are the Gordian knot cutters; they may undo the knot, but they ruin the rope.

Indeed, many features of the democratic process presuppose the multi-valued orientation. Even that most ancient of judicial procedures, the trial by jury, restricted to the conclusions "guilty" and "not guilty," is not as two-valued as it looks, since in the very selection of the charge to be brought against the defendant a choice is made among many possibilities, and also, in the jury's verdict as well as in the judge's sentence, guilt is often modified by recognition of "extenuating circumstances." Modern administrative tribunals and boards of mediation, not tied down by the necessity of arriving at clear verdicts of "guilty" and "not guilty" and empowered to issue "consent decrees" and to close agreements between litigants, are even more multi-valued than the trial by jury and therefore, for some purposes, considerably more efficient.

To take another example, very few bills ever pass a democratic parliamentary body in exactly the form in which they were proposed. Opposing parties argue back and forth, make bargains and compromises with each other, and by such a process tend to arrive at decisions that are more nearly adjusted to the needs of everyone in the community than the original proposals. The more fully developed a democracy, the more flexible become its orientations, and the more fully does it reconcile the conflicting desires of the people.

Even more multi-valued is the language of science. Instead of saying "hot" and "cold," we give the temperature in *degrees on a fixed and agreed-upon scale:* −20° F., 37° C., and so on. Instead of saying "strong" and "weak," we give strength in *horsepower* or *voltage;* instead of "fast" and "slow," we give speed in miles per hour or feet per second. Instead of being limited to two answers or even to several, we have an infinite number when we use these numerical methods. The language of science, therefore, can be said to offer an *infinite-valued orientation.* Having at its command the means to adjust one's action in an infinite number of ways according to the exact situation at hand, science travels rapidly and gets things done.

Two-Valued Orientation and Rhetoric

In spite of all that has been said to recommend multi- and infinite-valued orientation, it must not be overlooked that in the *expression of feelings,* the two-valued orientation is almost unavoidable. There is a profound "emotional" truth in the two-valued orientation that accounts for its adoption in strong expressions of feeling, especially those that call for sympathy, pity, or help in a struggle. "Fight polio!" "Down with slums and up with better housing!" "Throw out the crooks! Vote the Reform ticket!" The more spirited the expression, the more sharply will things be dichotomized into the "good" and the "bad."

As an expression of feeling and therefore as an affective element in speaking and writing, the two-valued orientation almost always appears. It is hardly possible to express strong feelings or to arouse the interest of an apathetic listener without conveying to some extent this sense of conflict. Everyone who is trying to promote a cause, therefore, shows the two-valued orientation somewhere in the course of his writing. It will be found, however, that the two-valued orientation is *qualified* in all conscientious attempts at presenting what is believed to be truth—qualified sometimes, in the ways explained above, by pointing out what can be said against the "good" and what can be said for the "bad"—qualified at other times by the introduction, elsewhere in the text, of a multi-valued approach to the problems.

The two-valued orientation, in short, can be compared to a paddle, which performs the functions, in primitive methods of navigation, both of starter and steering apparatus. In civilized life the two-valued orientation may be the starter, since it arouses interest with its affective power, but the multi-valued or infinite-valued orientation is our steering apparatus that directs us to our destination.

The Pitfalls of Debate

One of the principal points at which the two-valued orientation can seriously upset our thinking is in controversy. If *one* of the debaters has a two-valued orientation which leads him to feel that the Democrats, for example, are "entirely good" and the Republicans "entirely bad," he unconsciously forces his opponent into the position of maintaining that the Democrats are "entirely bad" and the Republicans "entirely good." If we argue with such a person at all, there is hardly any way to escape being put into a position as extreme on one side as his is on the other. This fact was well stated by Oliver Wendell Holmes in his *Autocrat of the Breakfast-Table,* where he speaks of the "hydrostatic paradox of controversy":

Don't you know what that means?—Well, I will tell you. You know that, if you had a bent tube, one arm of which was of the size of a pipe-stem, and the other big enough to hold the ocean, water would stand at the same height in one as in the other. Controversy equalizes fools and wise men in the same way—*and the fools know it.*

Disputes in which this "equalization" is likely to occur are, of course, a waste of time. The *reductio ad absurdum* of this kind of discussion is often to be found in the high school and college debate, as still practiced in many localities. Since both the "affirmative" and "negative" can do little other than exaggerate their own claims and belittle the claims of the opposition, the net intellectual result of such encounters is usually negligible, and decisions as to who "won" the debate must be made on such irrelevant points as skill of presentation and the pleasing personalities of the contestants. Parliaments and congresses, it will be observed, do not try to conduct much of their serious discussion on the floor. Speeches are made principally for the constituents back home and not for the other legislators. The main work of government is done in the committee room, where the traditional atmosphere of debate is absent. Freed from the necessity of standing resolutely on "affirmative" and "negative" positions, legislators in committee are able to thresh out problems, investigate facts, and arrive at workable conclusions that represent positions in between the possible extremes. It would seem that, in training students to become citizens in a democracy, practice in sitting on and testifying before committees of inquiry would be more suitable than debating, after the fashion of medieval schoolmen, for "victory."

In the course of everyday conversation, most of us need to watch for the two-valued orientation in ourselves. In a competitive society, conversation is often a battleground in disguise on which we are constantly (and unconsciously) trying to win victories—showing up the other fellow's errors, exposing his lack of information, confronting him (and all others present) with the superiority of our own erudition and logic. This habit of jousting for status is so deeply ingrained in most of us (especially in university and professional circles) that every literary cocktail party and every meeting of intellectuals is likely to include, as part of the entertainment, some sort of verbal dogfight among those present. Most people in such circles are so accustomed to this jousting that they rarely take offense at the remarks of their opponents. Nevertheless, they waste in argument a good deal of time that might more profitably be spent exchanging information and views.[3] An unconscious assumption, convenient for the purposes of those who are looking for occa-

---

[3] It is in such conversations that we all pretend to have read books that we know only by title, and to know about matters that we have never heard of before. People who don't know the rules and naïvely admit their ignorance are trampled upon or ignored; in either case they are left at the end of an evening with a crushing sense of inferiority. This, of course, is part of the purpose.

sions for argument and therefore underlying most of this kind of conversation, is that statements are either "true" or "false."

An important way to get the most out of conversation (and out of other forms of communication) is the following *systematic* application of the multi-valued orientation. Instead of assuming a statement to be "true" or "false," one should assume that it has a *truth-value* of somewhere *between* 0 and 100 per cent. For example, let us say that we are sympathetic to organized labor, and someone says to us, "Labor unions are rackets." Our immediate temptation is to say, "They are not"—and the battle would be on. But what is the truth-value of the man's statement? It is clearly neither 0 per cent ("No unions are rackets") nor 100 per cent ("All unions are rackets"). Let us then silently grant a *tentative* truth-value of 1 per cent ("One union out of 100 is a racket") and say to him, "Tell me more." If he has no more basis for his remark than the vague memory of something somebody once wrote in a newspaper column, he will fizzle out shortly, so that we need not be bothered with him any more. But if he does have experience with even *one* instance of union racketeering, he is talking about something quite real to him, although he may be vastly overgeneralizing his experience. If we listen sympathetically to his experience, the following are some of the things that may happen:

1. We may learn something we never knew before. We may, without giving up our pro-union sympathies, at least modify them so that they rest upon a clearer recognition of the shortcomings of unions as well as their advantages.

2. He may moderate his statement with such an admission as, "Of course, I haven't had experience with many unions." Again, if he tries to describe as extensionally as possible his experience with a labor union, he may find that some term other than "racketeering" more accurately fits the facts. In these and other ways he may make his remarks increasingly acceptable as he proceeds.

3. By inviting him to communicate to us, we establish lines of communication with him. This enables us later to say things to him which he may then be disposed to listen to.

4. Both may profit from the conversation.

To attempt to converse in this way is to make all our social contacts occasions for what we have earlier called the "pooling of knowledge." According to the "logic of probability" (one of the important instruments of scientific thought), even such a statement as "The sun will not rise tomorrow" has truth-value of an infinitesimal fraction of 1 per cent. The statements made in everyday life, even if based on slipshod inferences and hasty overgeneralizations, can usually be found to have *some* modest degree of truth-value. To find the needle of meaning in the haystacks of nonsense that the other fellow is talking is to learn something, even from the apparently prejudiced and uninformed. And if the other fellow is equally patient about looking for the needle of meaning in *our* haystacks of nonsense, he may learn something from us. Ultimately, all civilized life depends upon the willingness on the part of all of us to learn as well as to teach. To delay one's reactions and to be able to say "Tell me more," and then *to listen before reacting*— these are practical applications of some of the theoretical principles with which this book has been concerned: no statements, not even our own, say all about anything; inferences, such as one to the effect that the man who made the nasty remarks about unions is a "labor-hating reactionary," need to be checked before we react to them; a multi-valued orientation is necessary to democratic discussion and to human co-operation.

Orientations and Logic

The foregoing remarks about the two-valued *orientation* are not to be construed as being intended to apply to two-valued *logic*. Ordinary logic, such as we use in arithmetic, is strictly two-valued. Within the framework of ordinary arithmetic, two plus two are four. This is the "right" answer, and all other answers are "wrong." Many demonstrations in geometry are based on what is called "indirect proof": in order to prove a statement, you take its opposite and assume it to be "true" until you find in the course of further calculation that it leads to a flat contradiction; such a contradiction proves it to be "false," whereupon the original statement is regarded as "true." This too is an application of two-valued logic. The writer has no quarrel with arithmetic or geometry.

Logic is a set of rules governing *consistency in the use of language.* When we are being "logical," our statements are consistent *with each other;* they may be accurate "maps" of real "territories" *or they may not,* but the question whether they are or not is *outside the province of logic.* Logic is language about language, not language about things or events. The fact that two quarts of marbles plus two quarts of milk do not add up to four quarts of the mixture does not affect the "truth" of the statement, "Two plus two are four," because all that this statement says is that "four" *is the name of* "the sum of two and two." Of such a statement as "Two plus two are four," a two-valued question may be asked: "Is it true or false?"—meaning, "Is it or is it not consistent with the rest of our system? If we accept it, shall we be able to talk consistently without eventually contradicting ourselves?" As a set of rules for establishing discourse, a two-valued logic is one of the possible instruments for creating order out of linguistic chaos. It is indispensable, of course, to most of mathematics.

In some areas of discourse and within some special groups of people, it is possible, so to speak, to "police" the language so that it comes to have some of the clarity and freedom from ambiguity enjoyed by mathematics. In such cases, people may agree to call certain animals "cats," certain forms of government "democracy," and a certain gas "helium." They would also have clear agreements what *not* to call "cats," "democracy," or "helium." The two-valued rule of traditional (Aristotelian) logic, "A thing is either a cat or not a cat," and the Aristotelian "law of identity," "A cat is a cat," make a great deal of sense when we understand them as *devices for creating and maintaining order in one's vocabulary.* They may be translated, "We must, in order to understand one another, make up our minds whether we are going to call Tabby a 'cat' or 'not a cat.' *And once we have entered into an agreement as to what to call him, let's stick to it.*"

Such agreements do not, of course, *completely* solve the problem of what things to call by what names, nor do they guarantee the certainty of statements logically deduced. In other words, definitions, as stated in Chapter 10, say nothing about things, but only describe (and often prescribe) people's linguistic habits. Even with the strictest of agreements, therefore, as to what to call "cats" and what not to call "cats," whatever we may logically deduce about cats *may* turn out, on extensional examination of Tabby, Cinders, or Fluff, not to be true.

> Cats are creatures that meow.
> Tabby, Cinders, and Fluff are cats.
> Therefore Tabby, Cinders, and Fluff meow.

But what if Fluff has a sore throat and cannot meow? The *intensional* cat (the cat by definition, *whatever* our definition may be, "creatures that meow" *or any other*) IS NOT the *extensional* cat (Fluff, April 16, 2 P.M.). Each cat is different from every other cat; each cat also, like Bessie the Cow, is a *process,* undergoing constant change. Therefore, the only way to guarantee the "truth" of logically deduced statements and to arrive at agreements through logic alone is not to talk about actual cats at all, and to talk only about cats-by-definition. The nice thing about cats-by-definition is that, come hell or high water, they *always* meow (although, to be sure, they only meow-by-definition).

This principle is well understood in mathematics. The mathematical "point" (which "has position but occupies no space") and the mathematical "circle" (which is a "closed figure in which all points are equidistant from the center") exist *only as definitions;* actual points occupy *some* space, and actual circles are never *exactly* circular. Hence, as Einstein said, "As far as the laws of mathematics refer to reality, they are not certain; and as far as they are certain, they do not refer to reality." Therefore, even in an area such as chemistry, in which the vocabulary is quite strictly "policed," statements logically deduced *still have to be checked* against extensional observation. This is another reason why the rule for extensional orientation—cat_1 is not cat_2—is extremely important. No matter how carefully we have defined the word "cat," and no matter how logically we have reasoned, extensional cats still have to be examined.

The belief that logic will substantially reduce misunderstanding is widely and uncritically held, although, as a matter of common experience, we all know that people who pride themselves on their logic are usually, of all the people we know, the hardest to get along with. Logic can lead to agreement only when, as in mathematics or the sciences, there are *pre-existing*, hard-and-fast agreements as to what words stand for. But among our friends, business associates, and casual acquaintances—some of them Catholic and some Protestant, some of them scientists and some mystic sentimentalists, some sports fans and some interested in nothing but money—only the vaguest of linguistic agreements exist. In ordinary conversation, therefore, we have to learn people's vocabularies in the course of talking with them—which is what all sensible and tactful people do, without even being aware of the process.

On the whole, therefore, except in mathematics and other areas where clear-cut linguistic agreements either exist or can be brought into existence, the study and practice of traditional, two-valued logic is not recommended.[4] The habitual reliance on two-valued logic *in everyday life* quickly leads to a two-valued orientation—and we have already seen what *that* leads to.

Applications

I. The two-valued orientation appears in each of the following passages, in crude form as well as at higher levels of feeling; qualified as well as unqualified. Analyze each of them carefully, especially in the light of the questions: "How much confidence can I safely repose in the judgment of the author of this passage? A great deal? None at all? Or is there not enough evidence to be able to say?" Be on guard against the assumption that the two-valued orientation is always a bad thing.

1. "Politics, vacillation, the eternal straining after cleverness, a mind, as H. G. Wells observed of the President [Franklin Roosevelt], 'appallingly open,' open indeed at both ends, through which all sorts of half-baked ideas flow, love of the spectacular, preoccupation with war prob-

---

[4] It is interesting to note that even in mathematics, stress is laid today on the fact that two-valued logic is only one of many possible systems of logic. The logic of probability, on the basis of which insurance companies quote premiums, bookmakers quote odds, and physicists predict the behavior of neutrons, may be regarded as an infinite-valued logic.

lems and the affairs of Europe, and only a dim perception of the profound problems of economics and finance that dominate our scene, good
intentions mixed with confused ethical concepts—these have brought
the President to the tragic point where the only thing that can save his
regime is to take the country off into a war hysteria.

"Seven years after he took office there are eleven million unemployed,
private investment is dead, the farm problem is precisely where he
found it. He put through some social reforms that the country was
yelling for. But these social reforms have to be almost completely over-
hauled. As for recovery—the President has not one plan. The cost of
all this has been twenty-two billion dollars, all yet to be paid.

*"If it has all happened that way, it is because Franklin D. Roosevelt
is that way."*   —JOHN T. FLYNN, *Country Squire in the White House*

2.   *Preface to Milton*

And did those feet in ancient time
Walk upon England's mountains green?
And was the holy Lamb of God
On England's pleasant pastures seen?

And did the countenance divine
Shine forth upon our clouded hills?
And was Jerusalem builded here
Among these dark Satanic mills?

Bring me my bow of burning gold:
Bring me my arrows of desire:
Bring me my spear: O clouds, unfold!
Bring me my chariot of fire.

I will not cease from mental fight,
Nor shall my sword sleep in my hand,
Till we have built Jerusalem
In England's green and pleasant land.

—WILLIAM BLAKE

3.

WE ARE FOR THE STRIKING RAILROAD MEN 100 PER CENT—WE ARE
FOR A LIVING WAGE AND FAIR WORKING CONDITIONS.

These words on a card in a number of Emporia show windows
express a mild opinion of friendly sympathy with the strikers.

The cards have been ordered out by the Kansas Industrial Court. The order is an infamous infraction of the right of free press and free speech. Certainly it has not come to such a pass in this country that a man may not say what he thinks about an industrial controversy without disobeying the law.

One of these cards went up in THE GAZETTE window today. Instead of 100 per cent, we have started it at 49 per cent. If the strike lasts until tomorrow we shall change the per cent to fifty, and move it up a little every day. As a matter of fact, THE GAZETTE does not believe that anyone—not even THE GAZETTE—is 100 per cent right. But somewhere between forty-nine and 100 per cent the men are right. And if the Industrial Court desires to make a test case, here it is. This is not a question of whether the men are right or wrong, but a question of the right of an American citizen to say what he pleases about this strike. And if forty-nine per cent sympathy is permissible, in the next fifty days we shall all see where violation of the law begins. The Industrial Court which we have upheld from its conception, and still uphold, will have the nicest little chance to see just where it is lawful for a man to express sympathy with his friends and neighbors, even if in his heart he believes that they have made a mistake in the time of their strike.

Either we have free speech and a free press in this country, or we have not. Now is the time to find out.

—WILLIAM ALLEN WHITE, Editorial for
the Emporia *Gazette,* July 19, 1922 *

4. "I repeat, the conflicts about capitalism (and, really, about everything else as well) come from the two opposite views of the nature of man. The basic question is: Are all men endowed by the Creator with inalienable liberty? Or are all persons controlled, as wind and water are, by forces outside themselves?

"If everyone answered that question definitely and positively, for himself, and did all his thinking logically and soundly on the basis of his answer to that question, at least there would be no confusion in human affairs. The lines would be clearly drawn; the enemies would face each other in solid ranks; and the issue could be decided once for all. . . .

* From *Forty Years on Main Street.* Copyright, 1937, by William Allen White. Reprinted by permission of Rinehart & Company, Inc., publishers.

"Now, from the pagan belief that human beings are not free individuals, straight thinking leads directly to some kind of slavery. For if individuals do not control themselves, something else must control them; and in human society this Controller must have some kind of human form—a Living God, such as the Mikado; an autocrat, such as an Emperor, a King, a Leader, a Dictator; or a group of persons, such as a Ruling Class, a Party, a Parliament, or a Majority. . . .

"Whatever may be the political form that is established by the pagan view of man, the economy must always be a controlled economy. Of course, if individuals do not control their own actions, their actions are controlled by forces outside themselves; and since our first necessities are food, clothing and shelter, the major part of human activities will be farming, manufacturing, trading. Controlling anyone means controlling all their economic activities; that is, it means a controlled economy, now called a 'planned' economy. In other words, a controlled economy is a tyranny; a tyranny is a controlled economy.

"The tyrant may be a Mikado, an Emperor, a King, a Leader, a military dictator, a Ruling Class, a Party, or a Parliament (or Congress). The tyrant may control the economy in a number of ways: feudalism, communism, fascism, syndicalism, international or national socialism. The constant fact is that any controlled economy is some form of tyranny, and in it all men are slaves."

—ROSE WILDER LANE, Pittsburgh *Courier,* May 13, 1944

5. "One can imagine a semanticist in Poland, France, Norway, Greece, or any other country occupied by the Nazis. . . . Here, where revolutionary resistance to alien oppression was the only constructive therapy, the treacherous effects of the cult [of semantics] would have been clear. $Nazi_1$ was not the same as $Nazi_2$ or $Nazi_3$, to be sure, but more important for the victims was the functioning of all Nazis in a single pattern of destructive, anti-human behavior. In the coming period, with its sharpened imperialist rivalries so dreadfully jeopardizing our efforts toward world peace, there will no doubt be further destructive group actions which must be countered by positive and heroic struggles toward constructive ends. The alternatives are critical as never before in human history. In these times, harkening to the semantic cult is . . . rendering ourselves completely defenseless while we indulge in private games. For this reason I believe the vogue must not be dismissed as another curious but unimportant preoccupation of quasi-intellectuals.

It must be clearly revealed as a menace to the constructive social action so sorely needed today, and vigorously opposed.

—MARGARET SCHLAUCH, "The Cult of the Proper Word,"
New Masses, April 15, 1947

II. Consider the relative advantages and disadvantages of two-valued and multi-valued orientations in such situations as:

1. Trying to get parental consent to your marriage to someone outside your religious or racial group.

2. Deciding with the other members of the family where the family will spend the summer vacation.

3. Writing a script to be broadcast to the citizens of an enemy nation in time of war.

4. Leading an infantry combat unit into battle.

5. Getting elected mayor of your town or city.

6. Dealing, as mayor of your town or city, with the problem of traffic congestion on Main Street.

7. Increasing the efficiency and morale of the department, office, store, or factory unit in which you work.

8. Giving a speech urging support of the United Nations.

9. Trying to get your children to eat what you believe to be proper foods in what you believe to be the proper way.

III. One of the most effective ways of understanding and applying some of the key ideas in this chapter is to experiment, along with other people who have read it, in seeing how these ideas work.

For example, in a group of people who are familiar with the distinctions made here, choose some controversial subject of genuine interest to the group, such as the censorship of movies or of television, the abolition of college fraternities and sororities, world government, national health insurance by the federal government, pacifism, or the closed shop. Ask two members of the group to present a discussion of the chosen subject with one person persistently maintaining a two-valued orientation on the subject ("All censorship is bad," "The closed shop is undemocratic") and with the other person taking an opposing two-valued orientation.

Then ask two other members of the group to discuss the same subject, again with one of them maintaining a two-valued orientation but this time with the second person using the approach suggested in this chapter ("Tell me more," "Let's see").

The role-playing suggested here need not be lengthy—a three to five minute demonstration will usually suffice. A discussion of the demonstration, followed perhaps by another demonstration, will help to get the "feel" of "verbal jousting" as compared with the "systematic application of multi-valued orientation." In general discussion following such a demonstration, let the role-taker who has been most "on the spot" have the first chance to criticize what has been done, then his collaborator, and then those who were present as spectators.

15. The Great Snafu[1]

> *(Said Josie, the chimpanzee:)* *"No matter what names you humans give to things, we chimpanzees go right on enjoying life. It isn't so with humans. . . . The names you uncaged primates give things affect your attitude toward them forever after. You lose your insight because you are always holding up a screen of language between you and the real world."*
>
> RUTH HERSCHBERGER

> *In every cry of every man,*
> *In every infant's cry of fear,*
> *In every voice, in every ban,*
> *The mind-forg'd manacles I hear.*
>
> WILLIAM BLAKE

Freedom of Communication

We in the United States, who enjoy about as much freedom of press and freedom of speech as can be found anywhere in the world, frequently forget that information in the form of books, news, and education was long considered too valuable a commodity to be distributed freely among the common people. This is still the case, of course, in many countries. All tyrannies, ancient and modern, go on the assumption on the part of the rulers that they know best what is good for the people, who should only have what information the rulers think advisable. Until comparatively recent times, education was withheld from all but the privileged classes. In some states of the union, for example, it used to be a criminal offense to teach Negroes to read and write. The idea of universal education

[1] See Chapter 4: "The writer of a dictionary is a historian, not a lawgiver." The historians have caught up with this GI term. See *The American College Dictionary*, p. 1142.

was formerly regarded with as much horror by the "best people" as communism is today. Newspapers, during the early days of journalism, had to be bootlegged, because governments were unwilling to permit them to exist. Books formerly could be published only after official permission had been obtained. It is no accident that freedom of speech and freedom of press go hand in hand with democracy and that censorship and suppression always accompany tyranny and dictatorship.

The general suppression of information has rarely been completely successful over long periods of time in any nation. Human beings, for the purposes of their own well-being and survival, insist upon getting knowledge from as many people as possible, and also insist upon disseminating as widely as possible whatever knowledge they themselves may have found valuable. Even in the strictest of tyrannies, some form of "grapevine" communication continues to exist. Authority and aristocratic privilege gain temporary victories, but for the past three or four hundred years at least, universal access to information appears to have been, despite periodic censorship for military or political reasons, steadily increasing. In such a nation as the United States, the principles of universal education and freedom of the press are rarely openly questioned. We can deliver speeches without showing our manuscripts in advance to the chief of police. Except where considerations of "military security" stand in the way, we can print news stories and scientific papers without prior clearance with a governmental agency.[2] Power presses, cheaper methods of printing, public circulating libraries, elaborate systems of indexing and reference which make possible the quick finding of practically any information people might want—these and many other devices are now in operation in order that we need not depend solely on our own experience, but may utilize the experience of the rest of humanity.

It must not be forgotten, however, that technological advances in the communications industry, depending on what kind of economic or political control is exercised over them, may work either

[2] The exception is an extremely serious one. Overenergetic and overanxious measures in the interests of "security" can gravely impair the democracy that "security measures" are intended to protect.

for or against freedom of communication. There is little doubt that the invention of printing helped vastly the liberation of European people from the Renaissance onward. Pamphleteers disseminating new ideas have been important in every political movement. The freedom of the press traditional in democratic countries was established as a governing principle during a time when pamphleteers were still common and "the press" meant a large number of small newspapers produced in small print shops. It is often argued today that the enormous sums required to start a metropolitan daily newspaper effectively restrict freedom of the press to all but the very wealthy.[3] As an example of economic dangers to the freedom of the press, there is the fact that in the period immediately following the close of World War II, after the cessation of the wartime practice of governmental allocation of newsprint, thousands of small weeklies and special-interest papers were threatened with extinction as a result of the shortage of paper, the bulk of which went to the great newspapers. Again, radio is an amazingly efficient means of communication, but because the number of frequency channels is limited, and because stations can be linked up into vast nation-wide networks, it is (as totalitarian governments discovered) perhaps the easiest of all communication media to control centrally in the interests of one party or one powerful group of special interests. Every communication medium—press, radio, television, radio-transmitted facsimile newspaper—provides its own special problems as to how it is to be kept equally open to all important segments of public

[3] "I think almost everybody will grant that if candidates for the United States Senate were required to possess ten million dollars, and for the House one million, the year-in-year-out level of conservatism of those two bodies might be expected to rise sharply. We could still be said to have a freely elected Congress: anybody with ten million dollars (or one, if he tailored his ambition to fit his means) would be free to try to get himself nominated, and the rest of us would be free to vote for our favorite millionaires or even to abstain from voting. . . .

"In the same sense, we have a free press today. (I am thinking of big-city and middling-city publishers as members of an upper and lower house of American opinion.) Anybody in the ten-million-dollar category is free to try to buy or found a paper in a great city like New York or Chicago, and anybody with around a million (plus a lot of sporting blood) is free to try it in a place of mediocre size like Worcester, Mass. As to us, we are free to buy a paper or not, as we wish." A. J. Liebling, *The Wayward Pressman*, p. 265.

opinion. Unless these problems are thought about concretely, in terms of the technical peculiarities of each medium rather than in terms of abstract principles, important bodies of opinion can be kept from reaching the public at all.

Universal freedom of communication and the widest possible pooling of knowledge, even within the confines of the United States, is confronted by other difficulties as well. There are still millions of illiterates; good books, magazines, and newspapers are not everywhere available; there are many sections in our country without adequate schools; some communities have no libraries; other communities, having libraries, do not permit Negroes to use them. In all too many cities, there is only one newspaper (or two newspapers controlled by one firm). If, in such a city, the newspapers are partisan in their selection and editing of news and opinion, other sides are not heard at all.

Words as a Barrier

We are more concerned in this book, however, with the conditions within ourselves that stand in the way of universal communication. The idealistic proponents of universal education believed that people able to read and write would automatically be wiser and more capable of intelligent self-government than illiterates. But we are beginning to learn that literacy is not enough. Every drugstore newsstand in the country displays a collection of literature specially written for morons, and in most small towns there is no other place to buy reading matter. Furthermore, as the result of the necessary abstractness of our vocabulary, general literacy has often had the effect of merely making our folly more complicated and difficult to deal with than it was under conditions of illiteracy. And, as we have also seen, rapidity and ease of communication often make folly infectious. Universal literacy has brought new problems of its own.

Because words are such a powerful instrument, we have in many ways a superstitious awe rather than an understanding of them—

and even if we have no awe, we tend at least to have an undue respect for them. For example, when someone in the audience at a meeting asks the speaker a question, and when the speaker makes a long and plausible series of noises *without answering it, sometimes both the questioner and the speaker fail to notice that the question has not been answered; they both sit down perfectly satisfied.* That is to say, the mere fact that an appropriate-sounding set of noises has been made satisfies some people that a statement has been made; thereupon they accept and sometimes memorize that set of noises, serenely confident that it answers a question or solves a problem.

Many a cynical speaker and practical-minded clergyman has no doubt discovered the principle for himself: when someone asks a question that you can't answer, make an appropriate-sounding set of noises and all will be well. When Philip F. La Follette, then Governor of Wisconsin, forced the resignation of the late Dr. Glenn Frank from his post as president of the University of Wisconsin, the merits and demerits of Mr. La Follette's action were matters of heated discussion throughout the state. The writer, as an employee of the University of Wisconsin at the time, was traveling through the state and often encountered casual acquaintances and strangers who asked him, "Say, doc, what's the inside dope on that affair at the university? It's all politics, isn't it?" The writer never found out what anybody meant by "It's all politics," but in order to save trouble, he usually answered, "Yes, I suppose it is." Thereupon the questioner would look quite pleased with himself and say, "That's what I thought!" In short, the assurance that "politics" was the appropriate noise to make satisfied the questioner completely, in spite of the fact that the question which led to all the public discussion, namely, whether the governor had *abused his political office* or had *carried out his political duty,* had been left both unasked and unanswered. *This undue regard for words makes us tend to permit words to act as barriers between us and reality, instead of as guides to reality.*

Intensional Orientation

In previous chapters, we have analyzed particular kinds of mis-evaluation. All of these can now be summed up under one term: *intensional orientation*—the habit of guiding ourselves by *words alone,* rather than by the facts to which words should guide us. We all tend to assume, when professors, writers, politicians, or other apparently responsible individuals open their mouths, that they are saying something meaningful, simply because words have informative and affective connotations that arouse our feelings. When we open our own mouths, we are even more likely to make that assumption. As Wendell Johnson says, "Every man is his most interested and affected listener." The result of such indiscriminate lumping together of sense and nonsense is that "maps" pile up independently of "territory." And, in the course of a lifetime, we may pile up entire systems of meaningless noises, placidly unaware that they bear no relationship to reality whatever.

Intensional orientation may be regarded as a general term (at the next higher level of abstraction) covering the multitude of more specific errors already pointed out: the unawareness of contexts; the tendency toward automatic reactions; the confusion of levels of abstraction (of what is inside one's head with what is outside); the consciousness of similarities, but not of differences; the habit of being content to explain words by means of definitions, that is, more words. By intensional orientation, "capitalists," "Bolsheviks," "farmers," and "workingmen" "are" what we *say* they are; America "is" a democracy, because everybody *says* so; "atheists *must* be immoral" because it "logically follows" that if people do not fear God they have "no reason to behave themselves."

Ororverbalization

Let us take a term, such as "churchgoer," which *denotes* Smith$_1$, Smith$_2$, Smith$_3$ . . . , who attend divine services with moderate regularity. Note that the *denotation* says nothing about the "churchgoer's" character: his kindness to children or lack of it, the happiness or unhappiness of his married life, the honesty or dishonesty of his business practices. The term is applicable to a large number of people, some good, some bad, some poor, some rich, and so on. The *intensional* meanings or *connotations* of the term, however, are quite a different matter. "Churchgoer" *suggests* "good Christian"; "good Christian" *suggests* fidelity to wife and home, kindness to children, honesty in business, sobriety of living habits, and a whole range of admirable qualities. These suggestions further *suggest,* by two-valued orientation, that non-churchgoers are likely not to have these qualities.

If our intensional orientations are serious, therefore, we can manufacture verbally a whole system of values—a whole system for the classification of mankind into sheep and goats—out of the connotations, informative and affective, of the term "churchgoer." That is to say, once the term is given, we can, by proceeding from connotation to connotation, keep going indefinitely. A map is independent of territory, so that we can keep on adding mountains and rivers after we have drawn in all the mountains and rivers that actually exist in the territory. Once we get started, we can spin out whole essays, sermons, books, and even philosophical systems on the basis of the word "churchgoer" without paying a particle of further attention to Smith₁, Smith₂, Smith₃. . . .

Likewise, give a good Fourth of July orator the word "Americanism" to play with, and he can worry it for hours, exalting "Americanism," making dreadful thundering noises at "foreign-isms," and evoking great applause from his hearers. There is no way of stopping this process by which free associations, one word "implying" another, can be made to go on and on. That is why, of course, there are so many people in the world whom one calls windbags. That is why many orators, newspaper columnists, commencement day speakers, politicians, and high school elocutionists can speak at a moment's notice on any subject whatever. Indeed, a great many of the "English" and "speech" courses in our schools are merely training in this very thing—how to keep on talking importantly even when one hasn't a thing to say.

This kind of "thinking" which is the product of intensional

orientation, is called *circular,* because, since all the possible conclusions are contained in the connotations of the word to start with, we are bound, no matter how hard or how long we "think," to come back to our starting point. Indeed, we can hardly be said ever to leave our starting point. Of course, as soon as we are face to face with a fact, we are compelled to shut up, or start over again somewhere else. That is why it is so "rude" in certain kinds of meetings and conversations to bring up any facts. They spoil everybody's good time.[4]

Now let us go back to our "churchgoer." A certain Mr. William McDinsmore—the name is fictitious, of course—has had the term applied to him because of his habit of going to church. On examination, Mr. McDinsmore turns out to be, let us say, indifferent to his social obligations, unkind to his children, unfaithful to his wife, and dishonest in his trusteeship of other people's funds. If we have been habitually orientated towards Mr. McDinsmore by the intensional meanings of the word "churchgoer," this proves to be a shocking case. "How can a man be a churchgoer and so dishonest at the same time?" *The problem is completely incapable of solution for some people.* Unable to separate the intensional from the extensional "churchgoer," they are forced to one of three conclusions, all absurd:

1. "This is an exceptional case"—meaning, "I'm not changing my mind about churchgoers, who are *always* nice people *no matter how many exceptions you can find."*

2. "He isn't *really* that bad! He *can't* be!"—that is, *denying* the fact in order to escape the necessity of accounting for it.

3. "All my ideals are shattered! A man can't believe anything any more! My belief in human nature is destroyed!"[5]

---

[4] "When Harold Stassen in a 'Forum of the Air' radio debate the other day charged that no great advance like penicillin had ever come from a country with a medical-insurance plan, Oscar Ewing quietly pointed out that penicillin came from England." *New Republic,* January 24, 1949.

[5] When Sinclair Lewis's *Elmer Gantry* (1927) was published, it created much controversy. The disputants divided into two main factions. First, there were those who maintained that such a minister as Elmer Gantry—by intensional definition of "minister"—"couldn't possibly have existed," and that therefore Lewis had libeled the profession; secondly, there were the cynics who hailed the book as "an exposé of religion." Neither conclusion was, of course, justified by the novel.

An unfounded complacency, which can so easily be followed by "disillusionment," is perhaps the most serious consequence of intensional orientation. And, as we have seen, we all have intensional orientation regarding some subjects. In the 1930's the federal government, confronted by mass unemployment, created the Works Progress Administration, an agency which hired men and women and thought up public projects for them to work on. These WPA jobs were described scornfully by opponents of the administration as "made work," as distinguished from "real work" such as private industry was at that time failing to provide. It became a matter of pious faith on the part of these critics of the administration to believe that "WPA workers don't ever *really* work." The capacity for verbal autointoxication being as great as it is in some people, many of the believers in this faith were able to drive daily past gangs of WPA workers sweating over the construction of roads and bridges and still to declare quite honestly, "I've never yet seen a WPA worker do any work!" Another instance of this same self-induced blindness is to be found in widespread attitudes toward "women drivers." Many of us encounter daily hundreds of cars driven by women who handle them expertly; yet we declare, again quite honestly, "I never saw a woman yet who could *really* drive a car." By *definition,* women are "timid," "nervous," and "easily frightened"; therefore, they "can't drive." If we know women who have driven successfully for years, we maintain that "they've just been lucky," or that "they don't drive like women."

The important fact to be noticed about such attitudes towards "churchgoers," "WPA workers," and "women drivers" is that we should never have made such mistakes nor so blinded ourselves if we had never heard anything about them beforehand. Such attitudes are not the product of ignorance; genuine ignorance doesn't have attitudes. They are the result of false knowledge—false knowledge that robs us of whatever good sense we were born with. As we have already seen, part of this false knowledge we make up for ourselves with our confusions of levels of abstraction and other evaluative errors described in earlier chapters. However, a great deal of it is *manufactured* simply through our universal habit of *talking too much.*

Many people, indeed, are in a perpetual vicious circle. Because of intensional orientation, they are oververbalized; by oververbalization, they strengthen their intensional orientation. Such people burst into speech as automatically as juke boxes; a nickel in the slot, and they're off. With habits of this kind, it is possible for us to *talk ourselves into un-sane attitudes,* not only towards "women drivers," "Jews," "capitalists," "bankers," and "labor unions," but also towards our personal problems: "mother," "relatives," "money," "popularity," "success," "failure"—and, most of all, towards "love" and "sex."

Outside Sources of Intensional Orientation

In addition to our own habits, there are verbal influences from without that tend to increase our intensional orientations. Of these, only three will be dealt with here: education, magazine fiction, and advertising.

1. *Education.* Education really has two tasks. First, it is supposed to tell us facts about the world we live in: language is used *informatively.* Perhaps an even more important task, however, is that of inculcating ideals and "molding character"; that is, language is used *directively* in order that students should conform to the usages and traditions of the society in which they live. In their directive function, therefore, schools tell us the "principles" of democracy— how democracy *ought* to work. But often schools fail to perform adequately their informative function: that is, they may fail to tell us how democracy *does* work. What patronage privileges go with election to what offices; how the will of the people is sometimes subordinated to the will of insurance, railroad, real estate, labor, or gambling interests; how the fate of measures is sometimes determined not on their merits but by processes of legislative "logrolling" ("You vote for my bill and I'll vote for yours")—such topics are,

like sex, often regarded as not suitable for discussion before "impressionable young minds." [6]

Again, schools tell how "good English" *ought* to be spoken, but rarely take the trouble to describe how the English language *is* spoken. For example, we are all told that a double negative makes an affirmative, although nowhere is there any record of an officer of law holding a man on a charge of murder on the grounds that since the prisoner had said, "I ain't killed nobody," his words were actually a confession that he *had* killed *somebody*. The gap between the directives in the teaching of English and the realities of the English language are revealed in such a case as this: If a boy *ignores* his arithmetic teacher and states that 8 times 7 are 63, he will be laughed at by his friends; but if he *obeys* his English teacher and says, "With whom are you going to the party?" instead of, "Who are you going to the party with?" *he will also be laughed at.* Grammar, at least as taught by many old-fashioned teachers, is almost purely directive and bears little relation to the way English is actually spoken and written. Indeed, some teachers are so governed by two-valued rules of what expressions are "right" (under all circumstances) and "wrong" (under all circumstances), and so exclusively preoccupied with the problem of trying to get students to obey unrealistic grammatical directives, that they have long ago lost all sense of what language is for. These are the teachers who give the impression that the *only* important thing about any utter-

[6] Many parents react to the realistic discussion of politics in the classroom in exactly the same way as they react to the candid (informative) discussion of sex. In either case, they make no attempt to deny that the facts are as the teacher represents them to be; they simply insist that teachers "have no business telling children such things." Underlying such an attitude is, of course, the traditional educational theory to the effect that the way to bring up children is to keep them "innocent" (i.e., believing in biological, political, and socioeconomic fairy tales) as long as possible. The educational theory underlying this book, namely, that students should be given the best possible maps of the territories of experience in order that they may be prepared for life, is not as popular as might be assumed.

It should be remarked, however, that there is today a vigorous movement, especially on the part of social science teachers, to make secondary school education in such subjects as civics and government more informative than has been customary in the past. In sex education, too, most teachers and many parents have come to acknowledge the advantages of giving students "maps that accurately represent the territory."

ance is whether or not it is "grammatical." Since this is patently an absurd position, it is little wonder that students pay no attention to them.

Perhaps the greater part of education in some subjects is directive rather than informative. Law schools say much more about how law ought to work than about how it does work; the effects of the stomach ulcers, domestic troubles, and private economic views of judges upon their decisions are not regarded as fit topics for discussion in most law schools. History teachers of every nation often suppress or gloss over the disgraceful episodes in the histories of their nations. The reason for these silences and suppressions is that, although such statements may be informatively true, it is feared that they may, as directives, have bad effects on "impressionable minds."

Unfortunately, neither students nor teachers are in the habit of distinguishing between informative and directive utterances. Teachers issue such statements as "The United States is the greatest country in the world" and "Water is composed of oxygen and hydrogen" and ask their students to regard them as "true," *without telling them to distinguish between the two senses of the word "true."* Students thereupon find that some things their teachers say check with experience, while others are either questionable or false when examined as if they were informative statements. This creates among students, especially at around high school age, an uneasiness—a sense that their teachers are "stringing them along"—that leads many of them to leave school prematurely. Getting out of school, they feel that their suspicions about their teachers were correct, because, having mistaken the directive utterances they learned for informative, scientific utterances, they naturally find that they were "badly misinformed." Such experiences are probably the basis for that contempt for the "academic mind" which is so common in some circles. The fault is both the teacher's and the student's.

But those who continue in school are often no better off. Having indiscriminately lumped together directive and informative statements, they suffer shock and disillusionment when they get to a college where education is more realistic than that to which they have been accustomed. Other people continue all the way through college to confuse the directive and the informative; they may be aided in doing so by the unrealistic educational programs offered by the college. In such cases, the longer they go to school, the more badly adjusted they become to actualities. We have seen that directive language consists essentially of "maps" of "territories-to-be." We cannot attempt to cross a river on a bridge that is yet-to-be without falling into the water. Similarly students cannot be expected to guide their conduct exclusively by such statements as "Good always triumphs over evil" and "Our system of government ensures equality of opportunity to all men" without getting some terrible shocks. This may account in part for the fact that bitterness, disillusionment, and cynicism are particularly common among people during the first ten years after their graduation from college. Some people, indeed, never get over their shocks.

Education has to be, of course, both informative and directive. We cannot simply give information to students without giving them some "aspirations," "ideals," and "aims" so that they will know what to do with their information when they get it. But it is just as important to remember that we must not give them ideals alone without some factual information upon which to act; without such information they cannot even begin to bring their ideals to fruition. Information alone, students rightly insist, is "dry as dust." Directives alone, impressed upon the memory by frequent repetition, produce only intensional orientations that unfit students for the realities of life and leave them undefended against shock and cynicism in later years.

2. *Magazine fiction.* The next time the reader gets a printed slip giving "instructions for installation" with a car radio, a fog light, or similar piece of apparatus, he should notice how much close *attention* the reading of such a slip requires—how much constant checking with extensional facts: "The wires are distinguished from each other by colored threads in the insulation." We check and see if this is so. "Connect the positive wire, indicated by a red thread"—we find the wire—"with the terminal marked with the letter A. . . ."

He should then contrast such a task of reading with that of reading a story in one of the "pulp" magazines. This latter task can be performed with hardly any attention whatever; we can keep the radio going full blast, we can be munching chocolates, we can be teasing the cat with our feet, we can even carry on desultory conversations without being unduly distracted from the story. The reading of the average magazine story, that is, requires no extensional checking whatsoever, neither by looking at the extensional world around us nor by furrowing our foreheads in attempts to recall apposite facts. The story follows nice, easy paths of *already established intensional orientations.* As we have already seen, the expected judgments are accompanied by the expected facts. The straying hubby returns to his mate, and the little wife who is "true blue" triumphs over the beautiful but unscrupulous glamour girl; the little son is a "tousled, mischievous, but thoroughly irresistible little darling"; the big industrialist is "stern, but has a kindly twinkle in his eye." Such stories are sometimes cleverly contrived, but they never, if they can help it, disturb anyone's intensional orientations. Although in real life communists are sometimes charming people, they are never presented as such, because in the light of intensional orientations, anyone called "communist" cannot at the same time be "charming." Although in real life Negroes often occupy positions of dignity and professional responsibility, in magazine stories they are never permitted to appear except as comic characters or as servants, because, by intensional orientation, Negroes should never be anything else.

There are two important reasons for the maintenance of intensional orientation in mass-production fiction, political articles, books, and radio dramas. The first is that it is easy on the reader. The reader is, after all, seeking relaxation. The housewife has just got the kids to bed; the businessman has had "a hard day at the office." They do not want to try to account for unfamiliar or disturbing facts. They *want* to daydream.[7]

The other reason is, of course, that such writing is easy on the writer. In order to keep the market supplied, he has to produce so

---

[7] Persons deeply addicted to this narcotic, escape literature usually grow quite angry when, by mistake, they happen to read a novel which is sufficiently realistic to give a fairly extensional description of poverty, illness, or misfortune. "Isn't there enough unpleasantness in life," they ask, "without bringing it into literature too?"

many thousands of words a week. Proceeding by intension, as we have seen, the orator can go on talking for hours. Likewise proceeding by intension, the commercial story writer can, unencumbered by new facts to be explained or differences to be noted, keep on writing page after page. The resulting product is, to be sure, like paper towels, fit only to be used once and thrown away. Nobody reads a magazine story twice.

But, the reader may ask, since very few people take such stuff seriously anyway, why worry about it? The reason is that although we may not "take it seriously," our intensional orientations, which result from the word-deluge we live in, are deepened by such reading matter, although we may be quite unaware of the fact at the time. We must not forget that our excessive intensional orientations blind us to the realities around us.

3. *Advertising*. Perhaps the worst offender of all in the creation of intensional orientations is advertising as it is now practiced. The fundamental purpose of advertising, the announcing of products, prices, new inventions, and special sales, is not to be quarreled with; such announcements deliver needed information, which we are glad to get. But advertising long ago ceased to restrict itself to the giving of needed information, and its principal purpose, especially in so-called "national advertising," has become the creating, in as many of us as possible, of *automatic reactions*. That is to say, there is nothing that would profit the national advertiser more than to have us *automatically* ask for Coca-Cola whenever we walked to a soda fountain, *automatically* take Alka-Seltzer whenever we felt ill, *automatically* ask for Chesterfields whenever we wanted to smoke. Such automatic reactions are produced, of course, by investing "brand names" with all sorts of desirable affective connotations, suggestive of health, wealth, social prominence, domestic bliss, romance, personal popularity, fashion, and elegance. The process is one of creating in us *intensional orientations toward brand names:*

If you want love interest to thrive, then try this dainty way . . . For this way is glamorous! It's feminine! It's alluring! . . . Instinctively, you prefer this costly perfume of Verona Soap . . . It's a fragrance men love. Massage each tiny ripple of your body daily with this delicate, cleansing lather . . . Thrill as your senses are kissed by Verona's exquisite perfume. Be radiant.

Advertisers further promote intensional habits of mind by playing on words: the "extras" of skill and strength that enable champions to win games are equated with the "extras" of quality that certain products are claimed to have; the "protective blending" that harmonizes wild animals with their environment and makes them invisible to their enemies is equated with the "protective blending" of whiskies; a business association has for some time been publicizing this masterpiece of obfuscation: "If you work for a living you're in Business; what helps Business helps you!" Even the few facts that advertising gives us are charged with affective connotations: "It's got vitamins! It's chock-full of body-building, bone-building, energy-building VITAMINS!!" Meaningless facts are also charged with significance: "See the New Hy-Speed Electric Iron. It's STREAMLINED!"

When this advertising by verbal "glamorizing" succeeds in producing these intensional orientations, the act of washing with Verona Soap becomes, in our minds, a thrilling experience; brushing our teeth with Briten-Whyte tooth paste becomes, in our minds, a dramatic and timely warding off of terrible personal calamities, such as getting fired or losing one's girl friend; the smoking of cigarettes becomes, in our minds, the sharing of the luxuries of New York's Four Hundred; the taking of dangerous laxatives becomes, in our minds, "following the advice of a world-renowned Viennese specialist." [8] That is to say, we are sold daydreams with every bottle of mouthwash, and delusions of grandeur with every package of breakfast food.

Advertising has become, in short, the art of overcoming us with

[8] "But," some people are in the habit of saying, "surely nationally advertised products *must* be good! It stands to reason that a big advertiser couldn't afford to risk his reputation by selling inferior products!" A more perfect illustration of intensional orientation could hardly be found. Such people fail to realize, of course, that this is precisely the attitude that advertisers bank on. Yet these same people would hesitate to say, "Our public officials *must* be honest! It stands to reason that men in their position couldn't afford to risk their reputation by betraying the public interest." Such a trusting attitude toward public officials is prevented by intensional attitudes towards the *words* "politician" and "bureaucrat," more often than by experience with people in public office.

words. When the consumer demands that, as a step towards enabling him to orientate himself by facts rather than by the affective connotations of brand names, certain products be required by law to have informative labels and verifiable government grading, the advertising industry, backed by newspapers and magazines, raises a hue and cry about "government interference with business." For example, a pamphlet called "Your Bread and Butter: A Salesman's Handbook on the Subject of Brand Names," prepared by "Brand Names Research Foundation" (no address given), undertakes to explain "What's Behind All the Smoke" of the consumer movement, which, for many years, has demanded grade-labeling of consumer goods. Most of the members of women's organizations in the consumer movement, the pamphlet says, are "honestly concerned with solving the perennial problems of common sense buying," but a "vocal minority" of "self-appointed champions of the consumer" are the "spokesmen." This minority, it is explained, "want to standardize most consumer goods, to eliminate advertising and competing brands, to see government controls extended over production, distribution and profits. They believe in a planned economy, with a government brain trust doing all the planning." This is the sort of argument presented against grade-labeling *in spite of the fact that businessmen, both retailers and wholesalers, rely extensively on grading according to federally established standards when they do their own purchasing*. This is especially true in the case of canned foods, about which consumer groups have been especially insistent on grade-labeling.

Many advertisers *prefer* that we be governed by automatic reactions in favor of brand names rather than by consideration of the facts about their products. As the same pamphlet explains, it saves a lot of time: "her [the shopper's] time and the time of the overworked clerk. He has no need to sell her if she is already sold on a certain brand. All he has to do is wrap it up." Salesmen, in other words, may be as ignorant of what is in a product as the consumer.

Indeed, *the advertising of products under brand names has, within recent years, climbed to a higher level of abstraction*. In addition to the advertising of specific products by brand name, there is now *advertising of advertising*. The pamphlet also urges: "So it's up to you as a salesman for a brand name to keep pushing not only YOUR BRAND, but brands in general. *Get on the Brand Wagon!*" Says a whisky advertisement: "AMERICA IS NAMES . . . Seattle, Chicago, Kansas City . . . Elm Street, North Main, Times Square . . . Wrigley, Kellogg, Squibb, Ipana . . . Heinz, Calvert . . . Goodrich . . . Chevrolet. Names [the American has] always known . . . names of things he's bought and used . . . believed in . . . Yes, America is names. *Good* names. Familiar names that inspire confidence . . . For America *is* names . . . *good* names for good things to have. . . ." This sort of advertising of advertising has become increasingly common. The assumption is being dinned into us that if a brand name even *sounds* familiar, the product it stands for must be good. ("The best in the land if you buy by brand.") *A graver example of systematic public miseducation can hardly be imagined. Intensional orientation is elevated to a guiding principle in the life of the consumer.*

The writer is not opposed to advertising as such. Advertising is perhaps the greatest of the verbal forces shaping our daily living habits and our culture. It profoundly influences our looks, our manners, our economic life, our health, our ideas of art, and even our ethics. It enlists many of the best paid writers of our time and the majority of our artists and photographers. It takes up around 85 per cent of the space of mass circulation magazines, somewhat less of the space of newspapers, and sponsors something over 95 per cent of radio time, where it provides us with music, comedy, news commentary, and its own strange version of drama. It looks as if it is here to stay.

Furthermore, the basic functions performed by advertising are necessary to commerce. The writer finds it difficult to imagine an economic system under modern industrial methods of production that could operate without advertising in one form or another. Nor does the writer object to brand names as such. The advertising profession rightly tells us that distinguished brand names stand for years of conscientious service and manufacture, with scrupulous attention to high standards. The best brand names therefore stand for very high degrees of probability that a product will be outstandingly satisfactory. Brand names have the same kind of meaning that any other words may have, that is, varying degrees of probability that the connotations of the name are justified by the characteristics of the object named. The manufacturer who sees to it that a product "lives up to its name" performs a valuable social function, since in one small sector of experience he helps to create a language with a high degree of truth-value: "You are sure of a comfortable fit in XYZ shirts."

What is objected to in advertising, then, is *the promotion of pathological reactions to words and other symbols*. Because advertising is both so powerful and so widespread, it influences not only our choice of products; *it influences also our patterns of evaluation*. It can either increase or decrease the degree of sanity with which people respond to words. Therefore, if a product is sold through pushing people around with the affective connotations of words ("pin-point carbonation," "activated chlorophyll," "beware of gingivitis," "it contains *irium*"), such techniques, whether used in behalf of good products at fair prices or not, deepen the already grave intensional orientations widely prevalent in the public. The schizophrenic is the kind of person who attributes a greater reality to words, fantasies, daydreams, and "private worlds" than to the actualities around him. Surely it is possible for advertising to perform the functions necessary to commerce without going out of its way to promote schizophrenic patterns of evaluation.

The willingness to rely on words rather than on facts is a grave disorder of the evaluative process. If enough of our fellow-voters are afflicted with this disorder, it is at least as serious a threat to all of us as the widespread prevalence of smallpox.

Applications

I. Collect three or more samples of intensional orientation from each of the sources described in this chapter: (1) education; (2) magazine fiction; and (3) advertising. Note specifically your reasons for classifying each as an example of "intensional orientation."

II. Analyze the following selections, comparing and contrasting the evaluative habits of these various writers insofar as they are revealed by such short selections. Note especially automatic reactions, two-valued responses, confusion of levels of abstraction, and intensional orientation. Writing out such an analysis is recommended as a means of clarifying your own thinking.

1. "Socialism is thus for me not merely an economic doctrine which I favor; it is a vital creed which I hold with all my head and heart. I work for Indian independence because the nationalist in me cannot tolerate alien domination; I work for it even more because for me it is the inevitable step to social and economic change. I should like the Congress to become a socialist organization and to join hands with the other forces in the world who are working for the new civilization. But I realize that the majority in the Congress, as it is constituted today, may not be prepared to go thus far. We are a nationalist organization, and we think and work on the nationalist plane. . . .

"Much as I wish for the advancement of socialism in this country, I have no desire to force the issue in the Congress and thereby create difficulties in the way of our struggle for independence. I shall co-operate gladly and with all the strength in me with all those who work for independence even though they do not agree with the socialist solution. But I shall do so stating my position frankly and hoping in course of time to convert the Congress and the country to it, for only thus can I see it achieving independence. It should surely be possible for all of us who believe in independence to join our ranks together even though we might differ on the social issue. . . .

"How does socialism fit in with the present ideology of the Congress? I do not think it does. I believe in the rapid industrialization of the country. . . . Yet I have co-operated wholeheartedly in the past with the *khadi* program, and I hope to do so in the future because I believe that *khadi* and village industries have a definite place in our present economy. . . . But I look upon them more as temporary expedients of a transition stage rather than as solutions of our vital problems. That transition stage might be a long one, and in a country like India, village industries might well play an important, though subsidiary, role even after the development of industrialism. But, though I co-operate in the village-industries program, my ideological approach to it differs considerably from that of many others in the Congress who are opposed to industrialization and socialism. . . .

"The Congress is an all-inclusive body and represents many interests, but essentially it is a political organization with various subsidiary and allied organizations, like the Spinners' Association and the Village Industries Association. . . . It seems to me necessary that the Congress should encourage the formation of peasant unions as well as workers' unions, and co-operate with such as already exist, so that the day-to-day struggle of the masses might be continued on the basis of their economic demands and other grievances. This identification of the Congress with the economic struggle of the masses will bring us nearer to them and nearer to freedom than anything else."

—From the Presidential Address by Jawaharlal Nehru at the 49th session of the Indian National Congress, Lucknow, April 1936.

2. "I asked professors who teach the meaning of life to tell me what is happiness.

And I went to famous executives who boss the work of thousands of men.

They all shook their heads and gave me a smile as though I was trying to fool with them.

And then one Sunday afternoon I wandered out along the Desplaines River

And I saw a crowd of Hungarians under the trees with their women and children and a keg of beer and an accordion."

—CARL SANDBURG

3. "English-speaking peoples are all free-speaking peoples. Their Union would not be so much an English-speaking as a Free-speaking Union. English has long been the language of freedom, as of union. Indeed, English is a language in which *freedom* and *friend* have the same root. . . .

"These free-speaking peoples do not need to be convinced that no community, small or large, can long continue in a state of anarchy, or enjoy freedom, peace, and plenty unless it has dependable government. Nor need they be persuaded to choose democratic government and reject dictatorship. . . .

"Each of the great languages of mankind can be identified with some great field of human striving, in which the men who used it led the way for many others. Thus, Latin can be identified with law, Greek with knowledge, Hebrew and Arabian with religion, Hindu with philosophy, Persian with poetry, Chinese with wisdom, Italian with the Renaissance, Spanish with exploration, German with the Reformation, French with logic and reason, and Russian with economic collectivism. Similarly, the English language has become identified with freedom and union. . . .

"We English-speaking, free-speaking peoples face today a foe more ruthless than the Romans. Shall we go the way of the Sparta that was petty and the Athens that was proud? Or shall we outdo . . . the glory that was Greece?"   —CLARENCE K. STREIT, *Union Now with Britain*

4. "The pointing up of racial conflicts and injustices is important in a study of both the position of the Negro and the state of American culture. But the frictions are a healthy sign. They indicate a many-sided contact between the two races. The frictions are an evidence of the fact that the Negro and white man live in the same community and quarrel over the same values. As long as the two races are striving and disagreeing over the manifold issues of living in the same culture, then it means that they are engaged in the painful process of accommodation to each other and to the world. The real danger would be if the Negro managed to live in a vacuum where there was no friction between him and his white neighbors; then there would be real danger of the developing of a perpetual caste system. . . . It is desirable that nothing should remain static until the issues over which the friction arises have themselves ceased to trouble either the white or the blacks. To want peace when the contrasts are so great is to dream of an unreal world. To expect either the white or the Negro community to show neither anger nor hate, neither fear nor violence, when their values are challenged and their aspirations are frustrated is to ask for the impossible. . . . [Friction] shows that the evils complained of are alive, troublesome, and impelling. They force men to do something about them. They will do many wrong things about them, but, by the same token, many right ones.   —FRANK TANNENBAUM, "An American Dilemma" *Political Science Quarterly,* September 1944

5. "The bureaucrats in Washington are attempting to destroy the liberty and efficiency of the family doctor. In the name of public health, they are attempting to introduce socialized medicine such as is now in force in Germany and Russia. . . . These New Deal bureaucrats and politicians have played politics with hunger, they have played politics with cotton, wool, sugar; they have played politics with cattle, sheep, swine; they have played politics with highways, cement, droughts, river dams, but under God, are we American citizens going to be alert enough, to be sufficiently informed, are we going to be patriotic enough, are we going to see to it that they do not play politics with morphine, cocaine, anaesthetics, the birth of our little children, the physical ailments of our mothers and fathers, the intimate details of diseases which affect

our body and which are secrets that are held between us and our family physician? . . . A government that can regiment your family doctor can do what Germany has done; it can regiment your community Church. A government that can make a political jobholder out of your family physician is the same sort of dictatorial regime that can make a prisoner out of the minister of Christ."

—Newspaper editorial (around 1943-44)

6. "Ten prominent leaders of American labor . . . have published the most crushing indictment of the New Deal yet produced . . . : 'The most tragic result of the seven years of experiment has been the destruction of confidence, by incessant TINKERING with established forms and procedures.'

"There is probably no word in the English language better qualified to describe the experimental activities of the New Deal than TINKERING.

"According to the dictionary, a TINKERER is 'a butcher, a bungler.'

"The act of TINKERING is called 'an unskillful attempt to mend or improve.'

"To TINKER is 'to make futile attempts to mend, repair or improve; to potter fruitlessly.'

"To TINKER is to act 'in a makeshift, botching manner.'

"Now for seven years, according to the appraisal of these ten labor leaders, the New Deal has been:

" 'Tinkering with the wages and hours of labor under the NRA.

" 'Tinkering with the cost of labor's food under the AAA.

" 'Tinkering with property rights.

" 'Tinkering with the foundations of American government.' . . .

"In the light of this record, what else can be said of the New Deal than that it has been a 'botcher and a bungler'?

"What is the New Deal record, except 'An unskilled attempt to mend or improve'?

"What else has the New Deal done, except 'to potter fruitlessly' and to act 'in a makeshift, botching manner'?"

—Editorial, Chicago *Herald-American* (around 1940)

16. Rats and Men

The realization of the pathetic frailty of the knowledge or be-
liefs on which our life depends thus leads not to despair but to
open-eyed courage. But it also points to a most intimate connec-
tion between scientific method and liberal civilization. Science
is not, as is popularly conceived, a new set of dogmas taught by
a newer and better set of priests called scientists. It is rather a
method which is based on a critical attitude to all plausible and
self-evident propositions. It seeks not to reject them, but to
find out what evidence there is to support them rather than their
possible alternatives. This open eye for possible alternatives,
each to receive the same logical treatment before we can deter-
mine which is the better grounded, is the essence of liberalism
in art, morals, and politics. . . . Like science, liberalism insists
on a critical examination of the content of all our beliefs, prin-
ciples, or initial hypotheses and on subjecting them to a con-
tinuous process of verification so that they will be progressively
better founded in experience and reason.

MORRIS R. COHEN

"Insoluble" Problems

Professor N. R. F. Maier of the University of Michigan has performed a series of experiments in which "neurosis" is induced in
rats. The rats are first trained to jump off the edge of a platform at
one of two doors. If the rat jumps to the right, the door holds fast,
and it bumps its nose and falls into a net; if it jumps to the left,
the door opens, and the rat finds a dish of food. When the rats are
well trained to this reaction, the situation is changed. The food is
put behind the other door, so that in order to get their reward they
now have to jump to the right instead of to the left. (Other changes,
such as marking the two doors in different ways, may also be in-

troduced by the experimenter.) If the rat fails to figure out the new system, so that each time it jumps it never knows whether it is going to get food or bump its nose, it finally gives up and refuses to jump at all. At this stage, Dr. Maier says, "Many rats prefer to starve rather than make a choice."

Next, the rats are forced to make a choice, being driven to it by blasts of air or an electric shock. "Animals which are induced to respond in the insoluble problem situation," says Dr. Maier, "settle down to a specific reaction (such as jumping *solely* at the left-hand door) which they continue to execute regardless of consequences. . . . The response chosen under these conditions becomes fixated. . . . Once the fixation appears, the animal is incapable of learning an adaptive response in this situation." When a reaction to the left-hand door is thus fixated, *the right-hand door may be left open so that the food is plainly visible.* Yet the rat, when pushed, *continues to jump to the left,* becoming more panicky each time. When the experimenter persists in forcing the rat to make choices, it may go into convulsions, racing around wildly, injuring its claws, bumping into chairs and tables, then going into a state of violent trembling, until it falls into a coma. In this passive state, it refuses to eat, refuses to take any interest in anything: it can be rolled up into a ball or suspended in the air by its legs—the rat has ceased to care what happens to it. It has had a "nervous breakdown."[1]

It is the "insolubility" of the rat's problem that leads to its nervous breakdown, and, as Dr. Maier cautiously intimates, it is the "insolubility" of human problems that leads many human beings to have nervous breakdowns. Rats and men seem to go through pretty much the same stages. First, they are trained to make habitually a given choice when confronted by a given problem; secondly, they get a terrible shock when they find that the conditions have changed and that the choice doesn't produce the expected results; third, whether through shock, anxiety, or frustration, they may fixate on the original choice and continue to make that choice regardless of consequences; fourth, they sullenly refuse to act at all; fifth, when by external compulsion they are forced to make a choice, they again

[1] Norman R. F. Maier, "Two Types of Behavior Abnormality in the Rat," *Bulletin of the Menninger Clinic,* July 1943, pp. 141-47.

make the one they were originally trained to make—and again get a bump on the nose; finally, even *with the goal visible in front of them,* to be attained simply by making a different choice, they go crazy out of frustration. They tear around wildly; they sulk in corners and refuse to eat; bitter, cynical, disillusioned, they cease to care what happens to them.

Is this an exaggerated picture? It hardly seems so. The pattern recurs throughout human life, from the small tragedies of the home to the world-shaking tragedies among nations. In order to cure her husband's faults, a wife may nag him. His faults get worse, so she nags him some more. Naturally his faults get worse still—and she nags him even more. Governed, like the rat, by a fixated reaction to the problem of her husband's faults, she can meet it only in one way. The longer she continues, the worse it gets, until they are both nervous wrecks; their marriage is destroyed, and their lives are shattered.

Again, an industrialist, feeling that he has to increase the amount of production per worker, may order production increases peremptorily without adequate consultation with union officials and shop stewards to secure their co-operation. When they react to his orders with objections and countersuggestions—some of the objections will be genuine, of course, but some will arise from a simple determination not to be pushed around—he may, on the basis of intensional orientations about unions in general, decide to "get tough" to show them "who is boss." The workers, on the basis of intensional orientations about employers in general, may decide that he is trying to "bust their union" and respond to toughness with equal toughness. The employer, angered by this, makes even more rigid demands for "efficiency." The employees, equally angered, accuse him of trying to institute an unfair "speed-up" and deliberately slow down. When a fellow-industrialist suggests to him that the problem might be solved by inviting the union to take part in a joint labor-management committee, he snorts, "Not with those birds, you can't!" Every meeting between union and management becomes an increasingly acrimonious set-to, until both sides are unable to speak to each other except through the mediation of expensive and belligerent attorneys. Result: the lowest production

and the highest labor costs in the corporation's history, with "shattered nerves" on both sides.

Again, a nation may believe that the only way to secure peace
and dignity is through strong armaments. This makes neighboring
nations anxious, so that they increase their armaments too. There
is a war. The lesson of the war, the first nation declares when it is
all over, is that we were not strongly enough armed to preserve
peace; we must *double* our armaments. This naturally makes the
neighboring nations twice as anxious, so that they double their
armaments too. There is another war, bigger and bloodier. When
this is over, the first nation declares: "We have learned our lesson.
Never again shall we make the mistake of underestimating our defense needs. This time we must be *sure* to be sufficiently armed to
preserve peace. This time we must *triple* our armaments. . . ."

Of course these instances are purposely oversimplified, but are
not vicious circles of this kind responsible for the fact that we often
are unable to get at or do anything about the conditions that lead
to such tragedies? The pattern is frequently recognizable; the goal
may be in sight, attainable only by a change in methods. Nevertheless, governed by fixated reactions, the rat "cannot" get food, the
wife "cannot" cure her husband's faults, labor and management
"cannot" remain at peace, and wars "cannot" be prevented.

How about our other apparently insoluble problems? Why does
our nation want to manufacture and sell to the people within its
borders at higher prices the things it could import more cheaply
from elsewhere? Why, if it continues to send away more of its
natural resources, more of the products of its soil's fertility, more
of the products of its labor than it receives in exchange from other
nations, does it consider that it has a "favorable" balance of trade?
And why, when we are all agreed that lower trade barriers between
nations are necessary to world peace, do we have the difficulties we
do in lowering any of the barriers? Why do people speak bitterly
about the illiteracy and ignorance of Negroes and then use their
illiteracy and ignorance as grounds for opposing any measures for
ameliorating their condition? Why, above all, when every nation is
agreed that another world war would be unthinkably awful and
must be avoided at all costs, are the major powers breathlessly mak-

ing preparations for another war? The world is full of such para-
doxes.

Cultural Lag

A basic reason for such "insoluble" problems in society is what
might be called "institutional inertia." An "institution," as the
word is used in sociology, is "an organized pattern of group behavior, well-established and accepted as a fundamental part of a
culture" (*American College Dictionary*). Human beings are so
constituted that they inevitably organize their energies and activities into patterns of behavior more or less uniform throughout a
social group. In other words, the existence of a social institution
means that large numbers of people have accepted such patterns:
people in a communist (or capitalist) society accept and perpetuate
communist (or capitalist) habits of economic behavior; army men
acquire and perpetuate an army way of thinking and acting; priests
acquire and perpetuate priestly habits of thought and behavior;
veteran professional ballplayers pass on their behavior patterns to
the rookies.

A peculiar fact about institutions is that, once people have become accustomed to them, they eventually get to feeling that their
institutions represent the *only right and proper* way of doing things.
The institution of human slavery was, for example, claimed by its
defenders to be "divinely ordained," and attacks upon the institution were regarded as attacks upon natural law, reason, and the will
of God. Those who had contrary institutions, on the other hand,
regarded their system of free labor as "divinely ordained," and
slavery as contrary to natural law, reason, and the will of God. In
a similar way today, those who believe in corporate capitalist enterprise regard their way of organizing the distribution of goods as
the *only proper way;* while communists adhere to their way with
the same passionate conviction. This loyalty to one's own institutions is understandable: almost everyone in any culture feels that
his institutions are the very foundations of reasonable living. A
challenge to those institutions is almost inevitably felt to be a threat

to *all* orderly existence. (Ask a clergyman, "Is it necessary to have churches in order to maintain religion and the moral order?" Ask a general, "Is it necessary to have an army in order to maintain peace?" Ask a stock-broker, "Is the stock exchange necessary?" Ask a teacher, "Are schools necessary?" The first, unreflective answer will be "Yes," and after reflection, in the vast majority of cases, the answer will continue to be "Yes." The fact that almost everyone tends to defend his institutions against challenge or attack is the basis of social stability.)

Consequently, social institutions tend to change slowly—and, most importantly—they tend to continue to exist long after the necessity for their existence has disappeared, and sometimes even when their continued existence becomes a nuisance and a danger. Such continued existence of *obsolete* institutional habits and forms (like the systems of county government in many states of the Union, geographically arranged to suit the needs of a horse-drawn rural population) is called by sociologists "cultural lag." In everyday language, "cultural lag" is summed up in a peculiarly appropriate expression, "horse-and-buggy" ways.

The Fear of Change

The pressing problems of our world are then problems of cultural lag—problems arising from trying to organize a jet-propelled, supersonic, electronic, and atomic world with horse-and-buggy institutions.[2] The rate of technological advancement for almost two hundred years now, has been greater than the rate of the change of our social institutions and their accompanying loyalties and ideologies; and the disparity between the two rates is increasing rather than decreasing. Consequently, in every contemporary culture which has felt the impact of technology, people are questioning the applicability of nineteenth-century (or earlier) institutions to twentieth-century facts; they are progressively more alarmed at the dangers

[2] This is not to say, of course, that *all* contemporary institutions are obsolete. Many institutions are both very old and very satisfactory. Others are changing rapidly enough to keep up with changes in society.

arising from old-fashioned patriotism in a world that has become technologically one; they wonder with increasing anxiety about the possibility of attaining a sane world economic order with the instruments of nineteenth-century capitalism (or of nineteenth-century socialism). In Baltimore, Chungking, Cairo, Istanbul, Kyoto, Peoria, or Mexico City, wherever technologies are producing changes not adequately matched by changes in social institutions, there are people under strain and tension.

Some, of course, meet these strains and tensions in the only sensible way they can be met: they strive to change or abandon outmoded institutions and to bring into being new institutions or newer forms of old institutions. Changes in educational practice, in governmental organization, in the responsibilities of trades unions, in the structure of corporations, in the techniques of librarianship, in the marketing of agricultural commodities, and so on, go on all the time because extensional people are constantly striving to bring institutions into closer relationship with reality. An especially successful example of institutional adaptation is the Federal Deposit Insurance Corporation. Prior to 1934, bank failures resulted in the partial or total loss of the savings of depositors; panics, once started, were almost impossible to control. Since the setting up of FDIC, however, panics have disappeared; bank failures have been so reduced that in 1949 it was reported that there had not been a failure among banks insured under FDIC for five years. Today almost all banks are so insured, and there is more confidence in our banking system than at any previous time in the nation's history. The solution of banking problems was found in the adaptation of the institutions of insurance and the federal corporation to a new form of activity. The Tennessee Valley Authority is again an example of the successful creation of a vast new institution to solve problems left unsolved by older institutions. The ways in which the going patterns of behavior and the desires of farm organizations, river engineers, consumers of electrical power, shippers, chambers of commerce, county and state governments, public health authorities, and all other institutions concerned were extensionally examined and then skillfully taken account of and fitted into an over-all plan is vividly described by David Lilienthal in his book, *TVA: Democracy on the March*—an extraordinarily interesting description of the extensional approach to social problems and its possibilities when applied to a large-scale enterprise.

Some people, however, seeing the need for changes, agitate for cures which, on careful examination, appear to be no better than the ailment; still others agitate for changes that cannot possibly be brought about. However, in some of the most important areas of human life—especially in our ideas about international relations and in the deeply related problem of an equitable world economic order—areas in which our failure to find solutions threatens the future of civilization itself—we are, all over the world, in a state of cultural lag.

What causes this cultural lag? Obviously, in the case of many groups, the cause is ignorance. Some people manifestly don't know the score, so far as the realities of the modern world are concerned. Their "maps" represent "territories" that have long since passed out of existence. In other cases, the lag is due to fixed economic or political interests. Many individuals enjoy power and prestige within the framework of outmoded institutions—and with institutional inertia to support them, it is not hard for them to believe that their familiar institutions are beautiful and wonderful things. Indeed, there is little doubt that the desire of the wealthy and powerful to keep their wealth and power is a major reason for cultural lag in any society. Threatened with social change, they often act in such narrowly short-sighted and selfish ways that, like the Bourbons, they seem willing to destroy both the civilization they live in and themselves in grim, pigheaded attempts to hang on to their prerogatives.

But wealth and power are not in themselves guarantees either of social irresponsibility or of stupidity, and the existence of a powerful wealthy class in a culture is not in itself a guarantee that there will be cultural lag. At least some of the rich and powerful have known how to yield gracefully to institutional adjustments—sometimes they have even helped to introduce them—and by so doing they have maintained their favored position and have saved both society and themselves from the disasters that attend complete social disruption. When this happens, cultural lag is kept small enough to be manageable.

But when the rich and powerful are shortsighted and irresponsible, they are able to hold back necessary institutional adjustments only if they have enough support among those who are neither rich nor powerful. In accounting for cultural lag, then, we must account for the shortsightedness of the ordinary citizen who supports policies that are contrary to his own interests, in addition to accounting for the shortsightedness of the powerful. In addition to institutional inertia (which is a tremendous force keeping people busy doing things they should have stopped doing long ago), it appears that fear is another major force influencing both rulers and the ruled in the direction of institutional rigidity. Perhaps the ultimate strength of cultural lag comes from those persons in all walks of life whom change has made afraid.

The Revision of Group Habits

Whether the cultural lag arises from inertia, from shortsighted selfishness, from fear of change, or from a combination of these and other reasons, it is clear that the solution of social problems is basically a matter of adapting institutional habits to new conditions. The housing shortage following World War II was predicted by government authorities, by businessmen, and by ordinary citizens. It came as no surprise to anyone. Yet adequate measures were not taken to prevent its occurrence, and four years after the close of the war, most communities had still not taken adequate measures. The reason, of course, was not technological, but institutional. To build houses, especially on any large scale, requires dealing with innumerable institutions: special municipal, state, and federal legislation may be needed; delinquent taxes on vacant property have to be taken care of somehow and clear title obtained; zoning laws, insurance regulations, building ordinances, sanitary laws, and so on, have to be observed; the co-operation of banks and real estate firms has to be secured and agreements have to be made as to terms of financing; contractors, suppliers, and labor unions all have their going institutional habits governing who shall do what under what conditions; and the availability of everything needed in materials or services is governed by the condition of the market under the institutions of the profit economy and the price system. Each step in the building of houses (and there are thousands of steps) involves the intermeshing of dozens of institutions, each demanding that everything be done in the institutionally prescribed manner. Proposals on the part of progressive industrialists to mass-produce houses cannot be taken advantage of, not because of technological, but because of institutional, obstacles. Each of the institutional demands, at the time they had originated in the earlier history of the industry, had appeared reasonable and necessary. But the combination of all the demands in a period of acute shortage resulted in an almost complete throttling of production. (A similar housing shortage, originating from like causes, developed in the years following World War I.)

Perhaps the most dramatic thing about human behavior is how many problems which are "insoluble" for institutional reasons are promptly solved the moment a war breaks out. War is an institution the demands of which, at least in modern culture, take precedence over almost all other demands. Before the war, it would have been "impossible" to send the slum children of London to the country for the sake of their health. But when the air raids on London began, the evacuation of all the children took place over a week end. Institutionally-minded men, before the war, demonstrated time and again that it was "impossible" for either Germany or Japan to fight without an adequate gold supply. Nevertheless, Germany and Japan did manage to put up quite a fight in spite of the predictions of extremely reputable editorialists and news commentators. At Sydenham, England, and at Biarritz, France, the American government put together, almost overnight after the war closed, two great universities for GI's in Europe. Textbooks and equipment were flown over, luxurious quarters were provided for the thousands of students, and distinguished professors from the leading universities of America were hired at handsome salaries in order to provide, for a very short time, an educational Utopia for war-wearied American soldiers. In peacetime, is there any conceivable way in which a similar university could be set up, say, in

Mississippi, which, as the state that has the least per capita to spend on education, would be in greatest need of it?

If the United States were to go to war again tomorrow, and if it were shown to be a war necessity that housing in all the principal cities be immediately increased by 25 per cent, it is probable that the houses would be built in less than a year—with much the same determination with which the United States during World War II produced, in spite of all the statements from captains of industry that it was "impossible," the 50,000 planes a year which President Roosevelt said were necessary. Also, during the war, a degree of international co-operation among Allied nations that overturned all kinds of going institutional habits—the exchange of military secrets, the co-ordination of chiefs of staff, the joint carrying out of military and supply plans, the joint working out of diplomatic policies—was immediately achieved, only to be given up again when the war was over. One of the lessons of the war has been that institutions, while powerful and long-lasting, are often not insuperable *if the emergency is great enough.*

The problem, then, the world over, is to learn that the emergency in international affairs (as in so many other things) is great enough to require the modifying or abandoning of some of our institutions. And the problem for us as citizens, once we understand the emergency, is how we can contrive ways of adjusting our ways of thinking and acting so that institutional adjustments may be made both realistically and rapidly, with a minimum of human suffering and the maximum of general benefit.

The Extensional Approach

Every widely debated public issue—proposed changes in labor laws, proposed changes in the methods of distributing medical care, proposals for unifying the armed services under a single command, proposals to set up new ways of settling disputes between nations— is, then, a discussion of institutional adaptation. If we persist in discussing our social problems in terms of "justice" *versus* "injustice," "natural law, reason, and the will of God" *versus* "the forces of anarchy and chaos," reactions of fear and anger become general on both sides—and fear and anger paralyze the mind and make intelligent decision impossible. The escape from this two-valued debate lies in thinking about social problems as problems of institutional adaptation. Once we begin to do so, our questions with respect to hotly debated social issues begin automatically to become more extensional. We cease to ask whether a proposed institutional change is "right" or "wrong," "progressive" or "reactionary." We begin to ask instead, "What will be the results? Who would benefit, and by how much? Who would be harmed, and to what degree? What safeguards does the proposal contain to prevent further harm? Are people actually ready for such a measure? What will be the effect on prices, on the labor supply, on public health, or whatever? And who says so, on the basis of what kind of research and what kind of expert knowledge?" From extensional answers to such extensionally directed questions, decisions begin to flow.

The decisions that flow from extensional information are neither "left-wing" nor "right-wing." In science, which is the most systematically extensional of disciplines, there are neither "leftists" nor "rightists"; there are only degrees of competence. Who is the most competent scientist is determined not by debate but by comparing the accuracy of the predictions made. Those who make the most accurate predictions are universally conceded at once to be the best scientists. It is true that the accuracy of predictions on social issues leaves much to be desired compared with the accuracy of predictions obtainable in the physical sciences. But, in principle, increasing accuracy of prediction about the results of social actions is not impossible of attainment. When experts disagree on social issues, our present custom is to pour money into publicity campaigns to ballyhoo the opinions of those who testify on "our side." If, in such cases, we had the habit of pouring the same amount of money into scientific research (which would, if at all successful, bring experts into more and more agreement) every difference of opinion could be a starting point for further advances in knowledge, instead of, as at present, the source of further confusion.

Here, let us say, is a proposed municipal ordinance to permit trucks to pass over Oak Street bridge. Backing the measure are the truck lines who will save much time and money if the measure is passed. If our discussion of the proposal is reasonably extensional, our questions about it will be of the following kind: "Will the bridge structure stand the additional load? What will be the effect on traffic flow on Oak Street and streets approaching it? Is there danger of an increase in street accidents? Will the beauty of the city be adversely affected? What will be the effect on residences or businesses on and near Oak Street?" Such questions having been answered by persons of known ability in the making of accurate predictions in their several fields of knowledge, every voter has the materials with which to decide the question for himself according to his own interests and values, whether he is concerned with the safety of his children walking to school, with the beauty of the city, with trucking profits, with the effect on the tax rate, or whatever. Each voter's decision, made against a background of responsibly made predictions, will have some kind of reasonable relationship to his real desires.

Let us further suppose, however, that the measure is advantageous to practically no one in town *except* the truck lines. Then, if the truck lines want the measure passed, they will have to try to *prevent* the public from discussing the issue extensionally. The technique (familiar in the discussion of legislation affecting railroads, insurance, wartime price controls, housing, medical care, and so on) is immediately to move the discussion to higher levels of abstraction and to talk about "unreasonable restraints on business," the need for protecting "free enterprise" and "the American way" against harassment by "politicians," "officeholders," and "petty bureaucrats." By systematic confusion of levels of abstraction, the "freedom" of truck lines to operate over Oak Street bridge is made to appear one with the freedom fought and bled for at Valley Forge.

The tragedy is not only that many of us are innocent enough to be deceived by this sort of talk; a deeper tragedy is that in many communities the newspapers provide us with no more extensional materials for discussion. Partly because newspapers are large businesses themselves and often feel a community of interest with other large businesses; partly because some of them have long ago given up reporting in favor of printing material prepared for them by syndicated columnists, press agents, public relations counsels, and pressure groups; partly because sensational, two-valued utterances of extreme partisans make "livelier" stories than the factual testimony of extensionally-minded experts; and partly because some editors and publishers seem themselves to be even more susceptible to the razzle-dazzle of high-level abstractions than the least educated members of the general public, newspapers are in some communities almost worthless as sources of information on important public issues.

With respect to such questions as the federal control of tidelands oil or the federal control of grazing rights in national forests, the consequences of specific actions or regulations can be predicted, although the task will be greater than that of predicting the results of a change in traffic regulations over a local bridge. In neither the oil nor the grazing rights controversy is the point at issue a matter of "federal power" *versus* "states' rights," as is so often declared. "Federal power" is an extremely abstract term; so is "states' rights." By intensional orientation, "The greater the power of centralized government, the greater the threat to liberty. . . . Think of Germany under Hitler . . . think of Russia. . . . Do *you* want a police state?" By intensional orientation, the fight for "states' rights" is the fight of brave little local Davids against a huge federal Goliath. But the extensional facts are that "federal power" or "states' rights" may *both* be used *either for or against* the liberties of the individual. Federal power can tyrannize, but it can also protect individuals against the tyrannies of states, or states against the tyrannies of great national corporations or combines. States can also tyrannize, or protect against tyranny. Most of the uproar about "federal power" and "states' rights" has *no meaning* apart from specific proposals as to *what powers* (state or federal) are to be exercised in *what ways* for *what purposes*.

The discussion, then, of all such questions must be extensional. If federal control of tidelands oil is abandoned, what will happen? How will the availability of oil for commercial or defense needs be affected? What will be the effect on prices? Who will profit and to what degree? Who will be deprived and to what degree? If unlimited grazing of cattle on federal lands is permitted, who will profit and to what degree, and who will be harmed? What dangers are there to soil conservation, to the water level, to flood control, to the national food supply, to recreation areas, to game and wildlife management, in the alternative proposals of the contending parties? Once extensional answers to such questions are given and *widely publicized,* the need of people to line themselves up into "leftist" and "rightist" camps disappears. People become free to decide issues according to their real, rather than their imagined, interests, whether those interests be broad or narrow, selfish or idealistic.

But under present circumstances, the tenor of discussion (and therefore of public opinion) is such that the replacement of maladjustments by new maladjustments and the continuation of old maladjustments under new names are about as near as we can get to institutional adaptation with respect to some of our most pressing problems.

The End of the Road

When, as the result of protracted debate of a futile kind, years pass without the successful accomplishment of institutional adjustments, cultural lag grows progressively more serious. As social dislocations grow more serious, fear and confusion spread. As fear and confusion spread, societies, like individuals, grow increasingly disturbed at their failure to solve their problems. Lacking the confidence or the knowledge to try new patterns of behavior and at the same time panicky with the knowledge that their traditional methods no longer work, societies often appear to behave, to a greater or less degree, like Dr. Maier's rats, who, "induced to respond in the insoluble problem situation, settle down to a specific reaction which they continue to make regardless of circumstances. . . . The response under these conditions becomes fixated. . . . Once the fixation appears, the animal is incapable of learning an adaptive response in this situation." Thus do societies, as they have so often done in the past and continue to do today, fixate on *one* solution to their most pressing problem: the *only* way to appease the angry gods is to throw *still more* babies to the crocodiles; the *only* way to combat disease is to detect and hunt down *still more* people guilty of witchcraft; the *only* way to prosperity is to impose *still higher* protective tariffs; the *only* way to insure peace is to have *still greater* armaments.

Such are the mental blockages that prevent us from meeting our "insoluble" problems with the only approach which can ever help us solve them: the extensional approach—for we cannot distribute goods, feed people, or establish co-operation with our neighbors by intensional definitions and high-level abstractions. That which is done in the extensional world must be done by extensional means, no matter who does them. If we as citizens of a democracy are going to carry our share in the important decisions about the things that concern us so greatly, such as the problems of peace and a just world economic order, we must prepare ourselves to do so by coming down out of the clouds of high-level abstractions and learning to consider the problems of the world, whether at local, state, national, or international levels, as extensionally as we now consider the problems of getting food, clothing, and shelter.

If, however, we cling to our fixations and our intensional orientations, and the belligerent, two-valued sense of "I am right and you are wrong" which they produce, we have little before us but a fate similar to that of Dr. Maier's rat. We shall remain pathologically incapable of changing our ways of behavior, and there will be nothing for us to do but, like the rat, to try the same wrong solutions over and over again. After prolonged repetition of such futile conduct, would it be remarkable if we found ourselves finally in a condition of political "nervous breakdown"—sick of trying, and willing to permit dictators to dangle us upside down by our tails?

The Scientific Attitude

The most striking characteristic of science has been its continued success in the solving of "insoluble" problems. It was once considered "impossible" to devise means of traveling over twenty miles an hour, but now we have attained speeds of over six hundred miles an hour. It was "impossible" for man to fly—people "proved" it again and again—but now we fly across oceans as a matter of every-day routine. The writer was told repeatedly during the course of his education that the release of atomic energy was merely a *theoretical* possibility—of course, they would never actually *do* it. The scientist may almost be called the professional accomplisher of the "impossible." He does this because, as a scientist, he is extensionally orientated. He may be, and often is, intensionally orientated toward what he calls "nonscientific" subjects; therefore, the physical scientist talking about social or political problems is often no more sensible than the rest of us.

As we have seen, scientists have special ways of talking about the phenomena they deal with, special "maps" to describe the "territories" with which they are concerned. On the basis of these maps, they make predictions; when things turn out as predicted, they regard their maps as "true." If things do not turn out as predicted, however, they *discard* their maps and make new ones; that is, they act on *new sets of hypotheses* that suggest *new courses of action.* Again they check their map with the territory. If the new one does not check, they cheerfully discard it and make still more hypotheses, until they find some that *work.* These they regard as "true," but "true" *for the time being only.* When, later on, they find new situations in which they do not work, they are again ready to discard them, to re-examine the extensional world, and to make still more new maps that again suggest new courses of action.

When scientists work with a minimum of interference from pecuniary or political influences—when, that is, they are free to pool their knowledge with their co-workers all over the world and to check the accuracy of each other's maps by observations independently made and freely exchanged—they make rapid progress. Highly multi-valued and extensional in their orientations, they are troubled less than any other men by fixed dogmas and nonsense questions. In a way that is paradoxical in terms of traditional orientations but quite understandable in terms of the new, the conversation and the writings of scientific people are full of admissions of ignorance and declarations of partial knowledge. The writer has often been impressed by the frequency with which such expressions as the following appear in the conversation of the nuclear physicists with whom he has been acquainted: "According to Szilard's last paper—although there may be still later findings not yet published. . . ." "No one knows exactly what happens, but our guess is that it's something like this. . . ." "What I tell you is probably wrong, but it's the only plausible theory we've been able to construct. . . ." It has been said that knowledge is power, but *effective knowledge is that which includes knowledge of the limitations of one's knowledge.*

The last thing a scientist would do would be to cling to a map because he inherited it from his grandfather or because it was used by George Washington or Abraham Lincoln. By intensional orientation, "If it was good enough for Washington and Lincoln, it's good enough for me." By extensional orientation, *we don't know until we have checked.*

The Left-Hand Door Again

Notice the differences between the technological, scientific attitudes that we have toward some things and the intensional attitudes we have toward others. When we are having a car repaired, we think in terms of mechanisms. We do not ask: "Is the remedy you suggest consistent with the principles of thermodynamics? What would Faraday or Newton have done under similar circumstances? Are you sure that the remedy you suggest does not represent a degenerative, defeatist tendency in the technological traditions of our nation? What would happen if we did this to *every* car? What has Aristotle to say on this?" These are nonsense questions. We only ask, "What will be the *results?*"

But a different thing happens when we are trying to have society repaired. Few people have a sense of societies as mechanisms—as collections of going institutions. Accustomed to thinking of social problems in terms of simple moral indignation, we denounce the wickedness of labor unions (or of capitalists), we denounce the wickedness of those who clamor for Negro rights (or of those who persecute Negroes), we denounce Russia (or, if we are Russians, we denounce "American imperialism"). So doing, we miss entirely the basic requirement of "mapping" social problems, namely, the initial task of describing the *established patterns of group behavior* (i.e., the institutions) that constitute a society and create its social problems. Indignant at the wickedness of those with whom we disagree, we do not ask of a proposed institutional change what the results will be. We are usually more interested in "punishing the wicked" than in the practical results. And suggested social remedies are almost always discussed in the light of questions to which verifiable answers cannot be given: "Are your proposals consistent with sound economic policy? Do they accord with the principles of justice and reason? What would Alexander Hamilton, Thomas Jefferson, or Abraham Lincoln have said? Would it be a step in the direction of communism or fascism? What would happen if everybody followed your scheme? Why don't you read Aristotle?" And we spend so much time discussing nonsense questions that often we never get around to finding out exactly what the results of proposed actions would be.

During the course of our weary struggles with such nonsense questions, someone or other is sure to come along with a campaign to tell us, "Let's get *back* to normalcy. . . . Let's stick to the good *old-fashioned, tried-and-true* principles. . . . Let's *return* to *sound* economics and *sound* finance. . . . America must get *back* to this. . . . America must get *back* to that. . . ." Most of such appeals are, of course, merely invitations to take another jump at the left-hand door—in other words, INVITATIONS TO CONTINUE DRIVING OUR-SELVES CRAZY. In our confusion we accept those invitations—with the same old results.

Applications

I. Taking some community you know well, jot down some of its problems of cultural lag other than those mentioned in this chapter. What sort of questions would an extensionally orientated person be likely to ask if called upon to help in solving some one of these problems? What resource groups or persons would he be likely to consult?

II. Two friends of yours, both strongly opinionated but not at all well informed, one vigorously in favor of and the other vigorously opposed to "socialized medicine" (whatever either of them might mean by the term), are coming to your house tonight to spend the evening in conversation. Prepare some remarks you can throw into the discussion and some questions you might ask that might help make them see the problems of the distribution of medical care as a problem of institutional adjustment (of course, you will avoid using such fancy terms) and therefore help them keep the discussion at more extensional levels of discussion than they would otherwise employ. Warning: Do not start out by making them define "socialized medicine" (see pp. 171-173).

17. Towards Order Within and Without

> *But I say unto you, That every idle word that men shall speak, they shall give account thereof in the day of judgment. For by thy words thou shalt be justified, and by thy words thou shalt be condemned.*
>
> MATTHEW 12:36-37

Rules for Extensional Orientation

Just as a mechanic carries around a pair of pliers and a screw driver for use in an emergency—just as we all carry around in our heads tables of multiplication for daily use—so can we all carry with us in our heads convenient rules for extensional orientation. These rules need not be complicated; a short, rough-and-ready set of formulas will do. Their principal function will be to prevent us from going round in circles of intensional thinking, to prevent automatic reactions, to prevent us from trying to answer unanswerable questions, to prevent us from repeating old mistakes endlessly. They will *not* magically show us what better solutions are possible, but they will *start us looking* for better courses of action than the old ones. The following rules, then, are a brief summary of the parts of the book that directly apply to problems of evaluation. These rules should be memorized.

1. A map is NOT the territory it stands for; words are NOT things.

A map does not represent ALL of a territory; words never say ALL about anything.

Maps of maps, maps of maps of maps, and so on, can be made indefinitely, with or without relationship to a territory. (Chapters 2 and 10.)

2. The meanings of words are NOT in the words; they are in US. (Chapters 2 and 11.)

3. Contexts determine meaning (Chapter 4):
I like fish. (Cooked, edible fish.)
He caught a fish. (Live fish.)
You poor fish! (Not fish at all.)
To fish for compliments. (To seek.)

4. Beware of the word "is," which, when not simply used as an auxiliary verb ("he is coming"), can crystallize misevaluations:
The grass *is* green. (But what about the part our nervous system plays? Chapters 10 and 11.)
Mr. Miller *is* a Jew. (Beware of confusing levels of abstraction. Chapters 11 and 12.)
Business *is* business. (A directive. Chapter 7.)
A thing *is* what it *is*. (Unless this is understood as a rule of language, there is danger of ignoring alternative ways of classifying, as well as of ignoring the fact that everything is in process of change. Chapters 10, 13, and 14.)

5. Don't try to cross bridges that aren't built yet. Distinguish between directive and informative statements. (Chapter 7.)

6. Distinguish at least four senses of the word "true":
Some mushrooms are poisonous. (If we call this "true," it means that it is a *report that can be and has been verified*. Chapter 3.)
Sally is the sweetest girl in the world. (If we call this "true," it means that *we feel the same way* towards Sally. Chapters 6 and 8.)
All men are created equal. (If we call this "true," it means that this is *a directive which we believe should be obeyed*. Chapter 7.)
$(x + y)^2 = x^2 + 2xy + y^2$. (If we call this "true," it means that this statement is *consistent with the system of statements possible to be made in the language called algebra*. Chapter 14.)

7. When tempted to "fight fire with fire," remember that the fire department usually uses water. (Chapter 14.)

8. The two-valued orientation is the *starter, not the steering apparatus.* (Chapter 14.)

9. Beware of definitions, which are words about words. Think with examples rather than definitions wherever possible. (Chapter 10.)

10. Use INDEX NUMBERS and DATES as reminders that NO WORD EVER HAS EXACTLY THE SAME MEANING TWICE.

Cow$_1$ is *not* cow$_2$, cow$_2$ is *not* cow$_3$, . . .

Smith$_{1949}$ is *not* Smith$_{1950}$, Smith$_{1950}$ is *not* Smith$_{1951}$, . . .

If these rules are too much to remember, the reader is asked to memorize *at least* this much:

COW$_1$ IS NOT COW$_2$, COW$_2$ IS NOT COW$_3$, . . .

This is the simplest and most general of the rules for extensional orientation. The word "cow" gives us the intensional meanings, informative and affective; it calls up in our minds the features that this "cow" has *in common* with other "cows." The index number, however, reminds us that this one is *different;* it reminds us that "cow" does *not* tell us "all about" the event; it reminds us of the *characteristics left out* in the process of abstracting; it prevents us from equating the word with the thing, that is, from confusing the abstraction "cow" with the extensional cow.

Symptoms of Disorder

Not to observe, consciously or unconsciously, such principles of interpretation is to think and react in primitive and infantile ways. There are a number of ways in which we can detect unhealthy reactions in ourselves. One of the most obvious symptoms is sudden displays of temper. When blood pressure rises, quarrels become excited and feverish, and arguments end up in snarling and name-calling, there is a misevaluation somewhere in the background.

Another obvious symptom is worry—when we keep going round and round in circles. "I love her. . . . I love her. . . . Oh, if I could only forget that she is a *waitress!* . . . What will my friends think if I marry a *waitress?* . . . But I love her. . . . If only she weren't a *waitress!*" But waitress₁ is not waitress₂. "Gosh, what a terrible governor we've got! . . . We thought he was a businessman, but he proves to be only a *politician*. . . . Now that I think of it, the last governor wasn't too bad. . . . Oh, but he was a *politician* too, and how he *played politics!* . . . Can't we ever get a governor who isn't a *politician?*" But politician₁ is not politician₂. As soon as we break these circles and think about *facts* instead of *words,* new light is thrown on our problems.

Still another symptom of unhealthy reactions is a tendency to be oversensitive, easily hurt, and quick to resent insults. The infantile mind, equating words with things, regards unkind words as unkind acts. Attributing to harmless sets of noises a power of injuring, such a person is "insulted" when those noises are uttered at him. So-called "gentlemen" in semisavage and infantile societies used to dignify reactions of this kind into "codes of honor." By "honor," they meant extreme readiness to pull out swords or pistols whenever they imagined that they had been "insulted." Naturally, they killed each other off much faster than was necessary, illustrating again a principle often implied in this book: the lower the boiling point, the higher the mortality rate.

It has already been pointed out that the tendency to talk too much and too readily is an unhealthy sign. We should also be wary of "thinking too much." It is a mistake to believe that productive thinkers necessarily "think harder" than people who never get anywhere. They only think more efficiently. "Thinking too much" often means that somewhere in the back of our minds there is a "certainty"—an "incontrovertible fact," an "unalterable law," an "eternal principle"—some statement which we believe "says all" about something. Life, however, is constantly throwing into the face of our "incontrovertible certainties" facts that do not fit our preconceptions: "Politicians" who *aren't* corrupt, "friends" who *aren't* faithful, "benevolent societies" that *aren't* benevolent, "insurance companies" that *don't* insure. Refusing to give up our sense of "certainty" and yet unable to deny the facts that do not fit, we are forced to "think and think and think." And, as we have seen before, there are only two ways out of such dilemmas: first, to deny the facts altogether, and secondly, to reverse the principle altogether, so that we go from *"All* insurance companies are safe" to *"No* insurance companies are safe." Hence such infantile reactions as, "I'll *never* trust another woman!" "Don't *ever* say politics to me again!" "I'm through with newspapers for good!" "Men are all alike, the heels!"

The mature mind, on the other hand, knows that words never say all about anything, and it is therefore *adjusted to uncertainty.* In driving a car, for example, we never know what is going to happen next; no matter how often we have gone over the same road, we never find *exactly* the same traffic conditions. Nevertheless, a competent driver travels over all kinds of roads and even at high speeds without either fear or nervousness. As driver, he is *adjusted to uncertainty*—the unexpected blowout or the sudden hazard— and *he is not insecure.*

Similarly, the intellectually mature person does not "know all about" anything. And he is not insecure, because he knows that the only kind of security life offers is the *dynamic security that comes from within: the security derived from infinite flexibility of mind— from an infinite-valued orientation.*

"Knowing all" about this, "knowing all" about that, we have only ourselves to blame when we find certain problems "insoluble." With some working knowledge of how language acts, both in ourselves and others, we save both time and effort; we prevent ourselves from running around in verbal squirrel cages. With an extensional orientation, we are adjusted to the inevitable uncertainties of all our science and wisdom. And whatever other problems the world thrusts upon us, we at least escape those of our own making.

The Lost Children

Then there are the unhappy people who *don't* know "all about this" or "all about that," and *wish they did.* Being in a more or less chronic state of anxiety about not knowing all the answers, they are always looking for "the answer" that will forever still their anxieties. They drift from one church, political party, or "new thought" movement to another; they may drift from one psychiatrist to another if they are educated, or from one fortuneteller to another if they are not. Occasionally such people happen upon fortunetellers, political leaders, or systems of thought that hit them just right. Thereupon they are suddenly overwhelmed with relief and joy. Feeling that they have found *the* answer to all their problems, they become passionately devoted to spreading the news to everyone they know.

A major source both of the excessive anxiety which such people feel and of their excessive enthusiasm when they do find their problems "solved" has been described by psychiatrists. An adult—an emotionally mature person—is independent, able to work out his own answers to problems, and able to realize that there is no one answer to everything. If, however, we have not been brought up to be independent—if, for example, we were deprived of love and care at an age when we needed love and care, or if we had parents who did too much for us through excessive and misdirected love—we grow up physically mature but, as psychiatrists say, emotionally immature. We continue to need, no matter what our age, a *parent-symbol:* some figure of comforting authority to whom we can turn for "all the answers." Successively we will seek, if we are so troubled, one parent-symbol after another when we can no longer depend on our own parents—sometimes a kindly teacher, sometimes an authoritative and impressive clergyman, sometimes a fatherly employer, sometimes a political leader.

From our point of view as students of human linguistic behavior, the verbal aspects of this search for a parent-symbol deserve attention. Those who, for one reason or another, are unable to accept a priest, teacher, or political leader as a parent-symbol, may find a parent-symbol in a *big, systematic collection of words*—for example, a huge and difficult-to-understand philosophical work, a politico-economic philosophy, a system of "new thought," or the Hundred Great Books. "Here, here," they cry, "are all the answers in one place!" Finding "all the answers" in such collections of words is a sophisticated, and in our culture, a respectable form of both emotional immaturity and what we have earlier called naïveté regarding the symbolic process. It is emotional immaturity because it involves the giving up of independent thought in favor of dependence on a (verbal) parent-symbol. It is nevertheless respectable, because those who manifest their immaturity in this way acquire, in doing so, an impressively complicated and abstract vocabulary which they exhibit on all possible occasions—and our culture respects the fluent talker, especially one who talks at high levels of abstraction. This dependence on verbal parent-symbols is also naïve because it assumes what we have already seen to be an impossible assumption, namely, that a verbal "map" can "say all" about the "territory" of experience.

This is not to say, of course, that an enthusiasm for a "great book," or for a hundred of them, is necessarily a symptom of immaturity. However, there is a world of difference between the enthusiasm of the emotionally immature and that of the mature. An immature person, discovering a new intellectual system or philosophy that somehow meets his needs, tends to adopt it uncritically, to repeat endlessly the verbal formulas with which he has been provided, and *to resent any imputation that anything more needs to be discovered*. The mature reader, on the other hand, pleased and excited as he may be by the "great book" he has found, is *eager to test it*. Are these new and exciting principles or human insights as general as they appear to be? Are they true in many different cultural or historical contexts? Do they need revision or refinement or correction? How do the principles or attitudes apply in specific cases and under different conditions? As he asks himself these and other questions, he may find that his newly discovered system is quite as important as he originally thought it to be, but, along with his increased sense of power, he also gets a deep sense of *how much more there is to be learned*.

Indeed, the better and more widely useful a new philosophical or scientific synthesis is, the greater will be the number of fresh problems raised. The answers given to perplexing questions by Darwin in his *Origin of Species* did not stop biological inquiry; they gave biology the greatest spurt to fresh inquiry in modern times. The answers given by Freud to psychological questions did not stop psychology; they opened up whole new areas of investigation. "Great books" are those which open great new questions to which there is hope of finding fruitful answers. Great books are misread if their effect is to stop investigation.[1]

In other words, the wiser people become, whether in science, religion, politics, or art, the less dogmatic do they become. Apparently, the better we know the territory of human experience, the more aware do we become of the limitations of the verbal maps we can make of it. We have earlier (Chapter 11) called this awareness of the limitations of maps "consciousness of abstracting." The mature person retains "consciousness of abstracting" even with respect to philosophies or systems of thought about which he feels the greatest enthusiasm.

"Know Thyself"

Another area in which "consciousness of abstracting" is necessary is in *what we say to ourselves about ourselves*. We are all a great deal more complex than Bessie the Cow, and even more than Bessie, we are constantly undergoing change. Furthermore, we all describe ourselves to ourselves in some kind of language (or other abstractions, like "mental pictures," "idealizations," or "images"). These descriptions of ourselves are more or less clearly formulated: "I am the home-loving type," "I am beautiful," "I am hopelessly unattractive," "I believe in efficiency," "I am kind-hearted," "I'm not that kind of a girl," "I am not a snob," "I am a friend of the downtrodden," and so on. All such statements are *more or less* accurate "maps" of that "territory" which is ourselves. Some people make better maps of themselves than others. If a person makes a reasonably good map of himself, we say that he "knows himself"—that he accurately assesses his strengths and his limitations, his emotional

---

[1] The communist use of the writings of Marx and Lenin appears to the writer to be a misreading of books which were in their time important contributions to social science. The communists have treated all deviations from Marx and Lenin (or at least deviations from their interpretations of Marx and Lenin) as attacks upon "Truth," and seem thereby to have rendered the progress of social science in the Soviet Union almost impossible. See Anatol Rapoport, "Dialectical Materialism and General Semantics," in *ETC.: A Review of General Semantics,* Winter 1948, pp. 81-104.

powers and his emotional needs. The psychologist Carl R. Rogers refers to this "map" we make of ourselves as the "self-concept," which, according to his terminology, may be "realistic" or "unrealistic." What we do, how we dress, what manners or mannerisms we affect, what tasks we undertake and what tasks we decline, what kind of society we seek, and so on, are determined not so much by our *actual* powers and limitations as by what we *believe to be* our powers and limitations—i.e., our "self-concepts." [2]

All that has previously been said in this book about maps and territories applies with special relevance to our "self-concepts." A map *is not* the territory: one's self-concept *is not* one's self. A map represents *not all* of the territory: one's self-concept *omits* an enormous amount of one's actual self—we never know ourselves *completely*. Maps of maps of maps, and so on, can be made: one may describe oneself to oneself, and then make about oneself *any number of inferences and generalizations at higher levels of abstraction*.

The pitfalls of map-territory relationships therefore threaten the adequacy of our evaluations of ourselves just as much as they threaten the adequacy of our evaluations of other people and of external events. Indeed, as is suggested in the famous Socratic injunction, "Know thyself," it is more than probable that our wisdom in evaluating other people and external events rests largely upon our wisdom in evaluating ourselves. What kinds of "maps," then, do we make of ourselves?

Some people obviously have extremely unrealistic self-concepts. The person who says, "I have the ability to act as general manager" and accepts such a job, and then turns out not to have the ability, seriously disappoints himself and others. If another person says, "I'm not any good" and takes himself seriously when he says this, he may dissipate his talents, his opportunities, his entire life. The not uncommon sight of the middle-aged woman who dresses and acts like an eighteen-year-old is another instance of the kind of person who lives in terms of an extremely *unrealistic* self-concept.

---

[2] Carl R. Rogers, unpublished paper, "A Comprehensive Theory of Personality" (1948). See also Prescott Lecky, *Self-Consistency: A Theory of Personality*, Island Press, 1945, and Gardner Murphy, *Personality: A Biosocial Approach to Origins and Structure*, Harper, 1947.

Furthermore, there are those who do not seem to realize that their self-concepts do *not* include *all* the relevant facts about themselves. As psychiatrists have shown us time and again, we all have a way of concealing from others and from ourselves our deeper reasons for doing things; instead, we offer, in justification of our acts, more or less elaborate rationalizations. Let us suppose, for example, that a critic has given as his reason for attacking a book its "shoddy argument and bad prose style." Let us suppose, furthermore, that his deeper reasons are entirely different, such as professional jealousy, his psychological need not to believe the book because of its upsetting ideas, or a personal quarrel with the author ten years earlier. If the reviewer believes that his self-concept "says all" about himself, his picture of himself as "one who believes in rigorous logic and high standards of prose style" becomes to him a complete and adequate account of why he dislikes the book. In other words, the most common effect of not knowing that one's self-concept does not "say all" about one's self is *the tendency on the part of many people to believe their own rationalizations*. Some persons, indeed, believe their "self-concepts" so completely and sincerely—that is, they surround themselves with such airtight rationalizations—that they become incapable of any genuine self-knowledge.

Self-knowledge, of course, is often disturbing: statements of the kind "My real reason for not liking this book is that I'm jealous of the author," "The reason I am not getting ahead is that I am less intelligent than my colleagues," and so on, are extremely difficult to face if we are emotionally insecure. Therefore, we often *need* to believe our rationalizations: "The book is shoddy in its arguments," "The reason I am not getting ahead is that my colleagues are conspiring against me." If the need to believe in these inaccurate maps is strong enough, we can shut our eyes to any amount of evidence that contradicts them.

How do we prevent ourselves from getting into this emotional situation? Those who are already in it can probably be helped only by a professionally trained counselor or a psychiatrist. But for the rest of us, there remain the day-to-day problems of action and decision; the more realistic our self-concepts are, the more likelihood there is of fruitful action and sane decision. Can we do anything to achieve a greater realism about ourselves?

Reports and Judgments

There is at least one thing psychological counselors and many psychiatrists do which people who are capable of some degree of self-insight can, to a greater or lesser degree, do for themselves. As we have seen, we manufacture false self-concepts because truer statements are unbearable. The reason they are unbearable is often that they involve the uncritical acceptance from our environment (from what our friends and neighbors say, or what we think they are saying) of *other people's judgments*. Using the word "judgment" here as we have used it in Chapter 3, notice the difference between "I am a filling-station attendant" (which is a report) and "I am *only* a filling-station attendant" (which involves a judgment, implying that I ought to be something different and that it is disgraceful that I am what I am).

One of the most important aspects of a psychiatrist's or counselor's assistance is the fact that he *does not pass any judgments on us*. When we admit to him that we are "only" a filling-station attendant, or that, back in April 1943, we cracked up under the stress of battle, the psychiatrist or counselor helps us by indicating, by word or by manner, that, while he understands our feelings of shame or guilt, he does not in any way condemn us for being what we are or for having done what we have done. In other words, he helps us change the *judgment,* "I am only a filling-station attendant and *therefore I am not much good,*" back into the *report,* "I am a filling-station attendant." The judgment, "I cracked up in battle and *I am a coward,*" is changed into, "I cracked up in battle." As a result of the psychiatrist's or counselor's acceptance of us, we are better able to accept ourselves.

The fact that we permit other people's judgments (and what we believe to be their judgments) to influence us unduly is one of the commonest reasons for feelings of inferiority and guilt and insecurity. If a man says to himself, "I am a Negro," and simultaneously accepts the judgment of certain white people on Negroes, it is hard to be a Negro, and he may spend the rest of his life being jumpy and defensive and miserable. If a man makes fifty dollars a week and accepts the real or imagined judgment of others that if he were any good he would be making a hundred, it is difficult to face the fact of making fifty. The training suggested in Chapter 3 of *writing reports from which judgments are excluded* may be applied to writing *about ourselves.* Such self-descriptions are an especially helpful technique in arriving at more realistic self-concepts.

We should, in performing this exercise, put down facts about ourselves—especially the facts about which we feel some shame or embarrassment—and then ask with respect to each fact such questions as these: "Is it necessary to pass judgment at all on this fact?" "Who passes judgment on this fact, anyway, and should I also do so?" "Are no other judgments possible?" "What does an unfavorable judgment on one of my actions *in the past* prove about what I am *today?*" Reports of the following kind may lead to such re-evaluations as are indicated in the parentheses:

I am a filling-station attendant. (Some people think it is somehow "inferior" to be a filling-station attendant. Do *I* have to think so too?)

I am a Jew. (Is this good or bad? Or isn't this a silly question? Who says it's bad to be a Jew?)

I cracked up on the battlefield. (Who says I shouldn't have cracked up? Were they there? Did they have to go through what I did? I was psychologically wounded in battle; others were physically wounded. Why don't they give Purple Hearts to psychiatric casualties?)

I am a housewife. (Well?)

Naturally, if one's rationalizations are deeply rooted, this technique is difficult to practice. For example:

My real reason for disliking this book is professional jealousy. (Oh, no! The author's arguments *are* shoddy and his style *is* awful!)

But as we grow increasingly extensional about our own feelings —as we grow in our ability to accept ourselves, so that we are able to confront *without judgments of good or bad* such reports as, "I am below average in height," "I am not athletic," "I am the child of divorced parents," "My sister gets better grades than I do," "I never went to college," and so on—we progressively have less and less need to deceive ourselves. *In self-knowledge as in science, the conquest of little areas leads progressively to the conquest of larger and more difficult areas.* As our self-concepts grow more realistic, our actions and decisions become progressively wiser, since they are based on a more accurate "mapping" of that complex territory of our own personalities.

Institutionalized Attitudes

Another way in which we can increase our extensional awareness of ourselves is by distinguishing between attitudes *institutionally* arrived at and attitudes *extensionally* arrived at. As we have seen in Chapter 16, we are all members of institutions, and as members of institutions we incorporate into ourselves certain institutionally demanded attitudes. If we are Democrats, we are expected to support all Democratic candidates. If we belong to an employers' association, our fellow-members may expect us to be hostile to all labor unions. If we are Montagues, we are expected to be hostile to the Capulets.

A source of widespread misevaluation implicit in such institutionalized attitudes is that each of them involves a generalization at a high level of abstraction, while actual Democratic candidates, labor unions, and Capulets exist at the level of extensional fact. Many persons are, through emotional insecurity as well as through lack of an extensional orientation, unable to depart from institutionally expected attitudes. Seeking security by adopting the "official" point of view prevalent in the institutions of which they are members, they become excessively conventional and excessively given to commonplace ideas and emotions. They feel what they are expected to feel by their political party, their church, their social group, or their family; they think what they are expected to think. They find it both easier and safer not to examine too extensionally any *specific* Democratic candidate, any *specific* labor union, any *specific* Capulet, because extensional examination of any one of these *might* lead to an evaluation different from the institutionally accepted point of view.

But to have nothing but institutionalized attitudes is eventually to have no personality of one's own, and therefore to have nothing original or creative contribute to the institutions of which one is a member. Furthermore, there is the danger to one's personal adjustment implicit in continually living by high level generalizations and repressing (or avoiding) extensional evaluations.

The rule already suggested for the avoidance of excessively intensional attitudes is helpful for the avoidance of excessively conventional, institutionalized attitudes, because intensional attitudes are often the result of the uncritical acceptance of institutional dogmas. With the application of the cow_1 is not cow_2 rule, we begin to *look* in order to find out if $Democrat_1$ differs in any important respects from $Democrat_2$, if labor $union_1$ differs from labor $union_2$, if $Capulet_1$ differs from $Capulet_2$. As the result of such extensional examination we may find that the original institutional attitudes were the correct ones after all; or we may find it necessary, as Romeo and Juliet did, to depart from them. But whatever conclusions we may arrive at, the important thing is that they will be our own—the result of *our own* extensional examination of the events or objects to be evaluated.

People who are not accustomed to distinguishing between attitudes institutionally arrived at and those extensionally arrived at are capable of real self-deception. In a real sense, they don't know which of their opinions are simply a parrot-like repetition of institutional opinions, and which are the result of their own experience and their own thinking. Lacking that self-insight, they are unable to arrive at realistic self-concepts; they are unable to map accurately the territory of their own personalities.

Reading Towards Sanity

A few words, finally, need to be said on the subject of reading as an aid to extensional orientation. Studying books too often has the effect of producing excessive intensional orientation; this is espe-

cially true in literary study, for example, when the study of words
—novels, plays, poems, essays—becomes an end in itself. When
the study of literature is undertaken, however, not as an end in
itself, but as a guide to life, its effect is extensional in the best sense.

Literature works by intensional means; that is, by the manipulation of the informative and affective connotations of words. By
these means, it not only calls our attention to facts not previously
noticed, but it also is capable of arousing feelings not previously
experienced. These new feelings in turn call our attention to still
more facts not previously noticed. Both the new feelings and the
new facts, therefore, upset our intensional orientations, so that our
blindness is little by little removed.

The extensionally orientated person, as has been repeatedly said, is
governed not by words only, but by the facts to which the words
have guided him. But supposing there were no words to guide us?
Should we be able to guide ourselves to those facts? The answer is,
in the vast majority of cases, no. To begin with, our nervous systems are extremely imperfect, and we see things only in terms of
our training and interests. If our interests are limited, we see extremely little; a man looking for cigarette butts in the street sees
little else of the world passing by. Furthermore, as everyone knows,
when we travel, meet interesting people, or have adventures before
we are old enough to appreciate such experiences, we often feel that
we might just as well not have had them. Experience itself is an
extremely imperfect teacher. Experience does not tell us what it
is we are experiencing. Things simply happen. And if we do not
know *what to look for* in our experience, they often have no significance to us whatever.

Many people put a great deal of stock in experience as such; they
tend automatically to respect the person who has "done things."
"I don't want to sit around reading books," they say; "I want to
get out and do things! I want to travel! I want to have experiences!"
But often the experiences they go out and get do them no good
whatever. They go to London, and all they remember is their hotel
and the American Express Company office; they go to China, and
their total impression is that "there were a lot of Chinamen there";

they may have served in the South Pacific and remember only their dissatisfaction with their K-rations. The result often is that people who have never had these experiences, people who have never been to those places, know more about them than people who have. We all tend to go around the world with our eyes shut unless someone opens them for us.

This, then, is the tremendous function that language, in both its scientific and its affective uses, performs. In the light of abstract scientific generalizations, "trivial" facts lose their triviality. When we have studied, for example, surface tension, the alighting of a dragonfly on a pool of water is a subject for thought and explanation. In the light of reading *The Grapes of Wrath,* a trip through California is a doubly meaningful experience. And we turn and look at migrant families in all other parts of the country as well, because Steinbeck has created in us new ways of feeling about a subject that we may formerly have ignored. In the light of the subtleties of feeling aroused in us by the literature and poetry of the past, every human experience is filled with rich significances and relationships.

The communications we receive from others, insofar as they do not simply retrace our old patterns of feeling and tell us things we already know, increase the efficiency of our nervous systems. Poets, as well as scientists, have aptly been called "the window washers of the mind"; without their communications to widen our interests and increase the sensitivity of our perceptions, we could very well remain as blind as puppies.

Language, as has been repeatedly emphasized in these pages, is social.[3] Reading or listening, writing or talking, we are constantly involved in the processes of social interaction made possible by language. Sometimes, as we have seen, the result of that social

[3] Although the principles which have been explained throughout this book have as their purpose the establishment of agreement and the avoidance of conflict, some people may be tempted to use them as weapons with which to stir up arguments, as clubs with which to beat people over the head: "The trouble with you, Joe, is that you've got a bad case of two-valued orientation," "For God's sake, Mabel, stop being so intensional!" Those who use the formulations of this book in this way may be said to have understood it but dimly.

interaction is the sharing of knowledge, the enrichment of sympathies and insight, and the establishing of human co-operation. But at other times, the social interaction does not come out so well: every exchange of remarks, as between two drunks at a bar or between two hostile delegates at the United Nations Security Council, leads progressively to the conviction on the part of each that it is impossible to co-operate with the other.

We come back, then, to the judgments explicitly announced at the beginning of this book—the ethical judgments on which the argument has been based throughout—that widespread intraspecific co-operation through the use of language is the fundamental mechanism of human survival, and that, when the use of language results, as it so often does, in the creation or aggravation of disagreements and conflicts, there is something wrong with the speaker, the listener, or both. Sometimes, as we have seen, this "something wrong" is the result of ignorance of the territory which leads to the making of inaccurate maps; sometimes it is the result, through faulty evaluative habits, of refusing to look at the territory but insisting on talking anyway; sometimes it is the result of imperfections in language itself which neither speaker nor listener have taken the trouble to examine; often it has been the result, throughout the history of the human race, of using language not as an instrument of social cohesion, but as a weapon. The purpose of this book has been to lay before the reader some of the ways in which, whether as speakers or listeners, we may use or be used by the mechanisms of linguistic communication. What the reader may wish to do with these mechanisms is up to him.

Selected Bibliography

Alexander, Franz, and French, Thomas M., *Psychoanalytic Therapy,* Ronald Press, 1946.

Arnold, Thurman W., *The Symbols of Government,* Yale University Press, 1935.

—— *The Folklore of Capitalism,* Yale University Press, 1937.

Ayer, A. J., *Language, Truth and Logic,* Oxford University Press, 1936.

Bell, Eric Temple, *The Search for Truth,* Reynal and Hitchcock, 1934.

—— *Men of Mathematics,* Simon and Schuster, 1937.

Benedict, Ruth, *Patterns of Culture,* Houghton Mifflin, 1934; also Pelican Books, 1946.

Bentley, Arthur F., *Linguistic Analysis of Mathematics,* The Principia Press (Bloomington, Ind.), 1932.

Bloomfield, Leonard, *Language,* Henry Holt, 1933.

Bridgman, P. W., *The Logic of Modern Physics,* Macmillan, 1927.

Britton, Karl, *Communication: A Philosophical Study of Language,* Harcourt, Brace, 1939.

Burke, Kenneth, *The Philosophy of Literary Form,* Louisiana State University Press, 1941.

—— *A Grammar of Motives,* Prentice-Hall, 1945.

Burrow, Trigant, *The Social Basis of Consciousness,* Harcourt, Brace, 1927.

—— *The Biology of Human Conflict,* Macmillan, 1937.

Carnap, Rudolf, *Philosophy and Logical Syntax,* Psyche Miniatures (London), 1935.

Chase, Stuart, *The Tyranny of Words,* Harcourt, Brace, 1938.

Chisholm, Francis P., *Introductory Lectures on General Semantics,* Institute of General Semantics (Lakeville, Conn.), 1945.

Cohen, Felix S., "Transcendental Nonsense and the Functional Approach," *Columbia Law Review,* June 1935, pp. 809-49.

Cooper, Charles W., *Preface to Poetry,* Harcourt, Brace, 1946.

Dantzig, Tobias, *Number: The Language of Science,* Macmillan, 1933.

Doob, Leonard W., *Public Opinion and Propaganda,* Henry Holt, 1948.

Empson, William, *Seven Types of Ambiguity,* Chatto and Windus (London), 1930.

ETC.: A Review of General Semantics (quarterly), edited by S. I. Hayakawa. Published since 1943 by International Society for General Semantics, 549 W. Washington Blvd., Chicago 6, Ill.

Fenellosa, Ernest, *The Chinese Written Character,* ed. by Ezra Pound, Stanley Nott (London), 1936.

Frank, Jerome, *Law and the Modern Mind,* Brentano's, 1930 (also Tudor Publishing Company, 1936).

Fromm, Erich, *Escape from Freedom,* Rinehart, 1941.

Horney, Karen, *The Neurotic Personality of Our Time,* W. W. Norton, 1937.

Huse, H. R., *The Illiteracy of the Literate,* D. Appleton-Century, 1933.

Huxley, Aldous, *Words and Their Meanings,* Jake Zeitlin (Los Angeles), 1940.

Huxley, Julian, *Evolution: The Modern Synthesis,* Harper, 1942.

Johnson, Alexander Bryan, *A Treatise on Language* (1836), edited, with a critical essay on his philosophy of language, by David Rynin, University of California Press, 1947.

——— *The Meaning of Words* (1854), with an introduction by Irving J. Lee, John W. Chamberlin (Milwaukee), 1948.

Johnson, Wendell, *People in Quandaries: The Semantics of Personal Adjustment,* Harper, 1946.

Kepes, Gyorgy, *Language of Vision,* with introductory essays by Siegfried Giedion and S. I. Hayakawa, Paul Theobald (Chicago), 1944.

Köhler, Wolfgang, *Gestalt Psychology,* Liveright Publishing Corporation, 1947.

Korzybski, Alfred, *The Manhood of Humanity,* E. P. Dutton, 1921.

——— *Science and Sanity: An Introduction to Non-Aristotelian Systems and General Semantics,* Science Press Printing Company (Lancaster, Pa.), 1933.

Langer, Susanne K., *Philosophy in a New Key,* Harvard University Press, 1942; also Pelican Books, 1948.

Lasswell, Harold D., *Psychopathology and Politics,* University of Chicago Press, 1930.

Leavis, Q. D., *Fiction and the Reading Public,* Chatto and Windus (London), 1932.

Lecky, Prescott, *Self-Consistency: A Theory of Personality,* Island Workshop (New York), 1945.

Lee, Irving J., *Language Habits in Human Affairs,* Harper, 1941.

———— *The Language of Wisdom and Folly,* Harper, 1949.

Lee, Vernon, *The Handling of Words,* Dodd, Mead, 1923.

Lévy-Bruhl, Lucien, *How Natives Think,* Knopf, 1926.

Lewin, Kurt, *Principles of Topological Psychology,* McGraw-Hill, 1936.

Lieber, Lillian R., *The Einstein Theory of Relativity,* Farrar & Rinehart, 1945.

———— *The Education of T. C. Mits,* W. W. Norton, 1944.

Lilienthal, David E., *TVA: Democracy on the March,* Harper, 1944; also Pocket Books, 1945.

Malinowski, Bronislaw, *The Problem of Meaning in Primitive Languages,* Supplement I in Ogden and Richards, *The Meaning of Meaning.*

Masserman, Jules, *Behavior and Neurosis,* University of Chicago Press, 1943.

May, Mark A., and Doob, Leonard W., *Competition and Cooperation,* Social Science Research Council (New York), 1937.

Mead, Margaret, ed., *Cooperation and Competition among Primitive People,* McGraw-Hill, 1936.

Menninger, Karl, *Love Against Hate,* Harcourt, Brace, 1942.

Morris, Charles, *Signs, Language and Behavior,* Prentice-Hall, 1946.

Murphy, Gardner, *Personality: A Biosocial Approach to Origins and Structure,* Harper, 1947.

Ogden, C. K., and Richards, I. A., *The Meaning of Meaning,* 3rd ed., rev., Harcourt, Brace, 1930.

Piaget, Jean, *The Language and Thought of the Child,* Harcourt, Brace, 1926.

———— *The Child's Conception of the World,* Harcourt, Brace, 1929.

Pollock, Thomas Clark, *The Nature of Literature,* Princeton University Press, 1942.

Richards, I. A., *Science and Poetry,* W. W. Norton, 1926.

———— *Practical Criticism,* Harcourt, Brace, 1929.

———— *The Philosophy of Rhetoric,* Oxford University Press, 1936.

———— *Interpretation in Teaching,* Harcourt, Brace, 1938.

Rogers, Carl R., *Counseling and Psychotherapy,* Houghton Mifflin, 1942.

———— and Wallen, John, *Counseling with Returned Servicemen,* McGraw-Hill, 1946.

Sapir, Edward, *Language,* Harcourt, Brace, 1921.

Smith, Bruce L., Lasswell, Harold D., and Casey, Ralph D., *Propaganda, Communication, and Public Opinion: A Comprehensive Reference Guide,* Princeton University Press, 1946.

Stefansson, Vilhjalmur, *The Standardization of Error,* W. W. Norton, 1927.

Taylor, Edmond, *The Strategy of Terror,* Houghton Mifflin, 1940.

Upward, Allen, *The New Word: An Open Letter Addressed to the Swedish Academy in Stockholm on the Meaning of the Word IDEALIST,* Mitchell Kennerley (New York), 1910.

Vaihinger, Hans, *The Philosophy of "As If,"* Harcourt, Brace, 1924.

Veblen, Thorstein, *The Theory of the Leisure Class,* The Modern Library.

Walpole, Hugh R., *Semantics,* W. W. Norton, 1941.

Weiss, A. P., *The Theoretical Basis of Human Behavior,* R. G. Adams and Company (Columbus, Ohio), 1925; 2nd ed., rev., 1929.

Welby, V., *What Is Meaning?* Macmillan, 1903.

Yerkes, Robert M., *Chimpanzees: A Laboratory Colony,* Yale University Press, 1943.

Acknowledgments

Grateful acknowledgment is due to the following for permission to use selections quoted herein:

Appleton-Century Crofts, Inc.: Excerpts from *The Illiteracy of the Literate* by H. R. Huse, copyright, 1933, by D. Appleton-Century Company, Inc.; from *Political Ideals* by Bertrand Russell, copyright, 1917, by the Century Company.

The Bell Syndicate, Inc.: Excerpt from Dorothy Dix's column for December 15, 1948. Reprinted by special permission of the Bell Syndicate, Inc., and the Chicago *Sun-Times*.

Brandt & Brandt: Excerpt from "Rain after a Vaudeville Show" by Stephen Vincent Benét. Copyright, 1918, 1920, 1923, 1925, 1929, 1930, 1931, by Stephen Vincent Benét.

The John Day Company, Inc.: Excerpt from *Toward Freedom* by Jawaharlal Nehru.

Doubleday & Company, Inc.: Excerpts from *Literary Taste: How to Form It* by Arnold Bennett; from *Country Squire in the White House* by John T. Flynn.

E. P. Dutton & Co., Inc.: Excerpt from *Man and Society in Calamity* by Pitirim A. Sorokin, published and copyright, 1942, by E. P. Dutton & Co., Inc.

ETC.: A Review of General Semantics: Excerpts from the writings of Charles I. Glicksberg and S. I. Hayakawa.

Faher & Faher, Ltd.: "Salutation" from *Selected Poems* by Ezra Pound.

Fawcett Publications, Inc.: Excerpts from *True Confessions,* August 1948. Courtesy of *True Confessions.* Copyright 1948 Fawcett Publications, Inc.

Harcourt, Brace and Company, Inc.: Excerpts from T. S. Eliot; from *The Culture of Cities* by Lewis Mumford, copyright, 1938; from *The Meaning of Meaning,* 3rd ed., by C. K. Ogden and I. A. Richards; from *The Child's Conception of the World* by Jean Piaget; from *Theory of Literature* by René Wellek and Austin Warren, copyright, 1949; "Naming of Parts" from *A Map of Verona and Other Poems* by Henry Reed, copyright, 1947, by Henry Reed.

Harper & Brothers: Excerpts from *People in Quandries* by Wendell Johnson; from *The Mind in the Making* by James Harvey Robinson; from *Union Now with Britain* by Clarence Streit; from *Quo Vadimus* by E. B. White; "Commuter" from *The Lady Is Cold* by E. B. White.

Henry Holt and Company, Inc.: Excerpts from *Language* by Leonard Bloomfield; from *The Faith of a Liberal* by Morris Cohen; "Terence, This Is Stupid Stuff" from *A Shropshire Lad* by A. E. Housman; "Could Man Be Drunk Forever" from *Last Poems* by A. E. Housman, copyright, 1922, by Henry Holt and Company, Inc.; "Happiness" from *Chicago Poems* by Carl Sandburg, copyright, 1916, by Henry Holt and Company, Inc., copyright, 1943, by Carl Sandburg.

Houghton Mifflin Company: "Ars Poetica" from *Poems 1924-1933* by Archibald MacLeish.

King Features Syndicate: Excerpt from Westbrook Pegler's column of July 22, 1948.

Alfred A. Knopf, Inc.: Excerpt from "Miss Brill" by Katherine Mansfield.

A. J. Liebling: Excerpts from *The Wayward Pressman*.

J. B. Lippincott Company: Excerpt from *Handbook of Fresh Water Fishing* by Lee Wulff, published by the Frederick A. Stokes Company.

Liveright Publishing Corporation: Excerpts from *Lunacy Becomes Us* by Adolf Hitler and His Associates, edited by Clara Leiser, published by Liveright, copyright, 1939.

Longmans, Green & Company. Inc.: Excerpt from *Pragmatism* by William James, copyright, 1907.

Masses & Mainstream: Excerpt from "The Cult of the Proper Word" by Margaret Schlauch, *New Masses,* April 15, 1947.

Hughes Mearns: "The Man Who Wasn't There."

The Nation: Excerpts from *The Nation,* June 26, 1948 (book review by Rolfe Humphries, Jr.), and July 3, 1948 (account of the Republican Convention by Robert Bendiner).

New Directions: "Salutation" from *Selected Poems* by Ezra Pound.

New Republic: Excerpt from "Artists and Bureaucrats" by Joseph Lash, *New Republic,* January 10, 1949.

New Statesman & Nation: Excerpt from *New Statesman & Nation,* June 5, 1948.

Pittsburgh *Courier:* Excerpt from an article by Rose Wilder Lane, May 13, 1944.

Political Science Quarterly: Excerpt from "An American Dilemma" by Frank Tannenbaum, *Political Science Quarterly,* September 1944.

Prentice-Hall, Inc.: Excerpt from *Signs, Language and Behavior* by Charles Morris.

Random House Inc.: "Moving through the silent crowds" from *Poems* by Stephen Spender, copyright, 1934, by Modern Library; excerpt from *The Wisdom of Confucius* translated by Lin Yutang.

Rinehart and Company, Inc.: For editorial by William Allen White from *Forty Years on Main Street* by William Allen White.

W. B. Saunders Company: Excerpt from *Principles of Dynamic Psychiatry* by Jules Masserman.

Charles Scribner's Sons: "Invictus" by W. E. Henley; excerpts from "Haircut" in *Round Up* by Ring Lardner; from *A Farewell to Arms* by Ernest Hemingway.

Simon and Schuster, Inc.: Excerpts from *Try and Stop Me*, copyright, 1944, by Bennett Cerf; from *Mathematics and the Imagination,* copyright, 1940, by Edward Kasner and James Newman.

Time Inc.: Excerpts from *Time,* October 7, 1929, July 26, 1948, January 24, 1949, March 14, 1949. Courtesy of *Time,* Copyright Time Inc., 1929, 1948, and 1949.

The Viking Press, Inc.: Excerpt from "Morality and the Novel" (in *Phoenix*) by D. H. Lawrence.

The Ward Ritchie Press: Excerpt from *Words and Their Meanings* by Aldous Huxley.

Index